GUIDE TO GOODNESS

Dalāʾil al-khayrāt

(COMPLETE ARABIC-ENGLISH TEXTS)

AND THE ADVENT OF BLAZING LIGHTS
IN REMEMBERING TO ASK
FOR BLESSINGS UPON THE PROPHET

ʿAbū ʿAbd Allāh Muḥammad
ibn Sulaymān ibn Abū Bakr al-Jazūlī

TRANSLATED BY
ANDREY (HASSAN) ROSOWSKY

SERIES EDITOR
SEYYED HOSSEIN NASR

GREAT BOOKS OF THE ISLAMIC WORLD

Library of Congress Cataloging-in-Publication Data

ᶜAbū ᶜAbd Allāh Muḥammad ibn Sulaymān ibn Abū Bakr al-Jazūlī,
Guide to Goodness—Dalail al-khayrat—And the Advent of Blazing Lights in Remembering to Ask for Blessings upon the Prophet
1. Islam. 2. Prayer. I. Title.

ISBN: 1-930637-26-8

Cover design: Liaquat Ali
Cornerstones are Allah and Muhammad connected by *Bismillāh al-Raḥmān al-Raḥīm* (In the Name of God, the Merciful, the Compassionate).

Logo design by Mani Ardalan Farhadi
The cypress tree bending with the wind, the source for the paisley design, is a symbol of the perfect Muslim, who, as the tree, bends with the wind of God's Will.

Published by
Great Books of the Islamic World, Inc.

Distributed by
KAZI Publications, Inc.
3023 W. Belmont Avenue
Chicago IL 60618
Tel: 773-267-7001; FAX: 773-267-7002
email: info@kazi.org /www.kazi.org

Contents

Translator's Note

Of the various editions of *Dalāʾ'il al-khayrāt* available, this translation into English is based on the version of the text commonly available in Turkey and in the Indian sub-continent. Readers familiar with other editions, such as the Moroccan or Egyptian editions, will, therefore, notice some minor differences. These generally involve, on the one hand, the arrangement of the text of *Dalāʾ'il al-khayrāt* itself, and, on the other, the addition of certain other well known formulations of blessings and supplications which are traditionally placed either before or after the main text (eg. Shadhili's *Ḥizb al-bahr,* Ibn Mashshish's *Ṣalāt*, Aḥmad ibn Idris' *al-ᶜAstighfār al-kabir,* etc.). This translation is of the entire text of *Dalāʾ'il al-khayrāt* with only the minor additions of some verses ascribed to Imam Jazūlī towards the end of part eight.The translator hastens to point out that he is not a scholar of the Arabic language and welcomes comments on weaknesses in the translation and suggestions for improvements.

The title of the book is perhaps the most demanding problem the translator has had to deal with. Whilst the meaning of *dalāʾil* is now reasonably accurately conveyed by the modern term 'indices' and is roughly equivalent to the notion of 'pointers,' *khayrāt* is more problematic carrying with it both the sense of 'goodness' in an absolute sense, and also that which can be earned and stored, as in 'goods,' as a result of 'good actions.' The 'good actions' and the 'goods' in question here are the rewards to be had for the reader on uttering the various formulaic supplications in this book. I have settled on 'benefits' as being as good a word as any to convey the meaning of *khayrāt* though the reader should bear in mind the wider connotations of the word.

This work has been undertaken and made available with the approval of my Sheikh and Teacher, Sheikh Nazim Al-Qubrusi Al-Haqqani, Sheffield 1992.

Hassan Rosowsky

Note: This guide or prayer brings blessing in any language.

Editor's Note: As the first edition was entitled *Guide to Goodness,* the publishers have left this title for the second edition. The transator has translated it as *Indices of Benefits*.

About the Author

Imām Jazūlī's full name is Abū ᶜAbd Allāh Muḥammad ibn Sulaymān ibn Abū Bakr al-Jazūlī. According to his biographers he is a descendant of the Prophet, peace and the mercy of God be upon him. He belonged to the Berber tribe of Jazūla which was settled in the Sūs area of Morocco between the Atlantic Ocean and the Atlas Mountains. He studied locally and then went to the Madrasat al-Saffārīn in Fez where his room is still pointed out to visitors. After settling a tribal feud he left the area and spent the next forty years in Makkah, Madinah and Jerusalem. After this, he returned to Fez where he completed *Dalāᵓil al-khayrāt*.

He was initiated into the Shādhilī Sufi Order by Sharīf Abū ᶜAbd Allāh Muḥammad bin Amghar. He spent fourteen years in seclusion (*khalwah*) and then went to Āsfī where he gathered around him many followers. The governor of Āsfī felt obliged to expel him and, as a result, Jazūlī called down God's wrath on the town. It subsequently fell into the hands of the Portuguese for forty years. According to a tradition, it was the governor of Āsfī who poisoned Jazūlī and caused his death, while engaged in prayer, in 1464 AH/869 AH (or 870 or 873). Seventy-seven years after his death his body was exhumed for removal to Marrakesh and found to be uncorrupted (adapted from *The Encyclopedia of Islam*, 1957, Leiden).

It is said that the author of *Dalāᵓil al-khayrāt* once went on a journey. When in great need of water for performing ablution, he came upon a well but could not reach the water without a bucket and rope which he did not have. He became very worried. A young girl saw this and came to his assistance. She spat into the well whereupon the water rose to the top of its own accord. Seeing this miracle, he asked the girl, "And how is that possible?" The girl replied, "I was able to do this through my asking for blessings upon the Prophet, God's blessings and peace be upon him." Having thus seen the benefit of asking for blessings upon the Prophet, God's blessings and peace be upon him, he decided to write *Dalāᵓil al-khayrāt*.

دَلَآئِلُ الْخَيْرَات

بِسْمِ اللّٰهِ الرَّحْمٰنِ الرَّحِيْمِ ○

اَسْتَغْفِرُ اللّٰهَ الْعَظِيْمَ ○ ثَلٰثًا ○

سُبْحٰنَ اللّٰهِ وَالْحَمْدُ لِلّٰهِ ○ ثَلٰثًا ○

حَسْبِيَ اللّٰهُ وَنِعْمَ الْوَكِيْلُ ○ ثَلٰثًا ○

اَلْاِخْلَاصُ بِاَعُوْذُ مَعَ الْبَسْمَلَةِ ○ ثَلٰثًا ○

اَلْمُعَوَّذَتَيْنِ مَعَ الْبَسْمَلَةِ ○ اَلْفَاتِحَةُ مَعَ الْبَسْمَلَةِ ○

اَسْمَآءُ اللّٰهِ الْحُسْنٰى

بِسْمِ اللّٰهِ الرَّحْمٰنِ الرَّحِيْمِ

اَللّٰهُ جَلَّ جَلَالُهُ **اَلرَّحْمٰنُ** جَلَّ جَلَالُهُ **اَلرَّحِيْمُ** جَلَّ جَلَالُهُ **اَلْمَلِكُ** جَلَّ جَلَالُهُ **اَلْقُدُّوْسُ** جَلَّ جَلَالُهُ **اَلسَّلَامُ** جَلَّ جَلَالُهُ **اَلْمُؤْمِنُ** جَلَّ جَلَالُهُ **اَلْمُهَيْمِنُ** جَلَّ جَلَالُهُ **اَلْعَزِيْزُ** جَلَّ جَلَالُهُ **اَلْجَبَّارُ** جَلَّ جَلَالُهُ **اَلْمُتَكَبِّرُ** جَلَّ جَلَالُهُ **اَلْخَالِقُ** جَلَّ جَلَالُهُ **اَلْبَارِئُ** جَلَّ جَلَالُهُ **اَلْمُصَوِّرُ** جَلَّ جَلَالُهُ **اَلْغَفَّارُ** جَلَّ جَلَالُهُ **اَلْقَهَّارُ** جَلَّ جَلَالُهُ **اَلْوَهَّابُ** جَلَّ جَلَالُهُ **اَلرَّزَّاقُ** جَلَّ جَلَالُهُ **اَلْفَتَّاحُ** جَلَّ جَلَالُهُ **اَلْعَلِيْمُ** جَلَّ جَلَالُهُ **اَلْقَابِضُ** جَلَّ جَلَالُهُ **اَلْبَاسِطُ** جَلَّ جَلَالُهُ **اَلْخَافِضُ** جَلَّ جَلَالُهُ **اَلرَّافِعُ** جَلَّ جَلَالُهُ **اَلْمُعِزُّ** جَلَّ جَلَالُهُ **اَلْمُذِلُّ** جَلَّ جَلَالُهُ **اَلسَّمِيْعُ** جَلَّ جَلَالُهُ **اَلْبَصِيْرُ** جَلَّ جَلَالُهُ **اَلْحَكَمُ** جَلَّ جَلَالُهُ **اَلْعَدْلُ** جَلَّ جَلَالُهُ **اَللَّطِيْفُ** جَلَّ جَلَالُهُ **اَلْخَبِيْرُ** جَلَّ جَلَالُهُ **اَلْحَلِيْمُ** جَلَّ جَلَالُهُ **اَلْعَظِيْمُ** جَلَّ جَلَالُهُ **اَلْغَفُوْرُ** جَلَّ جَلَالُهُ **اَلشَّكُوْرُ** جَلَّ جَلَالُهُ **اَلْعَلِيُّ** جَلَّ جَلَالُهُ **اَلْكَبِيْرُ** جَلَّ جَلَالُهُ **اَلْحَفِيْظُ** جَلَّ جَلَالُهُ **اَلْمُقِيْتُ** دُ **اَلْحَسِيْبُ** جَلَّ جَلَالُهُ **اَلْجَلِيْلُ** جَلَّ جَلَالُهُ **اَلْكَرِيْمُ** جَلَّ جَلَالُهُ **اَلرَّقِيْبُ** جَلَّ جَلَالُهُ

The Opening of the Devotions

In the Name of God, the Merciful, the Compassionate
I ask God for forgiveness! (**three times**)
Glory be to God, Praise be to God! (**three times**)
God suffices me and He is the best Protector! (**three times**)
Surah Ikhlāṣ (**three times**) with in the Name of God
Surah al-Falaq and *al-Nās* with in the Name of God
Surah al-Fātihāh with in the Name of God

The Most Beautiful Names of God

In the Name of God, the Merciful, the Compassionate

Allāh (God) may He be glorified, **Al-Raḥmān** (The Merciful) may He be glorified, **Al-Raḥīm** (The Compassionate) may He be glorified, **Al-Malik** (The King) may He be glorified, **Al-Quddūs** (The Holy) may He be glorified, **Al-Salām** (The Peace) may He be glorified, **Al-Muʾmin** (The Guardian of Faith) may He be glorified, **Al-Muhaymin** (The Protector) may He be glorified, **Al-ʿAzīz** (The Mighty) may He be glorified, **Al-Jabbār** (The Compeller) may He be glorified, **Al-Mutakabbir** (The Victorious) may He be glorified, **Al-Khāliq** (The Creator) may He be glorified, **Al-Bāriʾ** (The Inventor) may He be glorified, **Al-Muṣawwir** (The Designer) may He be glorified, **Al-Ghaffār** (The Forgiver) may He be glorified, **Al-Qahhār** (The Subduer) may He be glorified, **Al-Wahhāb** (The Bestower) may He be glorified, **Al-Razzāq** (The Provider) may He be glorified, **Al-Fattāḥ** (The Opener) may He be glorified, **Al-ʿAlīm** (The Knower) may He be glorified, **Al-Qābiḍ** (The Straitener) may He be glorified, **Al-Bāsiṭ** (The Expander) may He be glorified, **Al-Khāfiḍ** (The Abaser) may He be glorified, **Al-Rāfiʿ** (The Exalter) may He be glorified, **Al-Muʿizz** (The Honorer) may He be glorified, **Al-Mudhill** (The Dishonorer) may He be glorified, **Al-Samīʿ** (The Hearing) may He be glorified, **Al-Baṣīr** (The Seeing) may He be glorified, **Al-Ḥakam** (The Judge) may He be glorified, **Al-ʿAdl** (The Just) may He be glorified, **Al-Laṭīf** (The Subtle) may He be glorified, **Al-Khabīr** (The Aware) may He be glorified, **Al-Ḥalīm** (The Forbearer) may He be glorified, **Al-ʿAẓīm** (The Magnificent) may He be glorified, **Al-Ghafūr** (The Forgiving) may He be glorified, **Al-Shakūr** (The Benefactor) may He be glorified, **Al-ʿAlī** (The High) may He be glorified, **Al-Kabīr** (The Greatest) may He be glorified, **Al-Ḥafīẓ** (The Preserver) may He be glorified, **Al-Muqīt** (The Nourisher) may He be glorified, **Al-Ḥasīb** (The Reckoner) may He be glorified, **Al-Jalīl** (The Glorious) may He be glorified, **Al-Karīm** (The Generous) may He be glorified, **Al-Raqīb** (The Observer) may He be glorified,

اَلْـمُجِيْبُ جَـلَّ جَلالُهٗ اَلْوَاسِعُ جَـلَّ جَلالُهٗ اَلْـحَكِيْمُ جَـلَّ جَلالُهٗ اَلْوَدُوْدُ جَـلَّ جَلالُهٗ
اَلْمَجِيْدُ جَلَّ جَلالُهٗ اَلْبَاعِثُ جَلَّ جَلالُهٗ اَلشَّهِيْدُ جَلَّ جَلالُهٗ اَلْحَقُّ جَلَّ جَلالُهٗ اَلْوَكِيْلُ
جَلَّ جَلالُهٗ اَلْقَوِىُّ جَلَّ جَلالُهٗ اَلْمَتِيْنُ جَلَّ جَلالُهٗ اَلْوَلِىُّ جَلَّ جَلالُهٗ اَلْحَمِيْدُ جَلَّ جَلالُهٗ
اَلْـمُحْصِىْ جَـلَّ جَلالُهٗ اَلْمُبْدِئُ جَـلَّ جَلالُهٗ اَلْمُعِيْدُ جَـلَّ جَلالُهٗ اَلْـمُحْىِ جَـلَّ جَلالُهٗ
اَلْمُمِيْتُ جَلَّ جَلالُهٗ اَلْحَىُّ جَلَّ جَلالُهٗ اَلْقَيُّوْمُ جَلَّ جَلالُهٗ اَلْوَاجِدُ جَلَّ جَلالُهٗ اَلْمَاجِدُ
جَلَّ جَلالُهٗ اَلْوَاحِدُ جَلَّ جَلالُهٗ اَلْاَحَدُ جَلَّ جَلالُهٗ اَلصَّمَدُ جَلَّ جَلالُهٗ اَلْقَادِرُ جَلَّ جَلالُهٗ
اَلْمُقْتَدِرُ جَلَّ جَلالُهٗ اَلْمُقَدِّمُ جَلَّ جَلالُهٗ اَلْمُؤَخِّرُ جَلَّ جَلالُهٗ اَلْاَوَّلُ جَلَّ جَلالُهٗ اَلْاٰخِرُ
جَلَّ جَلالُهٗ اَلظَّاهِرُ جَلَّ جَلالُهٗ اَلْبَاطِنُ جَلَّ جَلالُهٗ اَلْوَالِىْ جَلَّ جَلالُهٗ اَلْمُتَعَالِىْ جَلَّ جَلالُهٗ
اَلْبَرُّ جَلَّ جَلالُهٗ اَلتَّوَّابُ جَلَّ جَلالُهٗ اَلْمُنْتَقِمُ جَلَّ جَلالُهٗ اَلْعَفُوُّ جَلَّ جَلالُهٗ اَلرَّءُوْفُ جَلَّ
جَلالُهٗ مَالِكُ الْمُلْكِ جَلَّ جَلالُهٗ ذُوالْجَلَالِ وَالْاِكْرَامِ جَلَّ جَلالُهٗ اَلْمُقْسِطُ جَلَّ
جَلالُهٗ اَلْجَامِعُ جَلَّ جَلالُهٗ اَلْغَنِىُّ جَلَّ جَلالُهٗ اَلْمُغْنِىْ جَلَّ جَلالُهٗ اَلْمُعْطِىْ جَلَّ جَلالُهٗ
اَلْمَانِعُ جَلَّ جَلالُهٗ اَلضَّآرُّ جَلَّ جَلالُهٗ اَلنَّافِعُ جَلَّ جَلالُهٗ اَلنُّوْرُ جَلَّ جَلالُهٗ اَلْهَادِىْ جَلَّ
جَلالُهٗ اَلْبَدِيْعُ جَـلَّ جَلالُهٗ اَلْبَاقِىْ جَـلَّ جَلالُهٗ اَلْوَارِثُ جَـلَّ جَلالُهٗ اَلرَّشِيْدُ جَـلَّ جَلالُهٗ
اَلصَّبُوْرُ ۝

تَمَّتْ

وَاِذَا رَاَيْتَ النَّفْسَ مِنْكَ تَحَكَّمَتْ ۝
وَغَدَتْ تَقُوْدُكَ فِىْ لَظَى الشَّهَوَاتِ ۝
فَاصْرِفْ هَوَاهَا بِالصَّلٰوةِ مُوَاظِبًا ۝
لَا سِيَّمَا بِدَلَآئِلِ الْخَيْرٰتِ ۝

Al-Mujīb (The Responsive) may He be glorified, **Al-Wāsi**[c] (The Embracing) may He be glorified, **Al-Ḥakīm** (The Wise) may He be glorified, **Al-Wadūd** (The Loving) may He be glorified, **Al-Majīd** (The Majestic) may He be glorified, **Al-Bā**[c]**ith** (The Resurrector) may He be glorified, **Al-Shahīd** (The Witness) may He be glorified, **Al-Ḥaqq** (The Truth) may He be glorified, **Al-Wakīl** (The Provident) may He be glorified, **Al-Qawī** (The Strong) may He be glorified, **Al-Matīn** (The Firm) may He be glorified, **Al-Walī** (The Protecting Friend) may He be glorified, **Al-Ḥamīd** (The Praiseworthy) may He be glorified, **Al-Muḥṣī** (The Calculator) may He be glorified, **Al-Mubdi**ᵓ (The Originator) may He be glorified, **Al-Mu**[c]**īd** (The Renewer) may He be glorified, **Al-Muḥyī** (The Life-Giver) may He be glorified, **Al-Mumīt** (The Giver of Death) may He be glorified, **Al-Ḥayy** (The Living) may He be glorified, **Al-Qayyūm** (The Self-Existing) may He be glorified, **Al-Wājid** (The Present) may He be glorified, **Al-Mājid** (The Most Glorious) may He be glorified, **Al-Wāḥid** (The Unique) may He be glorified, **Al-Aḥad** (The One) may He be glorified, **Al-Ṣamad** (The Eternal) may He be glorified, **Al-Qādir** (The Able) may He be glorified, **Al-Muqtadir** (The Powerful) may He be glorified, **Al-Muqaddim** (The Expediter) may He be glorified, **Al-Mu**ᵓ**akhkhir** (The Delayer) may He be glorified, **Al-Awwal** (The First) may He be glorified, **Al-Ākhir** (The Last) may He be glorified, **Al-Ẓāhir** (The Manifest) may He be glorified, **Al-Bāṭin** (The Hidden) may He be glorified, **Al-Wālī** (The Governor) may He be glorified, **Al-Muta**[c]**ālī** (The Supreme) may He be glorified, **Al-Barr** (The Good) may He be glorified, **Al-Tawwāb** (The Acceptor of Repentance) may He be glorified, **Al-Muntaqim** (The Avenger) may He be glorified, **Al-**[c]**Afū** (The Pardoner) may He be glorified, **Al-Ra**ᵓ**ūf** (The Gentle) may He be glorified, **Mālik al-Mulk** (The Eternal Sovereign) may He be glorified, **Dhū -Jalāl wa-l-Ikrām** (The Lord of Glory and Nobility) may He be glorified, **Al-Muqsaṭ** (The Equitable) may He be glorified, **Al-Jāmi**[c] (The Gatherer) may He be glorified, **Al-Ghanī** (The Self-Sufficient) may He be glorified, **Al-Mughnī** (The Enricher) may He be glorified, **Al-Mu**[c]**ṭī** (The Giver) may He be glorified, **Al-Māni**[c] (The Withholder) may He be glorified, **Al-Ḍārr** (The Loss-Causer) may He be glorified, **Al-Nāfi**[c] (The Favorer) may He be glorified, **Al-Nūr** (The Light) may He be glorified, **Al-Hādī** (The Guide) may He be glorified, **Al-Badī**[c] (The Originator) may He be glorified, **Al-Bāqī** (The Everlasting) may He be glorified, **Al-Wārith** (The Inheritor) may He be glorified, **Al-Rashīd** (The Guide to the Right Path) may He be glorified, **Al-Sabūr** (The Patient). It is completed.

And if you see the Ego controlling you,
And it comes to lead you into the Fire of Desires,
Banish its desires by continuous blessing,
There is nothing to compare with *The Guide to Goodness*!

بِـدَلاَئِلِ الْـخَيْـرٰتِ كُـنْ مُّتَـمَسِّـكًـا ۝

وَالْـزِمْ قِـرَآءَتَهَـا تَـنَـلْ مَـا تَبْتَـغِـىْ ۝

فَشَـوَارِقُ الْاَنْـوَارِ لآئِـحَةٌ بِهَـا ۝

فَـالتَّـرْكُ مِنْكَ لَهَـا اَخِىْ لاَ يَنْبَغِـىْ ۝

دَلاَئِلُ الْخَيْرات

دُعَآءُ الْاِفْتِتَاحِ

بِسْمِ اللّٰهِ الرَّحْمٰنِ الرَّحِيْمِ ۝

وَصَلَّى اللّٰهُ عَلٰى سَيِّدِنَا مُحَمَّدٍ وَّآلِهٖ وَصَحْبِهٖ وَسَلَّمَ ۝ اِلٰهِىْ بِجَاهِ نَبِيِّكَ سَيِّدِنَا مُحَمَّدٍ صَلَّى اللّٰهُ عَلَيْهِ وَسَلَّمَ عِنْدَكَ وَمَكَانَتِهٖ لَدَيْكَ وَمَحَبَّتِكَ لَهٗ وَمَحَبَّتِهٖ لَكَ ۝ وَبِالسِّرِّ الَّذِىْ بَيْنَكَ وَبَيْنَهٗ ۝ اَسْئَلُكَ اَنْ تُصَلِّيَ وَتُسَلِّمَ عَلَيْهِ وَعَلٰى اٰلِهٖ وَصَحْبِهٖ وَضَاعِفِ اللّٰهُمَّ مَحَبَّتِىْ فِيْهِ وَعَرِّفْنِىْ بِحَقِّهٖ وَرُتَبِهٖ وَوَفِّقْنِىْ لِاتِّبَاعِهٖ وَالْقِيَامِ بِاَدَبِهٖ وَسُنَّتِهٖ وَاجْمَعْنِىْ عَلَيْهِ وَمَتِّعْنِىْ بِرُؤْيَتِهٖ وَاَسْعِدْنِىْ بِمُكَالَمَتِهٖ وَارْفَعْ عَنِّى الْعَوَآئِقَ وَالْعَلاَئِقَ وَالْوَسَآئِطَ وَالْحِجَابَ وَشَنِّفْ سَمْعِىْ مَعَهٗ بِلَذِيْذِ الْخِطَابِ ۝ وَهَيِّئْنِىْ لِلتَّلَقِّىْ مِنْهُ وَ اَهِّلْنِىْ لِخِدْمَتِهٖ ۝ وَاجْعَلْ صَلٰوتِىْ عَلَيْهِ نُوْرًا نَّيِّرًا كَامِلاً مُّكَمَّلاً طَاهِرًا مُّطَهِّرًا مَّاحِيًا كُلَّ ظُلْمٍ وَّظُلْمَةٍ وَّشَكٍّ وَّشِرْكٍ وَّ كُفْرٍ وَّ زُوْرٍ وَّ وِزْرٍ وَّاجْعَلْهَا سَبَبًا لِّلتَّمْحِيْصِ وَمَرْقًى لِّاَنَالَ بِهَآ اَعْلٰى مَقَامِ الْاِخْلاَصِ وَالتَّخْصِيْصِ حَتّٰى لاَ يَبْقٰى فِىَّ رَبَّانِيَّةٌ لِّغَيْرِكَ وَحَتّٰىٓ اَصْلُحَ لِحَضْرَتِكَ وَاَكُوْنَ مِنْ اَهْلِ خُصُوْصِيَّتِكَ مُسْتَمْسِكًا بِاَدَبِهٖ وَسُنَّتِهٖ صَلَّى اللّٰهُ عَلَيْهِ وَاٰلِهٖ وَاَصْحَابِهٖ وَاَهْلِ بَيْتِهٖٓ اَجْمَعِيْنَ فِىْ كُلِّ وَقْتٍ وَّحِيْنٍ ۝ يَآاَللّٰهُ يَا نُوْرُ يَا حَقُّ يَا مُبِيْنُ ۝ ثَلٰثًا ۝

With *The Guide to Goodness* you must be firm,
Read it to obtain your wishes,
Lights appear and blaze thereby,
It is never to be abandoned!

The Opening Supplication

In the Name of God, the Merciful, the Compassionate

The blessings and peace of God be upon our master Muḥammad, his Family and his Companions!

O my God, for the sake of the honor of Your Prophet, our master Muḥammad, God's blessings and peace be upon him, in the sight of You, and for the sake of his position in Your Presence, and for the sake of Your love for him and his love for You, and for the sake of the secret which is between You and him, I ask You to bless and grant peace to him, his family and his Companions, and that You multiply my love for him and acquaint me with his reality and rank, make me fit to follow him and uphold his manners and his way, join me with him and allow me a vision of him, and encourage me with his conversation free of all hindrances, attachments, means and veils pleasing my ears with the delights of his addressing me!

And prepare me to meet him and make me fit for his service! And make my request for Your blessing him a perfect and absolutely pure and purified shining light which dispels all darkness and gloom, all doubt and association, all unbelief, all falsehood and all iniquity, and make it a means of my increasing in sincerity and a way of obtaining the highest station of sincerity and distinction so that there remains for me no lord but You and so that I am fit for Your Presence and I am one of Your distinguished people holding firm to his manners and his way, God's blessings and peace be upon him, his Family, his Companions, and all the People of his House at every moment and on every occasion!

O God,
O Light,
O Truth,
O Manifest One!
(three times)

مُقَدِّمَة

اَلْحَمْدُ لِلّٰهِ وَالصَّلوٰةُ وَالسَّلَامُ عَلٰى سَيِّدِنَا مُحَمَّدٍ وَّاٰلِهٖ وَصَحْبِهٖ وَسَلَّمَ ۞ قَالَ الشَّيْخُ الْإِمَامُ الْوَلِيُّ الْكَبِيْرُ الْقُطْبُ الشَّهِيْرُ سُلْطَانُ الْمُقَرَّبِيْنَ وَقُطْبُ دَآئِرَةِ الْمُحَقِّقِيْنَ ۞ وَسَيِّدُ الْعَارِفِيْنَ ۞ صَاحِبُ الْكَرَامَاتِ الظَّاهِرَةِ وَالْاَسْرَارِ الْبَاهِرَةِ ۞ سَيِّدِيْ اَبُوْ عَبْدِ اللّٰهِ **مُحَمَّدُ** بْنُ سُلَيْمَانَ الْجَزُوْلِيْ رَضِيَ اللّٰهُ عَنْهُ ۞ اَلْحَمْدُ لِلّٰهِ الَّذِيْ هَدَانَا لِلْاِيْمَانِ وَالْاِسْلَامِ ۞ وَالصَّلوٰةُ وَالسَّلَامُ عَلٰى سَيِّدِنَا مُحَمَّدٍ نَّبِيِّهِ الَّذِى اسْتَنْقَذَنَا بِهٖ مِنْ عِبَادَةِ الْاَوْثَانِ وَالْاَصْنَامِ ۞ وَعَلٰى اٰلِهٖ وَاَصْحَابِهِ النُّجَبَآءِ الْبَرَرَةِ الْكِرَامِ ۞ **وَبَعْدَ هٰذَا** فَالْغَرَضُ فِيْ هٰذَا الْكِتَابِ ذِكْرُ الصَّلوٰةِ عَلَى النَّبِيِّ صَلَّى اللّٰهُ عَلَيْهِ وَسَلَّمَ وَفَضَآئِلُهَا نَذْكُرُهَا مَحْذُوْفَةَ الْاَسَانِيْدِ لِيَسْهَلَ حِفْظُهَا عَلَى الْقَارِءِ وَهِيَ مِنْ اَهَمِّ الْمُهِمَّاتِ لِمَنْ يُّرِيْدُ الْقُرْبَ مِنْ رَّبِّ الْاَرْبَابِ ۞ وَسَمَّيْتُهٗ بِكِتَابِ دَلَآئِلِ الْخَيْرَاتِ وَشَوَارِقِ الْاَنْوَارِ فِيْ ذِكْرِ الصَّلوٰةِ عَلَى النَّبِيِّ الْمُخْتَارِ ۞ اِبْتِغَآءً لِّمَرْضَاتِ اللّٰهِ تَعَالٰى وَمَحَبَّةً فِيْ رَسُوْلِهِ الْكَرِيْمِ سَيِّدِنَا مُحَمَّدٍ صَلَّى اللّٰهُ عَلَيْهِ وَسَلَّمَ تَسْلِيْمًا ۞ وَّاللّٰهُ الْمَسْئُوْلُ اَنْ يَّجْعَلَنَا لِسُنَّتِهٖ مِنَ التَّابِعِيْنَ ۞ وَلِذَاتِهِ الْكَامِلَةِ مِنَ الْمُحِبِّيْنَ ۞ فَاِنَّهٗ عَلٰى ذَالِكَ قَدِيْرٌ ۞ لَآ اِلٰهَ غَيْرُهٗ وَلَا خَيْرَ اِلَّا خَيْرُهٗ ۞ وَهُوَ نِعْمَ الْمَوْلٰى وَنِعْمَ النَّصِيْرُ ۞ وَلَا حَوْلَ وَلَا قُوَّةَ اِلَّا بِاللّٰهِ الْعَلِيِّ الْعَظِيْمِ ۞ **فَصْلٌ** فِيْ فَضْلِ الصَّلوٰةِ عَلَى النَّبِيِّ صَلَّى اللّٰهُ عَلَيْهِ وَسَلَّمَ ۞ قَالَ اللّٰهُ عَزَّوَجَلَّ اِنَّ اللّٰهَ وَمَلٰٓئِكَتَهٗ يُصَلُّوْنَ عَلَى النَّبِيِّ ط يٰٓاَيُّهَا الَّذِيْنَ اٰمَنُوْا صَلُّوْا عَلَيْهِ وَسَلِّمُوْا تَسْلِيْمًا ۞ وَيُرْوٰى اَنَّ رَسُوْلَ اللّٰهِ صَلَّى اللّٰهُ عَلَيْهِ وَسَلَّمَ جَآءَ ذَاتَ يَوْمٍ وَّالْبُشْرٰى تُرٰى فِيْ وَجْهِهٖ فَقَالَ اِنَّهٗ جَآءَنِيْ جِبْرِيْلُ عَلَيْهِ السَّلَامُ فَقَالَ لِيْ اَمَا

(AUTHOR'S) FOREWORD

Praise be to God and blessings and peace be upon our master Muḥammad, his family and his Companions!

The Sheikh, the Imam, the great saint, the renowned pole, the sultan of the near ones and pole of the true ones, the master of the gnostics, the possessor of open miracles and abundant secrets, Sayyidī Abū ᶜAbd Allāh Muḥammad ibn Sulaymān ibn Abū Bakr al-Jazūlī, may God be pleased with, said:

Praise be to God who has guided us to faith and to Islam!

And blessings and peace be upon our master Muḥammad, His Prophet, who has delivered us from worshipping graven images and idols!

The subject of this book is remembering to ask for blessings upon the Prophet, God's blessings and peace be upon him, and its benefits. We mention the traditions without the chains of transmission in order to make it easier for the reader to memorize them, this being one of the important essentials for the one seeking nearness to the Lord of Lords!I have named this book *The Guide to Goodness and the Advent of Blazing Lights in Remembering to ask for Blessings upon the Prophet* desiring the pleasure of God the Exalted and love for His noble Messenger, our master Muḥammad, God's blessings and abundant peace be upon him!

And God is responsible for making us follow his way, and making us love the perfect ones, for He is Able to do this. There is no god save He and there is no good save His good!

And He is the best Protector and best Helper! And there is no help nor power save through God, the High, the Mighty!

THE BENEFIT OF REQUESTING BLESSINGS UPON THE PROPHET, GOD'S BLESSINGS AND PEACE BE UPON HIM AND HIS FAMILY

God, Mighty and Sublime is He, said: "Verily, God and His angels bless the Prophet. O you who believe, ask (God) to bless him and grant him abundant peace!"

And it is related that the Messenger of God, God's blessings and peace be upon him, came one day with the signs of good tidings visible upon his face. He said: "Lo, Gabriel, peace be upon him, said to me, "Are

تَرْضٰى يَا مُحَمَّدُ اَنْ لَّا يُصَلِّىْ عَلَيْكَ اَحَدٌ مِّنْ اُمَّتِكَ اِلَّا صَلَّيْتُ عَلَيْهِ عَشْرًا ۝ وَّلَا يُسَلِّمَ عَلَيْكَ اَحَدٌ مِّنْ اُمَّتِكَ اِلَّا سَلَّمْتُ عَلَيْهِ عَشْرًا ۝ وَّقَالَ صَلَّى اللّٰهُ عَلَيْهِ وَسَلَّمَ اِنَّ اَوْلَى النَّاسِ بِىْ اَكْثَرُهُمْ عَلَىَّ صَلٰوةً ۝ وَّقَالَ صَلَّى اللّٰهُ عَلَيْهِ وَسَلَّمَ مَنْ صَلّٰى عَلَىَّ صَلَّتْ عَلَيْهِ الْمَلٰٓئِكَةُ مَا دَامَ يُصَلِّىْ عَلَىَّ فَلْيُقَلِّلْ عِنْدَ ذٰلِكَ اَوْ لِيُكَثِّرْ ۝ وَقَالَ صَلَّى اللّٰهُ عَلَيْهِ وَسَلَّمَ بِحَسْبِ الْمَرْءِ مِنَ الْبُخْلِ اَنْ اُذْكَرَ عِنْدَهٗ وَلَا يُصَلِّىْ عَلَىَّ ۝ وَقَالَ صَلَّى اللّٰهُ عَلَيْهِ وَسَلَّمَ اَكْثِرُوا الصَّلٰوةَ عَلَىَّ يَوْمَ الْجُمُعَةِ ۝ وَقَالَ صَلَّى اللّٰهُ عَلَيْهِ وَسَلَّمَ مَنْ صَلّٰى عَلَىَّ مِنْ اُمَّتِىْ مَرَّةً وَّاحِدَةً كُتِبَتْ لَهٗ عَشْرُ حَسَنَاتٍ وَّ مُحِيَتْ عَنْهُ عَشْرُ سَيِّاٰتٍ وَّقَالَ صَلَّى اللّٰهُ عَلَيْهِ وَسَلَّمَ مَنْ قَالَ حِيْنَ يَسْمَعُ الْاَذَانَ وَالْاِقَامَةَ ۝ اَللّٰهُمَّ رَبَّ هٰذِهِ الدَّعْوَةِ التَّآمَّةِ وَالصَّلٰوةِ الْقَآئِمَةِ اٰتِ مُحَمَّدًا نِ الْوَسِيْلَةَ وَالْفَضِيْلَةَ وَالدَّرَجَةَ الرَّفِيْعَةَ وَابْعَثْهُ مَقَامًا مَّحْمُوْدًا نِ الَّذِىْ وَعَدْتَّهٗ حَلَّتْ لَهٗ شَفَاعَتِىْ يَوْمَ الْقِيٰمَةِ ۝ وَقَالَ صَلَّى اللّٰهُ عَلَيْهِ وَسَلَّمَ مَنْ صَلّٰى عَلَىَّ فِىْ كِتَابٍ لَّمْ تَزَلِ الْمَلٰٓئِكَةُ تُصَلِّىْ عَلَيْهِ مَا دَامَ اِسْمِىْ فِىْ ذٰلِكَ الْكِتَابِ ۝ وَقَالَ اَبُوْ سُلَيْمٰنَ الدَّارَانِىُّ مَنْ اَرَادَ اَنْ يَّسْئَلَ اللّٰهَ حَاجَتَهٗ فَلْيُكْثِرْ بِالصَّلٰوةِ عَلَى النَّبِىِّ صَلَّى اللّٰهُ عَلَيْهِ وَسَلَّمَ ثُمَّ يَسْئَلُ اللّٰهَ حَاجَتَهٗ وَلْيَخْتِمْ بِالصَّلٰوةِ عَلَى النَّبِىِّ صَلَّى اللّٰهُ عَلَيْهِ وَسَلَّمَ فَاِنَّ اللّٰهَ يَقْبَلُ الصَّلٰوتَيْنِ وَهُوَ اَكْرَمُ مِنْ اَنْ يَّدَعَ مَا بَيْنَهُمَا ۝ وَرُوِىَ عَنْهُ صَلَّى اللّٰهُ عَلَيْهِ وَسَلَّمَ اَنَّهٗ قَالَ مَنْ صَلّٰى عَلَىَّ يَوْمَ الْجُمُعَةِ مِائَةَ مَرَّةٍ غُفِرَتْ لَهٗ خَطِيْئَةُ ثَمَانِيْنَ سَنَةً ۝ وَعَنْ اَبِىْ هُرَيْرَةَ رَضِىَ اللّٰهُ عَنْهُ اَنَّ رَسُوْلَ اللّٰهِ صَلَّى اللّٰهُ عَلَيْهِ وَسَلَّمَ قَالَ لِلْمُصَلِّىْ عَلَىَّ نُوْرٌ عَلَى الصِّرَاطِ وَمَنْ كَانَ عَلَى الصِّرَاطِ مِنْ اَهْلِ النُّوْرِ لَمْ يَكُنْ مِّنْ اَهْلِ النَّارِ ۝ وَقَالَ صَلَّى اللّٰهُ عَلَيْهِ

you not pleased, O Muḥammad, that whenever one of your nation asks God to bless you, God will bless him tenfold and that whenever one of your nation asks God to grant you peace, God will grant him peace tenfold."

And he said, God's blessings and peace be upon him: "The nearest person to me is the one who asks for blessings upon me the most."

And he said, God's blessings and peace be upon him: "Whoever asks for blessings upon me, angels are blessing him for as long as he asks, be it for a short time, be it for a long time."

And he said, God's blessings and peace be upon him: "A person is considered a miser if, when I am mentioned in his presence, he fails to ask for blessings upon me."

And he said, God's blessings and peace be upon him: "Ask for more blessings upon me on Fridays."

And he said, God's blessings and peace be upon him: "Whoever of my nation asks for blessings upon me once, ten good deeds are written down for him and ten sins are erased."

And he said, God's blessings and peace be upon him: "Whoever hears the call to prayer and says, 'O God, Lord of this perfect call and this established prayer, grant Muḥammad the closest access, the pre-eminence, the lofty rank and send him to the most praised station which You have promised him,' my intercession for him will be binding on the Day of Resurrection!" And he said, God's blessings and peace be upon him: "Whoever asks for blessings upon me in a book, the angels bless him for as long as my name is in that book."

And Abū Sulaymān al-Darānī said, "Whoever wishes to request something from God, let him increase his asking for blessings upon the Prophet, God's blessings and peace be upon him, and then he may ask God about his affair and then seal his request by once more asking for blessings upon the Prophet, God's blessings and peace be upon him. For God will accept the two requests for blessings upon the Prophet and this is something more noble than whatever he asks for in between."

And it is related that he said, God's blessings and peace be upon him: "Whoever asks God one hundred times to bless me on a Friday will be forgiven the sins of eighty years." And Abū Hurayrā, may God be pleased with him, said, "The Messenger of God, God's blessings and peace be upon him, said, 'For the one who asks for blessings upon me there is a light on the Bridge, and whoever is on the Bridge from the People of Light will not be among the People of the Fire.'"

And he said, God's blessings

وَسَلَّمَ مَنْ نَّسِيَ الصَّلٰوةَ عَلَيَّ فَقَدْ اَخطَا طَرِيْقَ الْجَنَّةِ وَاِنَّمَآ اَرَادَ بِالنِّسْيَانِ التَّرْكَ
وَاِذَا كَانَ التَّارِكُ يُخْطِئُ طَرِيْقَ الْجَنَّةِ كَانَ الْمُصَلِّيْ عَلَيْهِ سَالِكًا اِلَى الْجَنَّةِ ۝
وَفِيْ رِوَايَةِ عَبْدِالرَّحْمٰنِ ابْنِ عَوْفٍ رَّضِيَ اللّٰهُ عَنْهُ قَالَ رَسُوْلُ اللّٰهِ صَلَّى اللّٰهُ
عَلَيْهِ وَسَلَّمَ جَآءَنِيْ جِبْرِيْلُ عَلَيْهِ السَّلَامُ فَقَالَ يَا مُحَمَّدُ لَا يُصَلِّيْ عَلَيْكَ اَحَدٌ
مِّنْ اُمَّتِكَ اِلَّا صَلّٰى عَلَيْهِ سَبْعُوْنَ اَلْفَ مَلَكٍ وَّمَنْ صَلَّتْ عَلَيْهِ الْمَلٰٓئِكَةُ كَانَ مِنْ
اَهْلِ الْجَنَّةِ ۝ وَقَالَ صَلَّى اللّٰهُ عَلَيْهِ وَسَلَّمَ اَكْثَرُكُمْ عَلَيَّ صَلٰوةً اَكْثَرُكُمْ اَزْوَاجًا
فِي الْجَنَّةِ ۝ وَرُوِيَ عَنْهُ صَلَّى اللّٰهُ عَلَيْهِ وَسَلَّمَ اَنَّهٗ قَالَ مَنْ صَلّٰى عَلَيَّ صَلٰوةً
تَعْظِيْمًا لِّحَقِّيْ خَلَقَ اللّٰهُ عَزَّوَجَلَّ مِنْ ذٰلِكَ الْقَوْلِ مَلَكًا لَّهٗ جَنَاحٌ بِالْمَشْرِقِ
وَالْاٰخَرُ بِالْمَغْرِبِ وَرِجْلَاهُ مَقْرُوْرَتَانِ فِي الْاَرْضِ السَّابِعَةِ السُّفْلٰى وَعُنُقُهٗ مُلْتَوِيَةٌ
تَحْتَ الْعَرْشِ يَقُوْلُ اللّٰهُ عَزَّوَجَلَّ لَهٗ صَلِّ عَلٰى عَبْدِيْ كَمَا صَلّٰى عَلٰى نَبِيِّيْ فَهُوَ
يُصَلِّيْ عَلَيْهِ اِلٰى يَوْمِ الْقِيٰمَةِ ۝ وَرُوِيَ عَنْهُ صَلَّى اللّٰهُ عَلَيْهِ وَسَلَّمَ اَنَّهٗ قَالَ لَيَرِدَنَّ
عَلَيَّ الْحَوْضَ يَوْمَ الْقِيٰمَةِ اَقْوَامٌ مَّآ اَعْرِفُهُمْ اِلَّا بِكَثْرَةِ الصَّلٰوةِ عَلَيَّ ۝ وَرُوِيَ عَنْهُ
صَلَّى اللّٰهُ عَلَيْهِ وَسَلَّمَ اَنَّهٗ قَالَ مَنْ صَلّٰى عَلَيَّ مَرَّةً وَّاحِدَةً صَلَّى اللّٰهُ عَلَيْهِ عَشْرَ
مَرَّاتٍ وَّمَنْ صَلّٰى عَلَيَّ عَشْرَ مَرَّاتٍ صَلَّى اللّٰهُ عَلَيْهِ مِائَةَ مَرَّةٍ وَّمَنْ صَلّٰى عَلَيَّ
مِائَةَ مَرَّةٍ صَلَّى اللّٰهُ عَلَيْهِ اَلْفَ مَرَّةٍ وَّمَنْ صَلّٰى عَلَيَّ اَلْفَ مَرَّةٍ حَرَّمَ اللّٰهُ
جَسَدَهٗ عَلَى النَّارِ وَثَبَّتَهٗ بِالْقَوْلِ الثَّابِتِ فِي الْحَيٰوةِ الدُّنْيَا وَفِي الْاٰخِرَةِ عِنْدَ
الْمَسْئَلَةِ وَاَدْخَلَهُ الْجَنَّةَ وَجَآءَتْ صَلٰوتُهٗ عَلَيَّ نُوْرٌ لَّهٗ يَوْمَ الْقِيٰمَةِ عَلَى الصِّرَاطِ
مَسِيْرَةَ خَمْسِ مِائَةِ عَامٍ وَّاَعْطَاهُ اللّٰهُ بِكُلِّ صَلٰوةٍ صَلَّاهَا قَصْرًا فِي الْجَنَّةِ قَلَّ
ذٰلِكَ اَوْ كَثُرَ ۝ وَقَالَ النَّبِيُّ صَلَّى اللّٰهُ عَلَيْهِ وَسَلَّمَ مَا مِنْ عَبْدٍ صَلّٰى عَلَيَّ اِلَّا

and peace be upon him, "Whoever deliberately neglects to ask for blessings upon me has missed the path to the Garden, for the route to the Garden is barred for such a neglectful one, whereas it is open for him who asks blessings upon me."

"It is related by ᶜAbd al-Raḥmān ibn ᶜAwf, may God be pleased with him, that he said, "God's blessings and peace be upon him: "

Gabriel, peace be upon him, came to me and said,

"O Muḥammad, whenever someone from your nation asks for blessings upon you, seventy thousand angels bless him, and whomever is blessed by angels is one of the people of the Garden."

And he said, God's blessings and peace be upon him: "The more you ask for blessings upon me, the more you will have in the Garden."

It is related that he said, God's blessings and peace be upon him: "Whenever someone asks for blessings upon me, extolling my right, God, Mighty and Sublime is He, creates from his words an angel with wings stretching from the East to the West, with feet connected to the nethermost part of the seventh earth and a neck bent beneath the Throne. "

God, Mighty and Sublime is He, says to him, "Bless My servant as he asks for blessings upon My Prophet and thereupon the angel will bless him until the Day of Resurrection."

It is related that he said, God's blessings and peace be upon him: "There will come to my pool on the Day of Resurrection nations I will only know because of their frequent asking for blessings upon me."

It is related that he said, God's blessings and peace be upon him: "Whoever asks God to bless me, God will bless him ten times.

"And whoever asks God ten times to bless me, God will bless him one hundred times.

"And whoever asks God one hundred times to bless me, God will bless him one thousand times.

"And whoever asks God one thousand times to bless me, God will prohibit the Fire from touching his body. His word on any matter will be made enduring in this world and the next.

"He will enter the Garden, on the Day of Resurrection his request for blessings upon me will be a light for him on the Bridge, a light visible at a distance of five hundred years.

"And God will grant him, for every blessing upon me asked for, a palace in the Garden, regardless of how many."

And the Prophet said, God's blessings and peace be upon him:

"Whenever a servant asks for blessings upon me,

خَرَجَتِ الصَّلوٰةُ مُسْرِعَةً مِّنْ فِيْهِ فَلَا يَبْقٰى بَرٌّ وَّلَا بَحْرٌ وَّلَا شَرْقٌ وَّلَا غَرْبٌ اِلَّا وَتَمُرُّ بِهٖ وَتَقُوْلُ اَنَا صَلوٰةُ فُلَانِ بْنِ فُلَانٍ صَلّٰى عَلٰى مُحَمَّدِنِ الْمُخْتَارِ خَيْرِ خَلْقِ اللّٰهِ فَلَا يَبْقٰى شَيْءٌ اِلَّا وَصَلّٰى عَلَيْهِ وَيُخْلَقُ مِنْ تِلْكَ الصَّلوٰةِ طَآئِرٌ لَّهٗ سَبْعُوْنَ اَلْفَ جَنَاحٍ فِيْ كُلِّ جَنَاحٍ سَبْعُوْنَ اَلْفَ رِيْشَةٍ فِيْ كُلِّ رِيْشَةٍ سَبْعُوْنَ اَلْفَ رَاْسٍ فِيْ كُلِّ رَاْسٍ سَبْعُوْنَ اَلْفَ وَجْهٍ فِيْ كُلِّ وَجْهٍ سَبْعُوْنَ اَلْفَ فَمٍ فِيْ كُلِّ فَمٍ سَبْعُوْنَ اَلْفَ لِسَانٍ فِيْ كُلِّ لِسَانٍ يُّسَبِّحُ اللّٰهَ تَعَالٰى بِسَبْعِيْنَ اَلْفَ لُغَاتٍ وَّيَكْتُبُ اللّٰهُ لَهٗ ثَوَابَ ذٰلِكَ كُلِّهٖ ○ وَعَنْ عَلِيِّ بْنِ اَبِيْ طَالِبٍ رَضِيَ اللّٰهُ عَنْهُ قَالَ قَالَ رَسُوْلُ اللّٰهِ صَلَّى اللّٰهُ عَلَيْهِ وَسَلَّمَ مَنْ صَلّٰى عَلَيَّ يَوْمَ الْجُمُعَةِ مِائَةَ مَرَّةٍ جَاءَ يَوْمَ الْقِيٰمَةِ وَمَعَهٗ نُوْرٌ لَّوْ قُسِمَ ○ ذَالِكَ النُّوْرُ بَيْنَ الْخَلْقِ كُلِّهِمْ لَوَسِعَهُمْ ○ ذُكِرَ فِيْ بَعْضِ الْاَخْبَارِ مَكْتُوْبٌ عَلٰى سَاقِ الْعَرْشِ مَنِ اشْتَاقَ اِلَيَّ رَحِمْتُهٗ وَمَنْ سَاَلَنِيْ اَعْطَيْتُهٗ وَمَنْ تَقَرَّبَ اِلَيَّ بِالصَّلوٰةِ عَلٰى حَبِيْبِيْ مُحَمَّدٍ غَفَرْتُ لَهٗ ذُنُوْبَهٗ وَلَوْ كَانَتْ مِثْلَ زَبَدِ الْبَحْرِ ○ وَرُوِيَ عَنْ بَعْضِ الصَّحَابَةِ رِضْوَانُ اللّٰهِ عَلَيْهِمْ اَجْمَعِيْنَ اَنَّهٗ قَالَ مَا مِنْ مَّجْلِسٍ يُّصَلّٰى فِيْهِ عَلٰى مُحَمَّدٍ صَلَّى اللّٰهُ عَلَيْهِ وَسَلَّمَ اِلَّا قَامَتْ مِنْهُ رَآئِحَةٌ طَيِّبَةٌ حَتّٰى تَبْلُغَ عِنَانَ السَّمَآءِ فَتَقُوْلُ الْمَلٰٓئِكَةُ هٰذَا مَجْلِسٌ صُلِّيَ فِيْهِ عَلٰى مُحَمَّدٍ صَلَّى اللّٰهُ عَلَيْهِ وَسَلَّمَ ○ ذُكِرَ فِيْ بَعْضِ الْاَخْبَارِ اَنَّ الْعَبْدَ الْمُؤْمِنَ اَوِ الْاَمَةَ الْمُؤْمِنَةَ اِذَا بَدَاَ بِالصَّلوٰةِ عَلٰى مُحَمَّدٍ صَلَّى اللّٰهُ عَلَيْهِ وَسَلَّمَ فُتِحَتْ لَهٗ اَبْوَابُ السَّمَآءِ وَالسُّرَادِقَاتُ حَتّٰى اِلَى الْعَرْشِ فَلَا يَبْقٰى مَلَكٌ فِي السَّمٰوٰتِ اِلَّا صَلّٰى عَلٰى مُحَمَّدٍ صَلَّى اللّٰهُ عَلَيْهِ وَسَلَّمَ وَّيَسْتَغْفِرُوْنَ لِذَالِكَ الْعَبْدِ اَوِ لْاَمَةِ مَا شَآءَ اللّٰهُ ○ وَقَالَ صَلَّى اللّٰهُ عَلَيْهِ وَسَلَّمَ مَنْ عَسُرَتْ عَلَيْهِ حَاجَةٌ فَلْيُكْثِرْ

his request leaves him quickly and passes over land and sea, through East and West, saying,

'I am the blessing upon Muḥammad, the chosen one, the best of God's creation, asked for by so and so and everything asks for blessings upon him.

'A bird is created from these blessings with seventy thousand wings each of which has seventy thousand feathers.

'Each of the feathers has seventy thousand heads on each of which are seventy thousand faces.

'Each face has seventy thousand mouths and in every mouth there are seventy thousand tongues.

'Each tongue glorifies God the Exalted in seventy thousand languages and God will then write for him the reward for all of that!'"

ᶜAlī ibn Abī Ṭālib, may God be pleased with him, said: "The Messenger of God, God's blessings and peace be upon him, said,

'Whoever asks God one hundred times on a Friday to bless me, a light will come for him on the Day of Resurrection, a light which, were it to be divided among them, would be enough for the whole of creation.'"

It is mentioned in the good tidings, "It is written on the leg of the Throne 'Whoever yearns for Me, I am merciful to him. Whoever asks Me, I will grant him his wish.'

"Whoever draws near to Me by asking for blessings upon My beloved Muḥammad, I will forgive him, even if his sins were as plentiful as the foam on the surface of the ocean!"'

And it is related by one of the Companions, may God be pleased with them all, "There is no gathering in which blessings upon Muḥammad, God's blessings and peace be upon him, are asked for but that a beautiful fragrance rises from it which reaches the clouds in the sky and the angels say, 'This is a gathering in which blessings upon Muḥammad, God's blessings and peace be upon him, are being asked for."

Other reports mention that "The gates of the heavens are opened for a believing servant, male or female, who begins by asking for blessings upon Muḥammad, and the pavilions are opened as far as the Throne, and all the angels bless Muḥammad, God's blessings and peace be upon him, and ask for forgiveness for that servant for as long as God wishes."

And he said, God's blessings and peace be upon him: "Whoever is

بِالصَّلٰوةِ عَلَيَّ فَاِنَّهَا تَكْشِفُ الْهُمُوْمَ وَالْغُمُوْمَ وَالْكُرُوْبَ وَتُكْثِرُ الْاَرْزَاقَ وَتَقْضِي الْحَوَآئِجَ ۞ وَعَنْ بَعْضِ الصَّالِحِيْنَ اَنَّهُ قَالَ كَانَ لِيْ جَارٌ نَسَّاخٌ فَمَاتَ فَرَاَيْتُهُ فِي الْمَنَامِ فَقُلْتُ لَهُ مَا فَعَلَ اللّٰهُ بِكَ فَقَالَ غَفَرَلِيْ فَقُلْتُ لَهُ فَبِمَ ذَالِكَ فَقَالَ كُنْتُ اِذَا كَتَبْتُ اِسْمَ مُحَمَّدٍ صَلَّى اللّٰهُ عَلَيْهِ وَسَلَّمَ فِيْ كِتَابٍ صَلَّيْتُ عَلَيْهِ فَاَعْطَانِيْ رَبِّيْ مَا لَاعَيْنٌ رَاَتْ وَلَآ اُذُنٌ سَمِعَتْ وَلَا خَطَرَ عَلٰى قَلْبِ بَشَرٍ ۞ وَعَنْ اَنَسٍ رضـ اَنَّهُ قَالَ قَالَ رَسُوْلُ اللّٰهِ صَلَّى اللّٰهُ عَلَيْهِ وَسَلَّمَ لَا يُؤْمِنُ اَحَدُكُمْ حَتّٰٓى اَكُوْنَ اَحَبَّ اِلَيْهِ مِنْ نَفْسِهٖ وَمَا لِهٖ وَوَلَدِهٖ وَوَالِدِهٖ وَالنَّاسِ اَجْمَعِيْنَ ۞ وَفِيْ حَدِيْثِ عُمَرَ رضـ اَنْتَ اَحَبُّ اِلَيَّ يَا رَسُوْلَ اللّٰهِ مِنْ كُلِّ شَيْءٍ اِلَّا نَفْسِيَ الَّتِيْ بَيْنَ جَنْبَيَّ فَقَالَ لَهُ عَلَيْهِ الصَّلٰوةُ وَالسَّلَامُ لَا تَكُوْنُ مُؤْمِنًا حَتّٰٓى اَكُوْنَ اَحَبَّ اِلَيْكَ مِنْ نَفْسِكَ فَقَالَ عُمَرُ رضـ وَالَّذِيْٓ اَنْزَلَ عَلَيْكَ الْكِتَابَ لَاَنْتَ اَحَبُّ اِلَيَّ مِنْ نَفْسِيَ الَّتِيْ بَيْنَ جَنْبَيَّ فَقَالَ رَسُوْلُ اللّٰهِ صَلَّى اللّٰهُ عَلَيْهِ وَسَلَّمَ اَلْاٰنَ يَا عُمَرُ تَمَّ اِيْمَانُكَ ۞ وَقِيْلَ لِرَسُوْلِ اللّٰهِ صَلَّى اللّٰهُ عَلَيْهِ وَسَلَّمَ مَتٰى اَكُوْنُ مُؤْمِنًا وَفِيْ لَفْظٍ اٰخَرَ مُؤْمِنًا صَادِقًا قَالَ اِذَآ اَحْبَبْتَ اللّٰهَ فَقِيْلَ وَمَتٰى اُحِبُّ اللّٰهَ قَالَ اِذَآ اَحْبَبْتَ رَسُوْلَهُ فَقِيْلَ وَمَتٰى اُحِبُّ رَسُوْلَهُ قَالَ اِذَا اتَّبَعْتَ طَرِيْقَتَهُ وَاسْتَعْمَلْتَ بِسُنَّتِهٖ وَاَحْبَبْتَ بِحُبِّهٖ وَ اَبْغَضْتَ بِبُغْضِهٖ وَوَالَيْتَ بِوِلَايَتِهٖ وَعَادَيْتَ بِعَدَاوَتِهٖ وَيَتَفَاوَتُ النَّاسُ فِي الْاِيْمَانِ عَلٰى قَدْرِ تَفَاوُتِهِمْ فِيْ مَحَبَّتِيْ وَيَتَفَاوَتُوْنَ فِي الْكُفْرِ عَلٰى قَدْرِ تَفَاوُتِهِمْ فِيْ بُغْضِيْ ۞ اَلَا لَآ اِيْمَانَ لِمَنْ لَّا مَحَبَّةَ لَهُ ۞ اَلَا لَآ اِيْمَانَ لِمَنْ لَّا مَحَبَّةَ لَهُ ۞ اَلَا لَآ اِيْمَانَ لِمَنْ لَّا مَحَبَّةَ لَهُ ۞ وَ قِيْلَ لِرَسُوْلِ اللّٰهِ صَلَّى اللّٰهُ عَلَيْهِ وَسَلَّمَ نَرٰى مُؤْمِنًا يَّخْشَعُ وَ مُؤْمِنًا لَّا يَخْشَعُ مَا السَّبَبُ فِيْ ذٰلِكَ فَقَالَ مَنْ وَّجَدَ لِاِيْمَانِهٖ حَلَاوَةً خَشَعَ وَمَنْ

troubled by some matter should increase his asking for blessings upon me, and that will remove his anxieties, his sorrows and cares and will increase his provision and satisfy all his needs."

And one of the righteous said: "A neighbor of mine was a scribe and he died. I saw him in a dream and asked him how God had treated him. He replied, 'He has forgiven me.' I said, 'For what reason has He forgiven you?' and he replied, 'Whenever I wrote the name of Muḥammad, God's blessings and peace be upon him, in a book, I asked God to bless him and thus My Lord has given me what no eye has ever seen, no ear has ever heard and what no mortal has ever imagined!'"

And it is related from Anas, may God be pleased with him, that he said, God's blessings and peace be upon him:

"None of you truly believe until I am dearer to him than his own self, his wealth, his children, his parents and all other people." And it is related in the Tradition of ᶜUmar, may God be pleased with him, that he said: "You are dearer to me, O Messenger of God, than everything I possess except my own self which is within me."

The Messenger of God, God's blessings and peace be upon him, replied: "You will not be a believer until I am dearer to you than your own self." ᶜUmar said: "By Him who revealed to you the Book, you are dearer to me than my own self!" The Messenger of God, God's blessings and peace be upon him, said to him; "Now, O ᶜUmar, your faith is complete!"

And it was asked of the Messenger of God, God's blessings and peace be upon him: "When will I attain faith?" (and in another version, "When will I attain true faith?")

He replied:"When you love God." It was said: "And when will I love God?" He said: "When you love His Messenger." It was said: "And when will I love His Messenger?" He said: "When you follow his path, adhere to his way, love what he loves and hate what he hates, befriend whom he befriends and oppose whom he opposes—and people will be distinguished one from another in their unbelief according to their hate for me."

Can there be faith for the one who has no love for him?

Can there be faith for the one who has no love for him?

Can there be faith for the one who has no love for him?

It was said to the Messenger of God, God's blessings and peace be upon him: "We see believers who are humble and believers who are not humble. What is the reason for this?"

He said: "The one finds his faith adorned with humility whilst the

لَّمْ يَجِدْهَا لَمْ يَخْشَعْ فَقِيْلَ بِمَ تُوْجَدُ اَوْ بِمَ تُنَالُ وَتُكْتَسَبُ قَالَ بِصِدْقِ الْحُبِّ فِى اللّٰهِ فَقِيْلَ وَبِمَ يُوْجَدُ حُبُّ اللّٰهِ اَوْ بِمَ يُكْتَسَبُ فَقَالَ بِحُبِّ رَسُوْلِهٖ فَالْتَمِسُوْا رِضَآءَ اللّٰهِ وَ رِضَآءَ رَسُوْلِهٖ فِىْ حُبِّهِمَا ۝ وَقِيْلَ لِرَسُوْلِ اللّٰهِ صَلَّى اللّٰهُ عَلَيْهِ وَسَلَّمَ مَنْ اٰلُ مُحَمَّدٍ نِ الَّذِيْنَ اُمِرْنَا بِحُبِّهِمْ وَاِكْرَامِهِمْ وَ الْبُرُوْرِ بِهِمْ فَقَالَ اَهْلُ الصَّفَآءِ وَالْوَفَآءِ مَنْ اٰمَنَ بِىْ وَاَخْلَصَ فَقِيْلَ لَهٗ وَمَا عَلَامَاتُهُمْ فَقَالَ اِيْثَارُ مَحَبَّتِىْ عَلٰى كُلِّ مَحْبُوْبٍ وَّاشْتِغَالُ الْبَاطِنِ بِذِكْرِىْ بَعْدَ ذِكْرِ اللّٰهِ ۝ وَفِىْ اُخْرٰى عَلَامَتُهُمْ اِدْمَانُ ذِكْرِىْ وَالْاِكْثَارُ مِنَ الصَّلٰوةِ عَلَىَّ ۝ وَقِيْلَ لِرَسُوْلِ اللّٰهِ صَلَّى اللّٰهُ عَلَيْهِ وَسَلَّمَ مَنِ الْقَوِىُّ فِى الْاِيْمَانِ بِكَ فَقَالَ مَنْ اٰمَنَ بِىْ وَلَمْ يَرَنِىْ فَاِنَّهٗ مُؤْمِنٌ بِىْ عَلٰى شَوْقٍ مِّنْهُ وَصِدْقٍ فِىْ مَحَبَّتِىْ وَعَلَامَةُ ذٰلِكَ مِنْهُ اَنَّهٗ يَوَدُّ رُؤْيَتِىْ بِجَمِيْعِ مَا يَمْلِكُ ۝ وَفِىْ اُخْرٰى مِلْءُ الْاَرْضِ ذَهَبًا ذٰلِكَ الْمُؤْمِنُ بِىْ حَقًّا وَّالْمُخْلِصُ فِىْ مَحَبَّتِىْ صِدْقًا ۝ وَقِيْلَ لِرَسُوْلِ اللّٰهِ صَلَّى اللّٰهُ عَلَيْهِ وَسَلَّمَ اَرَاَيْتَ صَلٰوةَ الْمُصَلِّيْنَ عَلَيْكَ مِمَّنْ غَابَ عَنْكَ وَمَنْ يَّاْتِىْ بَعْدَكَ مَا حَالُهُمَا عِنْدَكَ فَقَالَ اَسْمَعُ صَلٰوةَ اَهْلِ مَحَبَّتِىْ وَاَعْرِفُهُمْ وَتُعْرَضُ عَلَىَّ صَلٰوةُ غَيْرِهِمْ عَرْضًا ۝

other does not."

It was said: "How can we find such faith, or obtain it or earn it?" He replied: "By sincerely loving God."

It was said: "How can the love of God be found or earned?"

He said: "By loving His Messenger! So seek out the pleasure of God and the pleasure of His Messenger by loving them!"

And it was said to the Messenger of God, God's blessings and peace be upon him: "

Who are the family of Muḥammad whom we are ordered to love and honor and treat with reverence?"

He replied: "The people of purity and fidelity, who believe in me sincerely." It was said: "What are their signs?"

He said: "The traces of my love are on every lover and their inner life is busy with remembering me and remembering God." (In another version the words are: "Their signs are being addicted to remembering me and constantly asking for blessings upon me.")

It was said to the Messenger of God, God's blessings and peace be upon him: "Who is he who is strong in his love for you?"

He replied: "The one who believes in me without seeing me for he is a believer in me through yearning and is sincere in his love for me. A sign of this is that he desires a vision of me more than anything he owns (in another version the words are: "than all the gold in the world.") This is a true believer in me whose love for me is true and sincere.

"It was said to the Messenger of God, God's blessings and peace be upon him: "

Are you aware of the blessings upon you asked for by those who are not with you or by those who will come after you? What is their state regarding you?"

He replied: "I hear the blessings of the people who love me and I know them! And the blessings of others than them are presented to me."

ذَالِكَ اَسْمَآءُ سَيِّدِنَا وَنَبِيِّنَا وَمَوْلَنَا **مُحَمَّدٍ** صَلَّى اللّٰهُ عَلَيْهِ وَسَلَّمَ مِائَتَانِ وَوَاحِدٌ وَّهِيَ هٰذِهِ اَللّٰهُمَّ صَلِّ وَسَلِّمْ وَبَارِكْ عَلٰى مَنِ اسْمُهُ سَيِّدُنَا **مُحَمَّدٌ** صَلَّى اللّٰهُ عَلَيْهِ وَسَلَّمَ ۝ اَللّٰهُمَّ صَلِّ وَسَلِّمْ وَبَارِكْ عَلٰى مَنِ اسْمُهُ سَيِّدُنَآ **اَحْمَدُ** صَلَّى اللّٰهُ عَلَيْهِ وَسَلَّمَ ۝ اَللّٰهُمَّ صَلِّ وَسَلِّمْ وَبَارِكْ عَلٰى مَنِ اسْمُهُ سَيِّدُنَا **حَامِدٌ** صَلَّى اللّٰهُ عَلَيْهِ وَسَلَّمَ ۝ اَللّٰهُمَّ صَلِّ وَسَلِّمْ وَبَارِكْ عَلٰى مَنِ اسْمُهُ سَيِّدُنَا وَمَوْلَنَا **مَحْمُوْدٌ** صَلَّى اللّٰهُ عَلَيْهِ وَسَلَّمَ- سَيِّدُنَا **اَحِيْدٌ** صَلَّى اللّٰهُ عَلَيْهِ وَسَلَّمَ- سَيِّدُنَا **وَحِيْدٌ** صَلَّى اللّٰهُ عَلَيْهِ وَسَلَّمَ- سَيِّدُنَا **مَاحٍ** صَلَّى اللّٰهُ عَلَيْهِ وَسَلَّمَ- سَيِّدُنَا **حَاشِرٌ** صَلَّى اللّٰهُ عَلَيْهِ وَسَلَّمَ- سَيِّدُنَا **عَاقِبٌ** صَلَّى اللّٰهُ عَلَيْهِ وَسَلَّمَ- سَيِّدُنَا **طٰهٰ** صَلَّى اللّٰهُ عَلَيْهِ وَسَلَّمَ- سَيِّدُنَا **يٰسٓ** صَلَّى اللّٰهُ عَلَيْهِ وَسَلَّمَ- سَيِّدُنَا **طَاهِرٌ** صَلَّى اللّٰهُ عَلَيْهِ وَسَلَّمَ- سَيِّدُنَا **مُطَهَّرٌ** صَلَّى اللّٰهُ عَلَيْهِ وَسَلَّمَ- سَيِّدُنَا **طَيِّبٌ** صَلَّى اللّٰهُ عَلَيْهِ وَسَلَّمَ- سَيِّدُنَا **سَيِّدٌ** صَلَّى اللّٰهُ عَلَيْهِ وَسَلَّمَ- سَيِّدُنَا **رَسُوْلٌ** صَلَّى اللّٰهُ عَلَيْهِ وَسَلَّمَ- سَيِّدُنَا **نَبِيٌّ** صَلَّى اللّٰهُ عَلَيْهِ وَسَلَّمَ- سَيِّدُنَا **رَسُوْلُ الرَّحْمَةِ** صَلَّى اللّٰهُ عَلَيْهِ وَسَلَّمَ- سَيِّدُنَا **قَيِّمٌ** صَلَّى اللّٰهُ عَلَيْهِ وَسَلَّمَ- سَيِّدُنَا **جَامِعٌ** صَلَّى اللّٰهُ عَلَيْهِ وَسَلَّمَ- سَيِّدُنَا **مُقْتَفٍ** صَلَّى اللّٰهُ عَلَيْهِ وَسَلَّمَ- سَيِّدُنَا **مُقَفِّى** صَلَّى اللّٰهُ عَلَيْهِ وَسَلَّمَ- سَيِّدُنَا **رَسُوْلُ الْمَلَاحِمِ** صَلَّى اللّٰهُ عَلَيْهِ وَسَلَّمَ- سَيِّدُنَا **رَسُوْلُ الرَّاحَةِ** صَلَّى اللّٰهُ عَلَيْهِ وَسَلَّمَ- سَيِّدُنَا **كَامِلٌ** صَلَّى اللّٰهُ عَلَيْهِ وَسَلَّمَ- سَيِّدُنَآ **اِكْلِيْلٌ** صَلَّى اللّٰهُ عَلَيْهِ وَسَلَّمَ- سَيِّدُنَا **مُدَّثِّرٌ** صَلَّى اللّٰهُ عَلَيْهِ وَسَلَّمَ- سَيِّدُنَا **مُزَّمِّلٌ** صَلَّى اللّٰهُ عَلَيْهِ وَسَلَّمَ- سَيِّدُنَا **عَبْدُاللّٰهِ** صَلَّى اللّٰهُ عَلَيْهِ وَسَلَّمَ- سَيِّدُنَا **حَبِيْبُ اللّٰهِ** صَلَّى اللّٰهُ عَلَيْهِ وَسَلَّمَ- سَيِّدُنَا **صَفِيُّ اللّٰهِ** صَلَّى اللّٰهُ عَلَيْهِ وَسَلَّمَ- سَيِّدُنَا **نَجِيٌّ**

The 201 names of our master and Prophet, Muḥammad, God's blessings and peace be upon him! O God, bless, sanctify and grant peace to the one named Muḥammad (the Praised One), God's blessings and peace be upon him!

O God, bless, sanctify and grant peace to the one named **Muḥammad** (Praised One), God's blessings and peace be upon him! O God, bless, sanctify and grant peace to the one named **Aḥmad** (Most Praised), God's blessings and peace be upon him! O God, bless, sanctify and grant peace to the one named **Ḥāmid** (Praiser), God's blessings and peace be upon him! O God, bless, sanctify and grant peace to the one named **Maḥmūd** (Most Highly Praised) God's blessings and peace be upon him! **Aḥīd** (name of the Prophet in the Torah), God's blessings and peace be upon him! **Waḥīd** (Unique), God's blessings and peace be upon him! **Māḥi** (Effacer), God's blessings and peace be upon him! **Ḥāshir** (Gatherer), God's blessings and peace be upon him! ^{c}**Āqib** (Last in Succession), God's blessings and peace be upon him! **Ṭāhā** (name of Surah 20 of the Holy Quran), God's blessings and peace be upon him! **Yāsīn** (name of Surah 36 of the Holy Quran), God's blessings and peace be upon him! **Ṭāhir** (Pure) God's blessings and peace be upon him! **Muṭahhir** (Purifier), God's blessings and peace be upon him! **Ṭayyib** (Good), God's blessings and peace be upon him! **Sayyid** (Master), God's blessings and peace be upon him! **Rasūl** (Messenger), God's blessings and peace be upon him! **Nabī** (Prophet), God's blessings and peace be upon him! **Rasūl al-Raḥmah** (Messenger of Mercy), God's blessings and peace be upon him! **Qayyim** (Straight One), God's blessings and peace be upon him! **Jāmi**^{c} (Collector), God's blessings and peace be upon him! **Muqtif** (Selected), God's blessings and peace be upon him! **Muqaffī** (Best Example), God's blessings and peace be upon him! **Rasūl al-Malāḥim** (Messenger of Fierce Battles), God's blessings and peace be upon him! **Rasūl al-Rāḥah** (Messenger of Rest), God's blessings and peace be upon him! **Kāmil** (Perfect), God's blessings and peace be upon him! **Iklīl** (Crown), God's blessings and peace be upon him! **Muddaththir** (Covered One), God's blessings and peace be upon him! **Muzzamil** (One Wrapped Up), God's blessings and peace be upon him! ^{c}**Abd Allāh** (Servant of God), God's blessings and peace be upon him! **Ḥabīb Allāh** (Beloved of God), God's blessings and peace be upon him! **Ṣāfīy Allāh** (Intimate of God), God's blessings and peace be upon him! **Najīy**

اللّٰهِ صَلَّى اللّٰهُ عَلَيْهِ وَسَلَّمَ۔ سَيِّدُنَا **كَلِيْمُ اللّٰهِ** صَلَّى اللّٰهُ عَلَيْهِ وَسَلَّمَ۔ سَيِّدُنَا **خَاتِمُ الْاَنْبِيَآءِ** صَلَّى اللّٰهُ عَلَيْهِ وَسَلَّمَ۔ سَيِّدُنَا **خَاتِمُ الرُّسُلِ** صَلَّى اللّٰهُ عَلَيْهِ وَسَلَّمَ۔ سَيِّدُنَا **مُحْيٍ** صَلَّى اللّٰهُ عَلَيْهِ وَسَلَّمَ۔ سَيِّدُنَا **مُنْجٍ** صَلَّى اللّٰهُ عَلَيْهِ وَسَلَّمَ۔ سَيِّدُنَا **مُذَكِّرٌ** صَلَّى اللّٰهُ عَلَيْهِ وَسَلَّمَ۔ سَيِّدُنَا **نَاصِرٌ** صَلَّى اللّٰهُ عَلَيْهِ وَسَلَّمَ۔ سَيِّدُنَا **مَنْصُوْرٌ** صَلَّى اللّٰهُ عَلَيْهِ وَسَلَّمَ۔ سَيِّدُنَا **نَبِيُّ الرَّحْمَةِ** صَلَّى اللّٰهُ عَلَيْهِ وَسَلَّمَ۔ سَيِّدُنَا **نَبِيُّ التَّوْبَةِ** صَلَّى اللّٰهُ عَلَيْهِ وَسَلَّمَ۔ سَيِّدُنَا **حَرِيْصٌ عَلَيْكُمْ** صَلَّى اللّٰهُ عَلَيْهِ وَسَلَّمَ۔ سَيِّدُنَا **مَعْلُوْمٌ** صَلَّى اللّٰهُ عَلَيْهِ وَسَلَّمَ۔ سَيِّدُنَا **شَهِيْرٌ** صَلَّى اللّٰهُ عَلَيْهِ وَسَلَّمَ۔ سَيِّدُنَا **شَاهِدٌ** صَلَّى اللّٰهُ عَلَيْهِ وَسَلَّمَ۔ سَيِّدُنَا **شَهِيْدٌ** صَلَّى اللّٰهُ عَلَيْهِ وَسَلَّمَ۔ سَيِّدُنَا **مَشْهُوْدٌ** صَلَّى اللّٰهُ عَلَيْهِ وَسَلَّمَ۔ سَيِّدُنَا **بَشِيْرٌ** صَلَّى اللّٰهُ عَلَيْهِ وَسَلَّمَ۔ سَيِّدُنَا **مُبَشِّرٌ** صَلَّى اللّٰهُ عَلَيْهِ وَسَلَّمَ۔ سَيِّدُنَا **نَذِيْرٌ** صَلَّى اللّٰهُ عَلَيْهِ وَسَلَّمَ۔ سَيِّدُنَا **مُنْذِرٌ** صَلَّى اللّٰهُ عَلَيْهِ وَسَلَّمَ۔ سَيِّدُنَا **نُوْرٌ** صَلَّى اللّٰهُ عَلَيْهِ وَسَلَّمَ۔ سَيِّدُنَا **سِرَاجٌ** صَلَّى اللّٰهُ عَلَيْهِ وَسَلَّمَ۔ سَيِّدُنَا **مِصْبَاحٌ** صَلَّى اللّٰهُ عَلَيْهِ وَسَلَّمَ۔ سَيِّدُنَا **هُدًى** صَلَّى اللّٰهُ عَلَيْهِ وَسَلَّمَ۔ سَيِّدُنَا **مَهْدِيٌّ** صَلَّى اللّٰهُ عَلَيْهِ وَسَلَّمَ۔ سَيِّدُنَا **مُنِيْرٌ** صَلَّى اللّٰهُ عَلَيْهِ وَسَلَّمَ۔ سَيِّدُنَا **دَاعٍ** صَلَّى اللّٰهُ عَلَيْهِ وَسَلَّمَ۔ سَيِّدُنَا **مَدْعُوٌّ** صَلَّى اللّٰهُ عَلَيْهِ وَسَلَّمَ۔ سَيِّدُنَا **مُجِيْبٌ** صَلَّى اللّٰهُ عَلَيْهِ وَسَلَّمَ۔ سَيِّدُنَا **مُجَابٌ** صَلَّى اللّٰهُ عَلَيْهِ وَسَلَّمَ۔ سَيِّدُنَا **حَفِيٌّ** صَلَّى اللّٰهُ عَلَيْهِ وَسَلَّمَ۔ سَيِّدُنَا **عَفُوٌّ** صَلَّى اللّٰهُ عَلَيْهِ وَسَلَّمَ۔ سَيِّدُنَا **وَلِيٌّ** صَلَّى اللّٰهُ عَلَيْهِ وَسَلَّمَ۔ سَيِّدُنَا **حَقٌّ** صَلَّى اللّٰهُ عَلَيْهِ وَسَلَّمَ۔ سَيِّدُنَا **قَوِيٌّ** صَلَّى اللّٰهُ عَلَيْهِ وَسَلَّمَ۔ سَيِّدُنَآ **اَمِيْنٌ** صَلَّى اللّٰهُ عَلَيْهِ وَسَلَّمَ۔ سَيِّدُنَا **مَأْمُوْنٌ** صَلَّى اللّٰهُ عَلَيْهِ وَسَلَّمَ۔ سَيِّدُنَا **كَرِيْمٌ** صَلَّى اللّٰهُ عَلَيْهِ

Allāh (Confidant of God), God's blessings and peace be upon him! **Kalīm Allāh** (Speaker with God), God's blessings and peace be upon him! **Khātim al-Anbiya** (Seal of the Prophets), God's blessings and peace be upon him! **Khātim al-Rusul** (Seal of the Messengers), God's blessings and peace be upon him! **Muḥyī** (Reviver), God's blessings and peace be upon him! **Munjī** (Rescuer), God's blessings and peace be upon him! **Mudhakkir** (Reminder), God's blessings and peace be upon him! **Nāṣir** (Helper), God's blessings and peace be upon him! **Manṣūr** (Victorious One), God's blessings and peace be upon him! **Nabīy al-Raḥmah** (Prophet of Mercy), God's blessings and peace be upon him! **Nabīy al-Tawbah** (Prophet of Repentance) God's blessings and peace be upon him! **Ḥarīṣ ᶜAlaykum** (Watchful Over You), God's blessings and peace be upon him! **Maᶜlūm** (Known One), God's blessings and peace be upon him! **Shahīr** (Famous), God's blessings and peace be upon him! **Shāhid** (Witnesser), God's blessings and peace be upon him! **Shahīd** (Witness), God's blessings and peace be upon him! **Mashhūd** (Attested), God's blessings and peace be upon him! **Bashīr** (Newsbringer), God's blessings and peace be upon him! **Mubashshir** (Spreader of Good News), God's blessings and peace be upon him! **Nadhīr** (Warner), God's blessings and peace be upon him! **Mundhir** (Admonisher), God's bless ings and peace be upon him! **Nūr** (Light), God's blessings and peace be upon him! **Sirāj** (Lamp), God's blessings and peace be upon him! **Miṣbāḥ** (Lantern), God's blessings and peace be upon him! **Huda** (Guidance), God's blessings and peace be upon him! **Mahdī** (Rightly Guided One), God's blessings and peace be upon him! **Munīr** (Illumined One), God's blessings and peace be upon him! **Dāᶜī** (Caller), God's blessings and peace be upon him! **Madᶜūw** (Called One), God's blessings and peace be upon him! **Mujīb** (Responsive), God's blessings and peace be upon him! **Mujāb** (One Responded To), God's blessings and peace be upon him! **Ḥafīy** (Welcoming), God's blessings and peace be upon him! **ᶜAfūw** (Overlooker of Sins), God's blessings and peace be upon him! **Walīy** (Friend), God's blessings and peace be upon him! **Ḥaqq** (Truth), God's blessings and peace be upon him! **Qawīy** (Powerful), God's blessings and peace be upon him! **Amīn** (Trustworthy), God's blessings and peace be upon him! **Maᵓmūn** (Trusted), God's blessings and peace be upon him! **Karīm** (the Noble,

God's blessings

وَسَلَّمَ۔ سَيِّدُنَا **مُكَرَّمٌ** صَلَّى اللّٰهُ عَلَيْهِ وَسَلَّمَ۔ سَيِّدُنَا **مَكِيْنٌ** صَلَّى اللّٰهُ عَلَيْهِ وَسَلَّمَ۔ سَيِّدُنَا **مَتِيْنٌ** صَلَّى اللّٰهُ عَلَيْهِ وَسَلَّمَ۔ سَيِّدُنَا **مُبِيْنٌ** صَلَّى اللّٰهُ عَلَيْهِ وَسَلَّمَ۔ سَيِّدُنَا **مُؤَمِّلٌ** صَلَّى اللّٰهُ عَلَيْهِ وَسَلَّمَ۔ سَيِّدُنَا **وَصُوْلٌ** صَلَّى اللّٰهُ عَلَيْهِ وَسَلَّمَ۔ سَيِّدُنَا **ذُوْقُوَّةٍ** صَلَّى اللّٰهُ عَلَيْهِ وَسَلَّمَ۔ سَيِّدُنَا **ذُوْحُرْمَةٍ** صَلَّى اللّٰهُ عَلَيْهِ وَسَلَّمَ۔ سَيِّدُنَا **ذُوْمَكَانَةٍ** صَلَّى اللّٰهُ عَلَيْهِ وَسَلَّمَ۔ سَيِّدُنَا **ذُوْعِزٍّ** صَلَّى اللّٰهُ عَلَيْهِ وَسَلَّمَ۔ سَيِّدُنَا **ذُوْفَضْلٍ** صَلَّى اللّٰهُ عَلَيْهِ وَسَلَّمَ۔ سَيِّدُنَا **مُطَاعٌ** صَلَّى اللّٰهُ عَلَيْهِ وَسَلَّمَ۔ سَيِّدُنَا **مُطِيْعٌ** صَلَّى اللّٰهُ عَلَيْهِ وَسَلَّمَ۔ سَيِّدُنَا **قَدَمُ صِدْقٍ** صَلَّى اللّٰهُ عَلَيْهِ وَسَلَّمَ۔ سَيِّدُنَا **رَحْمَةٌ** صَلَّى اللّٰهُ عَلَيْهِ وَسَلَّمَ۔ سَيِّدُنَا **بُشْرٰى** صَلَّى اللّٰهُ عَلَيْهِ وَسَلَّمَ۔ سَيِّدُنَا **غَوْثٌ** صَلَّى اللّٰهُ عَلَيْهِ وَسَلَّمَ۔ سَيِّدُنَا **غَيْثٌ** صَلَّى اللّٰهُ عَلَيْهِ وَسَلَّمَ۔ سَيِّدُنَا **غِيَاثٌ** صَلَّى اللّٰهُ عَلَيْهِ وَسَلَّمَ۔ سَيِّدُنَا **نِعْمَةُاللّٰهِ** صَلَّى اللّٰهُ عَلَيْهِ وَسَلَّمَ۔ سَيِّدُنَا **هَدِيَّةُ اللّٰهِ** صَلَّى اللّٰهُ عَلَيْهِ وَسَلَّمَ۔ سَيِّدُنَا **عُرْوَةٌ وُّثْقٰى** صَلَّى اللّٰهُ عَلَيْهِ وَسَلَّمَ۔ سَيِّدُنَا **صِرَاطُ اللّٰهِ** صَلَّى اللّٰهُ عَلَيْهِ وَسَلَّمَ۔ سَيِّدُنَا **صِرَاطٌ مُّسْتَقِيْمٌ** صَلَّى اللّٰهُ عَلَيْهِ وَسَلَّمَ۔ سَيِّدُنَا **ذِكْرُاللّٰهِ** صَلَّى اللّٰهُ عَلَيْهِ وَسَلَّمَ۔ سَيِّدُنَا **سَيْفُ اللّٰهِ** صَلَّى اللّٰهُ عَلَيْهِ وَسَلَّمَ۔ سَيِّدُنَا **حِزْبُ اللّٰهِ** صَلَّى اللّٰهُ عَلَيْهِ وَسَلَّمَ۔ سَيِّدُنَا **اَلنَّجْمُ الثَّاقِبُ** صَلَّى اللّٰهُ عَلَيْهِ وَسَلَّمَ۔ سَيِّدُنَا **مُصْطَفٰى** صَلَّى اللّٰهُ عَلَيْهِ وَسَلَّمَ۔ سَيِّدُنَا **مُجْتَبٰى** صَلَّى اللّٰهُ عَلَيْهِ وَسَلَّمَ۔ سَيِّدُنَا **مُنْتَقٰى** صَلَّى اللّٰهُ عَلَيْهِ وَسَلَّمَ۔ سَيِّدُنَا **اُمِّيٌّ** صَلَّى اللّٰهُ عَلَيْهِ وَسَلَّمَ۔ سَيِّدُنَا **مُخْتَارٌ** صَلَّى اللّٰهُ عَلَيْهِ وَسَلَّمَ۔ سَيِّدُنَآ **اَجِيْرٌ** صَلَّى اللّٰهُ عَلَيْهِ وَسَلَّمَ۔ سَيِّدُنَا **جَبَّارٌ** صَلَّى اللّٰهُ عَلَيْهِ وَسَلَّمَ۔ سَيِّدُنَآ **اَبُوالْقَاسِمِ** صَلَّى اللّٰهُ عَلَيْهِ وَسَلَّمَ۔ سَيِّدُنَآ **اَبُوالطَّاهِرِ** صَلَّى اللّٰهُ عَلَيْهِ وَسَلَّمَ۔

and peace be upon him! **Mukarram** (Honored), God's blessings and peace be upon him! **Makīn** (Firm), God's blessings and peace be upon him! **Matīn** (Stable), God's blessings and peace be upon him! **Mubīn** (Evident), God's blessings and peace be upon him! **Muʾammil** (Hoped For), God's blessings and peace be upon him! **Waṣūl** (Connection), God's blessings and peace be upon him! **Dhū Qūwah** (Possessor of Power), God's blessings and peace be upon him! **Dhū Ḥurmah** (Possessor of Honor), God's blessings and peace be upon him! **Dhū Makānah** (Possessor of Firmness), God's blessings and peace be upon him! **Dhū ʿIzz** (Possessor of Might), God's blessings and peace be upon him! **Dhū Faḍl** (Possessor of Grace), God's blessings and peace be upon him! **Muṭāʿ** (One Obeyed), God's blessings and peace be upon him! **Muṭīʿ** (Obedient), God's blessings and peace be upon him! **Qadamu Ṣidq** (Foot of Sincerity), God's blessings and peace be upon him! **Raḥmah** (Mercy), God's blessings and peace be upon him! **Bushrā** (the Good News), God's blessings and peace be upon him! **Ghawth** (Redeemer), God's blessings and peace be upon him! **Ghayth** (Succor), God's blessings and peace be upon him! **Ghiyāth** (Help), God's blessings and peace be upon him! **Niʿmat Allāh** (Blessing of God), God's blessings and peace be upon him! **Hadīyat Allāh** (Gift of God), God's blessings and peace be upon him! **ʿUrwatu Wuthqā** (Trusty Handhold), God's blessings and peace be upon him! **Ṣirāṭ Allāh** (Path to God), God's blessings and peace be upon him! **Ṣirāṭ al-Mustaqīm** (Straight Path), God's blessings and peace be upon him! **Dhikr Allāh** (Remembrance of God), God's blessings and peace be upon him! **Sayf Allāh** (Sword of God), God's blessings and peace be upon him! **Ḥizb Allāh** (Party of God), God's blessings and peace be upon him! **Najm al-Thāqib** (Piercing Star), God's blessings and peace be upon him! **Muṣṭafā** (Chosen One), God's blessings and peace be upon him! **Mujtabā** (Select), God's blessings and peace be upon him! **Muntaqā** (Eloquent), God's blessings and peace be upon him! **Ummīy** (Unlettered), God's blessings and peace be upon him! **Mukhtār** (Chosen), God's blessings and peace be upon him! **Ajīr** (God's Worker), God's blessings and peace be upon him! **Jabbār** (Compelling), God's blessings and peace be upon him! **Abū Qāsim** (Father of Qasim), God's blessings and peace be

upon him! **Abū al-Ṭāhir** (Pure Father), God's blessings and peace be

سَيِّدُنَآ **اَبُو الطَّيِّبِ** صَلَّى اللّٰهُ عَلَيْهِ وَسَلَّمَ۔ سَيِّدُنَآ **اَبُوْ اِبْرٰهِيمَ** صَلَّى اللّٰهُ عَلَيْهِ وَسَلَّمَ۔ سَيِّدُنَا **مُشَفَّعٌ** صَلَّى اللّٰهُ عَلَيْهِ وَسَلَّمَ۔ سَيِّدُنَا **شَفِيْعٌ** صَلَّى اللّٰهُ عَلَيْهِ وَسَلَّمَ۔ سَيِّدُنَا **صَالِحٌ** صَلَّى اللّٰهُ عَلَيْهِ وَسَلَّمَ۔ سَيِّدُنَا **مُصْلِحٌ** صَلَّى اللّٰهُ عَلَيْهِ وَسَلَّمَ۔ سَيِّدُنَا **مُهَيْمِنٌ** صَلَّى اللّٰهُ عَلَيْهِ وَسَلَّمَ۔ سَيِّدُنَا **صَادِقٌ** صَلَّى اللّٰهُ عَلَيْهِ وَسَلَّمَ۔ سَيِّدُنَا **مُصَدَّقٌ** صَلَّى اللّٰهُ عَلَيْهِ وَسَلَّمَ۔ سَيِّدُنَا **صِدْقٌ** صَلَّى اللّٰهُ عَلَيْهِ وَسَلَّمَ۔ سَيِّدُنَا **سَيِّدُالْمُرْسَلِيْنَ** صَلَّى اللّٰهُ عَلَيْهِ وَسَلَّمَ۔ سَيِّدُنَا **اِمَامُ الْمُتَّقِيْنَ** صَلَّى اللّٰهُ عَلَيْهِ وَسَلَّمَ۔ سَيِّدُنَا **قَآئِدُ الْغُرِّ الْمُحَجَّلِيْنَ** صَلَّى اللّٰهُ عَلَيْهِ وَسَلَّمَ۔ سَيِّدُنَا **خَلِيْلُ الرَّحْمٰنِ** صَلَّى اللّٰهُ عَلَيْهِ وَسَلَّمَ۔ سَيِّدُنَا **بَرٌّ** صَلَّى اللّٰهُ عَلَيْهِ وَسَلَّمَ۔ سَيِّدُنَا **مُبَرٌّ** صَلَّى اللّٰهُ عَلَيْهِ وَسَلَّمَ۔ سَيِّدُنَا **وَجِيْهٌ** صَلَّى اللّٰهُ عَلَيْهِ وَسَلَّمَ۔ سَيِّدُنَا **نَصِيْحٌ** صَلَّى اللّٰهُ عَلَيْهِ وَسَلَّمَ۔ سَيِّدُنَا **نَاصِحٌ** صَلَّى اللّٰهُ عَلَيْهِ وَسَلَّمَ۔ سَيِّدُنَا **وَكِيْلٌ** صَلَّى اللّٰهُ عَلَيْهِ وَسَلَّمَ۔ سَيِّدُنَا **مُتَوَكِّلٌ** صَلَّى اللّٰهُ عَلَيْهِ وَسَلَّمَ۔ سَيِّدُنَا **كَفِيْلٌ** صَلَّى اللّٰهُ عَلَيْهِ وَسَلَّمَ۔ سَيِّدُنَا **شَفِيْقٌ** صَلَّى اللّٰهُ عَلَيْهِ وَسَلَّمَ۔ سَيِّدُنَا **مُقِيْمُ السُّنَّةِ** صَلَّى اللّٰهُ عَلَيْهِ وَسَلَّمَ۔ سَيِّدُنَا **مُقَدَّسٌ** صَلَّى اللّٰهُ عَلَيْهِ وَسَلَّمَ۔ سَيِّدُنَا **رُوْحُ الْقُدُسِ** صَلَّى اللّٰهُ عَلَيْهِ وَسَلَّمَ۔ سَيِّدُنَا **رُوْحُ الْحَقِّ** صَلَّى اللّٰهُ عَلَيْهِ وَسَلَّمَ۔ سَيِّدُنَا **رُوْحُ الْقِسْطِ** صَلَّى اللّٰهُ عَلَيْهِ وَسَلَّمَ۔ سَيِّدُنَا **كَافٍ** صَلَّى اللّٰهُ عَلَيْهِ وَسَلَّمَ۔ سَيِّدُنَا **مُكْتَفٍ** صَلَّى اللّٰهُ عَلَيْهِ وَسَلَّمَ۔ سَيِّدُنَا **بَالِغٌ** صَلَّى اللّٰهُ عَلَيْهِ وَسَلَّمَ۔ سَيِّدُنَا **مُبَلِّغٌ** صَلَّى اللّٰهُ عَلَيْهِ وَسَلَّمَ۔ سَيِّدُنَا **شَافٍ** صَلَّى اللّٰهُ عَلَيْهِ وَسَلَّمَ۔ سَيِّدُنَا **وَاصِلٌ** صَلَّى اللّٰهُ عَلَيْهِ وَسَلَّمَ۔ سَيِّدُنَا **مَوْصُوْلٌ** صَلَّى اللّٰهُ عَلَيْهِ وَسَلَّمَ۔ سَيِّدُنَا **سَابِقٌ** صَلَّى اللّٰهُ عَلَيْهِ وَسَلَّمَ۔ سَيِّدُنَا **سَآئِقٌ** صَلَّى اللّٰهُ عَلَيْهِ

upon him! **Abū al-Ṭayyib** (Good Father), God's blessings and peace be upon him! **Abū Ibrāhīm** (Father of Ibrahim), God's blessings and peace be upon him! **Mushaffa**^{c} (One Whose Intercession is Accepted), God's blessings and peace be upon him! **Shafi**^{c} (Interceder), God's blessings and peace be upon him! **Ṣāliḥ** (Righteous), God's blessings and peace be upon him! **Muṣliḥ** (Conciliator), God's blessings and peace be upon him! **Muhaymin** (Guardian), God's blessings and peace be upon him! **Ṣādiq** (Truthful), God's blessings and peace be upon him! **Muṣaddaq** (Confirmer), God's blessings and peace be upon him! **Ṣidq** (Sincerity), God's blessings and peace be upon him! **Sayyid al-Mursalīn** (Master of the Messengers), God's blessings and peace be upon him! **Imām al-Muttaqīn** (Leader of the Godfearing), God's blessings and peace be upon him! **Qā**^{ɔ}**id al-Ghurr il-Muḥajjilīn** (Guide of the Brightly Shining Ones), God's blessings and peace be upon him! **Khalīl al-Raḥmān** (Friend of the Merciful), God's blessings and peace be upon him! **Barr** (Pious), God's blessings and peace be upon him! **Mubirr** (Venerated), God's blessings and peace be upon him! **Wajīh** (Eminent), God's blessings and peace be upon him! **Naṣīh** (Adviser), God's blessings and peace be upon him! **Nāṣih** (Counselor), God's blessings and peace be upon him! **Wakīl** (Advocate), God's blessings and peace be upon him! **Mutawwakkil** (Reliant on God), God's blessings and peace be upon him! **Kafīl** (Guarantor), God's blessings and peace be upon him! **Shafīq** (Tender), God's blessings and peace be upon him! **Muqīm al-Sunnah** (Establisher of the Way), God's blessings and peace be upon him! **Muqaddis** (Sacred), God's blessings and peace be upon him! **Rūḥ al-Qudus** (the Holy Spirit), God's blessings and peace be upon him! **Rūḥ al-Ḥaqq** (the Spirit of Truth), God's blessings and peace be upon him! **Rūḥ al-Qisṭ** (Spirit of Justice), God's blessings and peace be upon him! **Kāfi** (Qualified), God's blessings and peace be upon him! **Muktafi** (Broad-shouldered), God's blessings and peace be upon him! **Bāligh** (Proclaimer) God's blessings and peace be upon him! **Muballigh** (Informer), God's blessings and peace be upon him! **Shāfi** (Healing), God's blessings and peace be upon him! **Wāṣil** (Inseparable Friend), God's blessings and peace be upon him! **Mawṣūl** (One Bound to God), God's blessings and peace be upon him! **Sābiq** (Foremost), God's blessings and peace be upon him!

Sā^{ɔ}**iq** (Driver), God's blessings

وَسَلَّمَ۔ سَيِّدُنَا **هَادٍ** صَلَّى اللّٰهُ عَلَيْهِ وَسَلَّمَ۔ سَيِّدُنَا **مُهْدٍ** صَلَّى اللّٰهُ عَلَيْهِ وَسَلَّمَ۔ سَيِّدُنَا **مُقَدَّمٌ** صَلَّى اللّٰهُ عَلَيْهِ وَسَلَّمَ۔ سَيِّدُنَا **عَزِيزٌ** صَلَّى اللّٰهُ عَلَيْهِ وَسَلَّمَ۔ سَيِّدُنَا **فَاضِلٌ** صَلَّى اللّٰهُ عَلَيْهِ وَسَلَّمَ۔ سَيِّدُنَا **مُفَضَّلٌ** صَلَّى اللّٰهُ عَلَيْهِ وَسَلَّمَ۔ سَيِّدُنَا **فَاتِحٌ** صَلَّى اللّٰهُ عَلَيْهِ وَسَلَّمَ۔ سَيِّدُنَا **مِفْتَاحٌ** صَلَّى اللّٰهُ عَلَيْهِ وَسَلَّمَ۔ سَيِّدُنَا **مِفْتَاحُ الرَّحْمَةِ** صَلَّى اللّٰهُ عَلَيْهِ وَسَلَّمَ۔ سَيِّدُنَا **مِفْتَاحُ الْجَنَّةِ** صَلَّى اللّٰهُ عَلَيْهِ وَسَلَّمَ۔ سَيِّدُنَا **عَلَمُ الْإِيمَانِ** صَلَّى اللّٰهُ عَلَيْهِ وَسَلَّمَ۔ سَيِّدُنَا **عَلَمُ الْيَقِينِ** صَلَّى اللّٰهُ عَلَيْهِ وَسَلَّمَ۔ سَيِّدُنَا **دَلِيلُ الْخَيْرَاتِ** صَلَّى اللّٰهُ عَلَيْهِ وَسَلَّمَ۔ سَيِّدُنَا **مُصَحِّحُ الْحَسَنَاتِ** صَلَّى اللّٰهُ عَلَيْهِ وَسَلَّمَ۔ سَيِّدُنَا **مُقِيلُ الْعَثَرَاتِ** صَلَّى اللّٰهُ عَلَيْهِ وَسَلَّمَ۔ سَيِّدُنَا **صَفُوحٌ عَنِ الزَّلَّاتِ** صَلَّى اللّٰهُ عَلَيْهِ وَسَلَّمَ۔ سَيِّدُنَا **صَاحِبُ الشَّفَاعَةِ** صَلَّى اللّٰهُ عَلَيْهِ وَسَلَّمَ۔ سَيِّدُنَا **صَاحِبُ الْمَقَامِ** صَلَّى اللّٰهُ عَلَيْهِ وَسَلَّمَ۔ سَيِّدُنَا **صَاحِبُ الْقَدَمِ** صَلَّى اللّٰهُ عَلَيْهِ وَسَلَّمَ۔ سَيِّدُنَا **مَخْصُوصٌ بِالْعِزِّ** صَلَّى اللّٰهُ عَلَيْهِ وَسَلَّمَ۔ سَيِّدُنَا **مَخْصُوصٌ بِالْمَجْدِ** صَلَّى اللّٰهُ عَلَيْهِ وَسَلَّمَ۔ سَيِّدُنَا **مَخْصُوصٌ بِالشَّرَفِ** صَلَّى اللّٰهُ عَلَيْهِ وَسَلَّمَ۔ سَيِّدُنَا **صَاحِبُ الْوَسِيلَةِ** صَلَّى اللّٰهُ عَلَيْهِ وَسَلَّمَ۔ سَيِّدُنَا **صَاحِبُ السَّيْفِ** صَلَّى اللّٰهُ عَلَيْهِ وَسَلَّمَ۔ سَيِّدُنَا **صَاحِبُ الْفَضِيلَةِ** صَلَّى اللّٰهُ عَلَيْهِ وَسَلَّمَ۔ سَيِّدُنَا **صَاحِبُ الْإِزَارِ** صَلَّى اللّٰهُ عَلَيْهِ وَسَلَّمَ۔ سَيِّدُنَا **صَاحِبُ الْحُجَّةِ** صَلَّى اللّٰهُ عَلَيْهِ وَسَلَّمَ۔ سَيِّدُنَا **صَاحِبُ السُّلْطَانِ** صَلَّى اللّٰهُ عَلَيْهِ وَسَلَّمَ۔ سَيِّدُنَا **صَاحِبُ الرِّدَآءِ** صَلَّى اللّٰهُ عَلَيْهِ وَسَلَّمَ۔ سَيِّدُنَا **صَاحِبُ الدَّرَجَةِ الرَّفِيعَةِ** صَلَّى اللّٰهُ عَلَيْهِ وَسَلَّمَ۔ سَيِّدُنَا **صَاحِبُ التَّاجِ** صَلَّى اللّٰهُ عَلَيْهِ وَسَلَّمَ۔ سَيِّدُنَا **صَاحِبُ الْمِغْفَرِ** صَلَّى اللّٰهُ

and peace be upon him! **Hādi** (Guide), God's blessings and peace be upon him! **Muhdi** (Guided), God's blessings and peace be upon him! **Muqaddam** (Overseer), God's blessings and peace be upon him! **ᶜAzīz** (Mighty), God's blessings and peace be upon him! **Fāḍil** (the Outstanding), God's blessings and peace be upon him! **Mufaḍḍil** (Favored), God's blessings and peace be upon him! **Fātiḥ** (Opener), God's blessings and peace be upon him! **Miftāḥ** (Key), God's blessings and peace be upon him! **Miftāḥ al-Raḥmah** (Key to Mercy), God's blessings and peace be upon him! **Miftāḥ al-Jannah** (Key to the Garden), God's blessings and peace be upon him! **ᶜAlam al-Īmān** (Banner of the Faith), God's blessings and peace be upon him! **ᶜAlam al-Yaqīn** (Banner of Certainty), God's blessings and peace be upon him! **Dalāᵓil al-Khayrāt** (Guide to Goodness), God's blessings and peace be upon him! **Musaḥḥih al-Ḥasanāt** (Verifier of Good Deeds), God's blessings and peace be upon him! **Muqīl al-ᶜAtharāt** (Forewarner of False Steps), God's blessings and peace be upon him! **Ṣafūḥ ᵓan al-Zallāt** (Pardoner of Oppressions), God's blessings and peace be upon him! **Ṣāḥib al-Shafāᶜah** (Possessor of Intercession), God's blessings and peace be upon him! **Ṣāḥib al-Maqām** (Possessor of the Honored Station), God's blessings and peace be upon him! **Ṣāḥib al-Qadam** (Owner of the Footprint), God's blessings and peace be upon him! **Makhṣūṣ bil-ᶜIzz** (Distinguished with Might), God's blessings and peace be upon him! **Makhṣūṣ bil-Majd** (Distinguished with Glory), God's blessings and peace be upon him! **Makhṣūṣ bil-Sharaf** (Distinguished with Nobility), God's blessings and peace be upon him! **Ṣāḥib al-Wasīlah** (Possessor of the Closest Access), God's blessings and peace be upon him! **Ṣāḥib us-Sayf** (Owner of the Sword), God's blessings and peace be upon him! **Ṣāḥib al-Faḍīlah** (Possessor of Pre-eminence), God's blessings and peace be upon him! **Ṣāḥib al-Izār** (Owner of the Cloth), God's blessings and peace be upon him! **Ṣāḥib al-Ḥujjah** (Possessor of Proof), God's blessings and peace be upon him! **Ṣāḥib al-Sulṭān** (Possessor of Authority), God's blessings and peace be upon him! **Ṣāḥib al-Riḍā** (Owner of the Robe), God's blessings and peace be upon him! **Ṣāḥib al-Darajat al-Rafīᶜ** (Possessor of the Lofty Rank), God's blessings and peace be upon him! **Ṣāḥib al-Tāj** (Possessor of the Crown) God's blessings and peace be upon him! **Ṣāḥib al-Maghfir**

(Possessor of Forgiveness), God's blessings

عَلَيْهِ وَسَلَّمَ ـ سَيِّدُنَا **صَاحِبُ اللِّوَآءِ** صَلَّى اللّٰهُ عَلَيْهِ وَسَلَّمَ ـ سَيِّدُنَا **صَاحِبُ الْمِعْرَاجِ** صَلَّى اللّٰهُ عَلَيْهِ وَسَلَّمَ ـ سَيِّدُنَا **صَاحِبُ الْقَضِيْبِ** صَلَّى اللّٰهُ عَلَيْهِ وَسَلَّمَ ـ سَيِّدُنَا **صَاحِبُ الْبُرَاقِ** صَلَّى اللّٰهُ عَلَيْهِ وَسَلَّمَ ـ سَيِّدُنَا **صَاحِبُ الْخَاتَمِ** صَلَّى اللّٰهُ عَلَيْهِ وَسَلَّمَ ـ سَيِّدُنَا **صَاحِبُ الْعَلَامَةِ** صَلَّى اللّٰهُ عَلَيْهِ وَسَلَّمَ ـ سَيِّدُنَا **صَاحِبُ الْبُرْهَانِ** صَلَّى اللّٰهُ عَلَيْهِ وَسَلَّمَ ـ سَيِّدُنَا **صَاحِبُ الْبَيَانِ** صَلَّى اللّٰهُ عَلَيْهِ وَسَلَّمَ ـ سَيِّدُنَا **فَصِيْحُ اللِّسَانِ** صَلَّى اللّٰهُ عَلَيْهِ وَسَلَّمَ ـ سَيِّدُنَا **مُطَهَّرُ الْجَنَانِ** صَلَّى اللّٰهُ عَلَيْهِ وَسَلَّمَ ـ سَيِّدُنَا **رَءُوْفٌ** صَلَّى اللّٰهُ عَلَيْهِ وَسَلَّمَ ـ سَيِّدُنَا **رَحِيْمٌ** صَلَّى اللّٰهُ عَلَيْهِ وَسَلَّمَ ـ سَيِّدُنَا **اُذُنُ خَيْرٍ** صَلَّى اللّٰهُ عَلَيْهِ وَسَلَّمَ ـ سَيِّدُنَا **صَحِيْحُ الْاِسْلَامِ** صَلَّى اللّٰهُ عَلَيْهِ وَسَلَّمَ ـ سَيِّدُنَا **سَيِّدُالْكَوْنَيْنِ** صَلَّى اللّٰهُ عَلَيْهِ وَسَلَّمَ ـ سَيِّدُنَا **عَيْنُ النَّعِيْمِ** صَلَّى اللّٰهُ عَلَيْهِ وَسَلَّمَ ـ سَيِّدُنَا **عَيْنُ الْغُرِّ** صَلَّى اللّٰهُ عَلَيْهِ وَسَلَّمَ ـ سَيِّدُنَا **سَعْدُاللّٰهِ** صَلَّى اللّٰهُ عَلَيْهِ وَسَلَّمَ ـ سَيِّدُنَا **سَعْدُالْخَلْقِ** صَلَّى اللّٰهُ عَلَيْهِ وَسَلَّمَ ـ سَيِّدُنَا **خَطِيْبُ الْاُمَمِ** صَلَّى اللّٰهُ عَلَيْهِ وَسَلَّمَ ـ سَيِّدُنَا **عَلَمُ الْهُدٰى** صَلَّى اللّٰهُ عَلَيْهِ وَسَلَّمَ ـ سَيِّدُنَا **كَاشِفُ الْكُرَبِ** صَلَّى اللّٰهُ عَلَيْهِ وَسَلَّمَ ـ سَيِّدُنَا **رَافِعُ الرُّتَبِ** صَلَّى اللّٰهُ عَلَيْهِ وَسَلَّمَ ـ سَيِّدُنَا **عِزُّالْعَرَبِ** صَلَّى اللّٰهُ عَلَيْهِ وَسَلَّمَ ـ سَيِّدُنَا **صَاحِبُ الْفَرَجِ** صَلَّى اللّٰهُ عَلَيْهِ وَعَلٰى اٰلِهٖ ۝ **اَللّٰهُمَّ** يَا رَبِّ بِجَاهِ نَبِيِّكَ الْمُصْطَفٰى ۝ وَرَسُوْلِكَ الْمُرْتَضٰى ۝ طَهِّرْ قُلُوْبَنَا مِنْ كُلِّ وَصْفٍ يُّبَاعِدُنَا عَنْ مُّشَاهَدَتِكَ وَمَحَبَّتِكَ وَاَمِتْنَا عَلَى السُّنَّةِ وَالْجَمَاعَةِ وَالشَّوْقِ اِلٰى لِقَآئِكَ يَا ذَاالْجَلَالِ وَالْاِكْرَامِ ۝ وَصَلَّى اللّٰهُ عَلٰى سَيِّدِنَا وَمَوْلٰنَا **مُحَمَّدٍ** وَّعَلٰى اٰلِهٖ وَصَحْبِهٖ وَسَلَّمَ تَسْلِيْمًا ۝ وَالْحَمْدُ لِلّٰهِ رَبِّ الْعٰلَمِيْنَ ۝

and peace be upon him! **Ṣāḥib al-Liwā** (Possessor of the Flag), God's blessings and peace be upon him! **Ṣāḥib al-Mi^crāj** (Master of the Night Journey), God's blessings and peace be upon him! **Ṣāḥib al-Qaḍīb** (Possessor of the Staff) God's blessings and peace be upon him! **Ṣāḥib al-Burāq** (Owner of Buraq), God's blessings and peace be upon him! **Ṣāḥib al-Khātam** (Owner of the Ring), God's blessings and peace be upon him! **Ṣāḥib al-ᶜAlāmah** (Owner of the Sign), God's blessings and peace be upon him! **Ṣāḥib al-Burhān** (Possessor of the Evidence), God's blessings and peace be upon him! **Ṣāḥib al-Bayān** (Possessor of Evident Proofs), God's blessings and peace be upon him! **Fasīḥ al-Lisān** (Good Communicator), God's blessings and peace be upon him! **Muṭahhir al-Jannān** (Purifier of the Soul), God's blessings and peace be upon him! **Raᵓūf** (Kind), God's blessings and peace be upon him! **Raḥīm** (Mercy-giving), God's blessings and peace be upon him! **Udhun Khayr** (Good Listener), God's blessings and peace be upon him! **Ṣaḥīḥ al-Islām** (the Completer of Islam), God's blessings and peace be upon him! **Sayyid al-Kawnayn** (Master of the Two Universes), God's blessings and peace be upon him! **ᶜAyn al-Naᶜīm** (Spring of Bliss), God's blessings and peace be upon him! **ᶜAyn al-Ghurr** (Spring of Beauty), God's blessings and peace be upon him! **Saᶜd Allāh** (Joy of God), God's blessings and peace be upon him! **Saᶜd al-Khalq** (Joy of the Creator), God's blessings and peace be upon him! **Khaṭīb al-Umam** (Preacher to Nations), God's blessings and peace be upon him! **ᶜAlam al-Hudā** (Teacher of Guidance), God's blessings and peace be upon him! **Kāshif al-Kurab** (Remover of Worries), God's blessings and peace be upon him! **Rāfiᶜ al-Rutab** (Raiser of Ranks), God's blessings and peace be upon him! **ᶜIzz al-ᶜArab** (Might of the Arabs), God's blessings and peace be upon him! **Ṣāḥib al-Faraj** (Possessor of Happiness), God's blessings and peace be upon him!

O God, O Lord, for the honor of Your Prophet, al-Muṣṭafā, and Your Messenger, al-Murtadā, purify our hearts from every characteristic which keeps us away from Your Presence and Your Love, and have us pass away following his way and in his community, longing to meet You, O Owner of Majesty and Nobility! And the blessings and abundant peace of God be upon our master Muḥammad, his family and his Companions and praise be to God, Lord of the Worlds!

هَذَا الدُّعَآءُ النِّيَّةِ

بِسْمِ اللّٰهِ الرَّحْمٰنِ الرَّحِيْمِ۝

اَلْحَمْدُ لِلّٰهِ رَبِّ الْعٰلَمِيْنَ ۝ وَحَسْبِىَ اللّٰهُ وَنِعْمَ الْوَكِيْلُ۝ وَلَا حَوْلَ وَلَا قُوَّةَ اِلَّا بِاللّٰهِ الْعَلِيِّ الْعَظِيْمِ ۝ **اَللّٰهُمَّ** اِنِّىٓ اَبْرَءُ اِلَيْكَ مِنْ حَوْلِىْ وَقُوَّتِىٓ اِلٰى حَوْلِكَ وَقُوَّتِكَ۝ **اَللّٰهُمَّ** اِنِّىْ نَوَيْتُ بِصَلٰوةِ عَلَى النَّبِيِّ صَلَّى اللّٰهُ عَلَيْهِ وَسَلَّمَ اِمْتِثَالاً لِّاَمْرِكَ وَتَصْدِيْقًا لِّنَبِيِّكَ سَيِّدِنَا مُحَمَّدٍ صَلَّى اللّٰهُ عَلَيْهِ وَسَلَّمَ وَمَحَبَّةً فِيْهِ وَشَوْقًا اِلَيْهِ وَتَعْظِيْمًا لِّقَدْرِهٖ وَلِكَوْنِهٖ اَهْلاً لِّذٰلِكَ فَتَقَبَّلْهَا مِنِّىْ بِفَضْلِكَ وَاِحْسَانِكَ وَاَزِلْ حِجَابَ الْغَفْلَةِ عَنْ قَلْبِىْ وَاجْعَلْنِىْ مِنْ عِبَادِكَ الصّٰلِحِيْنَ ۝ **اَللّٰهُمَّ** زِدْهُ شَرَفًا عَلٰى شَرَفِهِ الَّذِىْٓ اَوْلَيْتَهٗ۝ وَعِزًّا عَلٰى عِزِّهِ الَّذِىْٓ اَعْطَيْتَهٗ ۝ وَنُوْرًا عَلٰى نُوْرِهِ الَّذِىْ مِنْهُ خَلَقْتَهٗ۝ وَاَعْلِ مَقَامَهٗ فِىْ مَقَامَاتِ الْمُرْسَلِيْنَ ۝ وَدَرَجَتَهٗ فِىْ دَرَجَاتِ النَّبِيِّيْنَ ۝ وَاَسْئَلُكَ رِضَاكَ وَرِضَاهُ يَا رَبَّ الْعٰلَمِيْنَ مَعَ الْعَافِيَةِ الدَّآئِمَةِ وَالْمَوْتَ عَلَى الْكِتَابِ وَالسُّنَّةِ وَالْجَمَاعَةِ وَكَلِمَتِى الشَّهَادَةِ عَلٰى تَحْقِيْقِهَا مِنْ غَيْرِ تَغْيِيْرٍ وَّ تَبْدِيْلٍ وَّاغْفِرْلِىْ مَا ارْتَكَبْتُهٗ بِمَنِّكَ وَفَضْلِكَ وَجُوْدِكَ وَكَرَمِكَ يَآ اَرْحَمَ الرّٰحِمِيْنَ وَصَلَّى اللّٰهُ عَلٰى سَيِّدِنَا مُحَمَّدٍ وَّاٰلِهٖ وَصَحْبِهٖ وَسَلَّمَ۝

هَذِهٖ صِفَةُ الرَّوْضَةِ الَّتِىْ دُفِنَ فِيْهَا رَسُوْلُ اللّٰهِ صَلَّى اللّٰهُ عَلَيْهِ وَسَلَّمَ وَصَاحِبَاهُ اَبُوْبَكْرٍ وَعُمَرُ رَضِىَ اللّٰهُ عَنْهُمَا

هٰكَذَا ذَكَرَهٗ عُرْوَةُ ابْنُ الزُّبَيْرِ رَضِىَ اللّٰهُ تَعَالٰى عَنْهُ قَالَ دُفِنَ رَسُوْلُ اللّٰهِ صَلَّى اللّٰهُ عَلَيْهِ وَسَلَّمَ فِى السَّهْوَةِ وَ دُفِنَ اَبُوْبَكْرٍ رَّضِىَ اللّٰهُ عَنْهُ خَلْفَ رَسُوْلِ اللّٰهِ صَلَّى اللّٰهُ عَلَيْهِ وَسَلَّمَ وَدُفِنَ عُمَرُ بْنُ الْخَطَّابِ رَضِىَ اللّٰهُ عَنْهُ عِنْدَ رِجْلَىْ اَبِىْ

The Supplication of Intention

In the Name of God, The Merciful, The Compassionate

Praise be to God, Lord of the Worlds! God suffices me, and He is the best Protector! There is no help or power save in God, the High, the Mighty! **O God**, I rid myself of reliance upon any help or power save Your Help and Your Power. **O God**, I intend to ask for blessings upon the Prophet, God's blessings and peace be upon him, in obedience to Your Command and with faith in Your Prophet, our master Muḥammad, God's blessings and peace be upon him, loving him and longing for him, extolling the greatness of his rank and because he is deserving of this! Accept this from us through Your Favors and Your Grace, and make the veil of forgetfulness fall from my heart and make me one of Your righteous servants! **O God**, make him more noble than he is already! And make him mightier than he is already! And make his light greater than the light from which You created him! And make his station higher than all the stations of the Messengers! And his rank higher than all the ranks of the Prophets! And I ask You for Your Pleasure and his pleasure, O Lord of the Worlds, and eternal well-being and a death following The Book and the *sunna*, and that my witnessing of faith is truly without modification or innovation! Forgive me, through Your Grace, Your Favor, Your Generosity and Your Nobility, for what I have done, O Merciful of the Merciful, and the blessings and peace of God be upon our master Muḥammad, his family and his Companions!

The Description of the Rawḍah
(the tomb of the Prophet, God's blessings and peace be upon him!)

This is a description of the *Rawḍah* (Paradisal Garden) in which are buried the Messenger of God, God's blessings and peace be upon him, and his Companions, Abū Bakr and ᶜUmar, may God be pleased with them both! Thus ᶜUrwah ibn al-Zubayr, may God be pleased with him, mentioned: "The Messenger of God, God's blessings and peace be upon him, is buried in an alcove, and Abū Bakr, may God be pleased with him, is behind the Messenger of God, God's blessings and peace be upon him. ᶜUmār ibn al-Khattāb, may God be pleased with him, is buried at the feet of Abū

بَكْرٍ وَّبَقِيَتِ السَّهْوَةُ الشَّرْقِيَّةُ فَارِغَةً فِيْهَا مَوْضِعُ قَبْرٍ يُّقَالُ لَهٗ وَاللّٰهُ اَعْلَمُ اَنَّ عِيْسَى ابْنَ مَرْيَمَ عَلَيْهِ السَّلَامُ يُدْفَنُ فِيْهِ وَكَذٰلِكَ جَآءَ فِي الْخَبَرِ عَنْ رَّسُوْلِ اللّٰهِ صَلَّى اللّٰهُ عَلَيْهِ وَسَلَّمَ وَقَالَتْ عَآئِشَةُ رَضِيَ اللّٰهُ عَنْهَا رَاَيْتُ ثَلٰثَةَ اَقْمَارٍ سُقُوْطًا فِيْ حُجْرَتِيْ فَقَصَصْتُ رُءْيَايَ عَلَى اَبِيْ بَكْرٍ رض فَقَالَ لِيْ يَاعَآئِشَةُ لَيُدْفَنَنَّ فِيْ بَيْتِكِ ثَلٰثَةٌ هُمْ خَيْرُ اَهْلِ الْاَرْضِ فَلَمَّا تُوُفِّيَ رَسُوْلُ اللّٰهِ صَلَّى اللّٰهُ عَلَيْهِ وَسَلَّمَ وَدُفِنَ فِيْ بَيْتِيْ قَالَ لِيْ اَبُوْبَكْرٍ رض هٰذَا وَاحِدٌ مِّنْ اَقْمَارِكِ وَهُوَ خَيْرُهُمْ صَلَّى اللّٰهُ عَلَيْهِ وَعَلٰى اٰلِهٖ وَسَلَّمَ كَثِيْرًا ۝

فَصْلٌ فِيْ كَيْفِيَّةِ الصَّلٰوةِ

عَلَى النَّبِيِّ صَلَّى اللّٰهُ عَلَيْهِ وَاٰلِهٖ وَسَلَّمَ ۝

اَلْحِزْبُ الْاَوَّلُ

بِسْمِ اللّٰهِ الرَّحْمٰنِ الرَّحِيْمِ ۝

صَلَّى اللّٰهُ عَلٰى سَيِّدِنَا وَمَوْلٰنَا مُحَمَّدٍ وَّعَلٰى اٰلِهٖ وَصَحْبِهٖ وَسَلَّمَ ۝ **اَللّٰهُمَّ** صَلِّ عَلٰى سَيِّدِنَا مُحَمَّدٍ وَّاَزْوَاجِهٖ وَذُرِّيَّتِهٖ كَمَا صَلَّيْتَ عَلٰى سَيِّدِنَآ اِبْرٰهِيْمَ وَبَارِكْ عَلٰى سَيِّدِنَا مُحَمَّدٍ وَّاَزْوَاجِهٖ وَذُرِّيَّتِهٖ كَمَا بَارَكْتَ عَلٰى اٰلِ سَيِّدِنَآ اِبْرٰهِيْمَ اِنَّكَ حَمِيْدٌ مَّجِيْدٌ ۝ **اَللّٰهُمَّ** صَلِّ عَلٰى سَيِّدِنَا مُحَمَّدٍ وَّعَلٰى اٰلِهٖ كَمَا صَلَّيْتَ عَلٰى سَيِّدِنَآ اِبْرٰهِيْمَ وَبَارِكْ عَلٰى سَيِّدِنَا مُحَمَّدٍ وَّعَلٰى اٰلِ سَيِّدِنَا مُحَمَّدٍ كَمَا بَارَكْتَ عَلٰى اٰلِ سَيِّدِنَآ اِبْرٰهِيْمَ فِي الْعٰلَمِيْنَ اِنَّكَ حَمِيْدٌ مَّجِيْدٌ ۝ **اَللّٰهُمَّ** صَلِّ عَلٰى سَيِّدِنَا مُحَمَّدٍ وَّاٰلِ سَيِّدِنَا مُحَمَّدٍ كَمَا صَلَّيْتَ عَلٰى سَيِّدِنَآ اِبْرٰهِيْمَ وَبَارِكْ عَلٰى سَيِّدِنَا مُحَمَّدٍ وَّاٰلِ سَيِّدِنَا مُحَمَّدٍ كَمَا بَارَكْتَ عَلٰى سَيِّدِنَآ اِبْرٰهِيْمَ اِنَّكَ حَمِيْدٌ

Bakr and the eastern side of the alcove is left empty. There is a place for another tomb. They say, and God knows best, that Jesus son of Mary, peace be upon him, will be buried there, and this is part of the good news brought by the Messenger of God, God's blessings and peace be upon him."

ᶜAyishah, may God be pleased with her, said: "I saw three moons falling into my room. I told my vision to Abū Bakr, may God be pleased with him. He told me, 'O ᶜAyishah, there will be three buried in your house. They are better than all the people of the earth.'

"When the Messenger of God, God's blessings and peace be upon him, passed away, he was buried in my house. Abū Bakr, may God be pleased with him, said to me, 'This is one of your moons and he is the best of them, God's blessings and peace be upon him and his family!'"

The Method of Requesting Blessings upon the Prophet, God's blessings and peace be upon him and his Family

The First Part to be Read on Monday

In the Name of God, the Merciful, The Compassionate

God's blessings and peace be upon our liege and master Muḥammad and on his family and Companions!

O God, bless our master Muḥammad and his wives and his descendants just as You blessed our master Abraham and sanctify our master Muḥammad and his wives and descendants just as You sanctified our master Abraham, for You are the Praiseworthy, the Mighty!

O God, bless our master Muḥammad and his family just as You blessed our master Abraham and sanctify our master Muḥammad and the family of Muḥammad just as You sanctified Abraham and the family of Abraham in all the worlds, for You are the Praiseworthy, the Mighty!

O God, bless our master Muḥammad and the family of our master Muḥammad just as You blessed our master Abraham and sanctify our master Muḥammad and the family of Muḥammad just as You sanctified our master Abraham, for You are the Praiseworthy,

مَّجِيْدٌ ○ **اَللّٰهُمَّ** صَلِّ عَلٰى سَيِّدِنَا مُحَمَّدِنِ النَّبِيِّ الْاُمِّيِّ وَعَلٰٓى اٰلِ سَيِّدِنَا مُحَمَّدٍ ○ **اَللّٰهُمَّ** صَلِّ عَلٰى سَيِّدِنَا مُحَمَّدٍ عَبْدِكَ وَرَسُوْلِكَ ○ **اَللّٰهُمَّ** صَلِّ عَلٰى سَيِّدِنَا مُحَمَّدٍ وَّعَلٰٓى اٰلِ سَيِّدِنَا مُحَمَّدٍ كَمَا صَلَّيْتَ عَلٰى سَيِّدِنَآ اِبْرٰهِيْمَ وَعَلٰٓى اٰلِ سَيِّدِنَآ اِبْرٰهِيْمَ اِنَّكَ حَمِيْدٌ مَّجِيْدٌ ○ **اَللّٰهُمَّ** بَارِكْ عَلٰى سَيِّدِنَا مُحَمَّدٍ وَّعَلٰٓى اٰلِ سَيِّدِنَا مُحَمَّدٍ كَمَا بَارَكْتَ عَلٰى سَيِّدِنَآ اِبْرٰهِيْمَ وَعَلٰٓى اٰلِ سَيِّدِنَآ اِبْرٰهِيْمَ اِنَّكَ حَمِيْدٌ مَّجِيْدٌ ○ **اَللّٰهُمَّ** وَتَرَحَّمْ عَلٰى سَيِّدِنَا مُحَمَّدٍ وَّعَلٰٓى اٰلِ سَيِّدِنَا مُحَمَّدٍ كَمَا تَرَحَّمْتَ عَلٰى سَيِّدِنَآ اِبْرٰهِيْمَ وَعَلٰٓى اٰلِ سَيِّدِنَآ اِبْرٰهِيْمَ اِنَّكَ حَمِيْدٌ مَّجِيْدٌ ○ **اَللّٰهُمَّ** وَتَحَنَّنْ عَلٰى سَيِّدِنَا مُحَمَّدٍ وَّعَلٰٓى اٰلِ سَيِّدِنَا مُحَمَّدٍ كَمَا تَحَنَّنْتَ عَلٰى سَيِّدِنَآ اِبْرٰهِيْمَ وَعَلٰٓى اٰلِ سَيِّدِنَآ اِبْرٰهِيْمَ اِنَّكَ حَمِيْدٌ مَّجِيْدٌ ○ **اَللّٰهُمَّ** وَسَلِّمْ عَلٰى سَيِّدِنَا مُحَمَّدٍ وَّعَلٰٓى اٰلِ سَيِّدِنَا مُحَمَّدٍ كَمَا سَلَّمْتَ عَلٰى سَيِّدِنَآ اِبْرٰهِيْمَ وَعَلٰٓى اٰلِ سَيِّدِنَآ اِبْرٰهِيْمَ اِنَّكَ حَمِيْدٌ مَّجِيْدٌ ○ **اَللّٰهُمَّ** صَلِّ عَلٰى سَيِّدِنَا مُحَمَّدٍ وَّعَلٰٓى اٰلِ سَيِّدِنَا مُحَمَّدٍ وَّارْحَمْ سَيِّدِنَا مُحَمَّدً وَّاٰلَ سَيِّدِنَا مُحَمَّدٍ وَّبَارِكْ عَلٰى سَيِّدِنَا مُحَمَّدٍ وَّعَلٰٓى اٰلِ سَيِّدِنَا مُحَمَّدٍ كَمَا صَلَّيْتَ وَرَحِمْتَ وَبَارَكْتَ عَلٰى سَيِّدِنَآ اِبْرٰهِيْمَ وَعَلٰٓى اٰلِ سَيِّدِنَآ اِبْرٰهِيْمَ فِى الْعٰلَمِيْنَ اِنَّكَ حَمِيْدٌ مَّجِيْدٌ ○ **اَللّٰهُمَّ** صَلِّ عَلٰى سَيِّدِنَا مُحَمَّدِنِ النَّبِيِّ وَاَزْوَاجِهٖ اُمَّهَاتِ الْمُؤْمِنِيْنَ وَذُرِّيَّتِهٖ وَاَهْلِ بَيْتِهٖ كَمَا صَلَّيْتَ عَلٰى سَيِّدِنَآ اِبْرٰهِيْمَ اِنَّكَ حَمِيْدٌ مَّجِيْدٌ ○ **اَللّٰهُمَّ** بَارِكْ عَلٰى سَيِّدِنَا مُحَمَّدٍ وَّعَلٰٓى اٰلِ سَيِّدِنَا مُحَمَّدٍ كَمَا بَارَكْتَ عَلٰى سَيِّدِنَآ اِبْرٰهِيْمَ اِنَّكَ حَمِيْدٌ مَّجِيْدٌ ○ **اَللّٰهُمَّ** دَاحِىَ الْمَدْحُوَّاتِ وَبَارِئَ الْمَسْمُوْكَاتِ وَجَبَّارَ الْقُلُوْبِ عَلٰى فِطْرَتِهَا شَقِيِّهَا وَسَعِيْدِهَا اجْعَلْ شَرَآئِفَ صَلَوَاتِكَ وَنَوَامِىَ بَرَكَاتِكَ وَرَأْفَةَ تَحَنُّنِكَ عَلٰى

the Mighty! **O God**, bless our master **Muḥammad**, the unlettered Prophet and the family of our master **Muḥammad**! **O God**, bless our master **Muḥammad**, Your servant, Your Messenger! **O God**, bless our master **Muḥammad** and the family of our master **Muḥammad** just as You blessed our master Abraham and the family of our master Abraham, for You are the Praiseworthy, the Mighty!

O God, sanctify our master **Muḥammad** and the family of our master **Muḥammad** just as You sanctified our master Abraham and the family of Abraham, for You are the Praiseworthy, the Mighty!

O God, show mercy to our master **Muḥammad** and the family of our master **Muḥammad** just as You showed mercy to our master Abraham and the family of Abraham, for You are the Praiseworthy, the Mighty!

O God, be kind to our master **Muḥammad** and the family of our master **Muḥammad** just as You were kind to our master Abraham and the family of our master Abraham, for You are the Praiseworthy, the Mighty!

O God, grant peace to our master **Muḥammad** and the family of our master **Muḥammad** just as You granted peace to our master Abraham and the family of our master Abraham, for You are the Praiseworthy, the Mighty!

O God, bless our master **Muḥammad** and the family of our master **Muḥammad**, and be merciful to our master **Muḥammad** and the family of our master **Muḥammad**, and sanctify our master **Muḥammad** and the family of our master **Muḥammad** just as You blessed, and showed mercy to, and sanctified our master Abraham and the family of our master Abraham in the worlds, for You are the Praiseworthy, the Mighty!

O God, bless our master **Muḥammad**, the Prophet, and his wives, the Mothers of the Believers, and his descendants and the People of his House just as You blessed our master Abraham, for You are the Praiseworthy, the Mighty!

O God, bless our master **Muḥammad** and the family of our master **Muḥammad** just as You blessed our master Abraham, for You are the Praiseworthy, the Mighty!

O God, the Leveller of the Plains, the Maker of the Firmament, and the Molder of Hearts into the good and the bad, grant Your noblest blessings, most fruitful favors and most loving kindness to our

سَيِّدِنَا مُحَمَّدٍ عَبْدِكَ وَرَسُوْلِكَ الْفَاتِحِ لِمَآ اُغْلِقَ وَالْخَاتِمِ لِمَا سَبَقَ وَالْمُعْلِنِ الْحَقَّ بِالْحَقِّ وَالدَّامِغِ لِجَيْشَاتِ الْاَبَاطِيْلِ كَمَا حُمِّلَ فَاضْطَلَعَ بِاَمْرِكَ لِطَاعَتِكَ مُسْتَوْفِزًا فِى مَرْضَاتِكَ وَاعِيًا لِّوَحْيِكَ حَافِظًا لِّعَهْدِكَ مَاضِيًا عَلٰى نِفَاذِ اَمْرِكَ حَتّٰى اَوْرٰى قَبَسًا لِّقَابِسٍ اٰلَآءُ اللّٰهِ تَصِلُ بِاَهْلِهٖ اَسْبَابَهٗ بِهٖ هُدِيَتِ الْقُلُوْبُ بَعْدَ خَوْضَاتِ الْفِتَنِ وَالْاِثْمِ وَاَبْهَجَ مُوْضِحَاتِ الْاَعْلَامِ وَنَآئِرَاتِ الْاَحْكَامِ وَمُنِيْرَاتِ الْاِسْلَامِ فَهُوَ اَمِيْنُكَ الْمَأْمُوْنُ وَخَازِنُ عِلْمِكَ الْمَخْزُوْنِ وَشَهِيْدُكَ يَوْمَ الدِّيْنِ وَبَعِيْثُكَ نِعْمَةً وَّرَسُوْلُكَ بِالْحَقِّ رَحْمَةً ۝ **اَللّٰهُمَّ** افْسَحْ لَهٗ فِىْ عَدْنِكَ وَاجْزِهٖ مُضَاعَفَاتِ الْخَيْرِ مِنْ فَضْلِكَ مُهَنَّاتٍ لَّهٗ غَيْرَ مُكَدَّرَاتٍ مِّنْ فَوْزِ ثَوَابِكَ الْمَحْلُوْلِ وَجَزِيْلِ عَطَآئِكَ الْمَعْلُوْلِ ۝ **اَللّٰهُمَّ** اَعْلِ عَلٰى بِنَاءِ النَّاسِ بِنَآئَهٗ وَاَكْرِمْ مَّثْوَاهُ لَدَيْكَ وَنُزُلَهٗ وَاَتْمِمْ لَهٗ نُوْرَهٗ وَاجْزِهٖ مِنِ ابْتِعَاثِكَ لَهٗ مَقْبُوْلَ الشَّهَادَةِ وَمَرْضِيَّ الْمَقَالَةِ ذَا مَنْطِقٍ عَدْلٍ وَّخُطَّةٍ فَصْلٍ وَّبُرْهَانٍ عَظِيْمٍ ۝ اِنَّ اللّٰهَ وَمَلٰٓئِكَتَهٗ يُصَلُّوْنَ عَلَى النَّبِيِّ ط يَآ اَيُّهَا الَّذِيْنَ آمَنُوْا صَلُّوْا عَلَيْهِ وَسَلِّمُوْا تَسْلِيْمًا ۝ لَبَّيْكَ اَللّٰهُمَّ رَبِّىْ وَسَعْدَيْكَ صَلَوَاتُ اللّٰهِ الْبَرِّ الرَّحِيْمِ وَالْمَلٰٓئِكَةِ الْمُقَرَّبِيْنَ وَالنَّبِيّٖنَ وَالصِّدِّيْقِيْنَ وَالشُّهَدَآءِ وَالصَّالِحِيْنَ وَمَا سَبَّحَ لَكَ مِنْ شَىْءٍ يَّا رَبَّ الْعٰلَمِيْنَ عَلٰى سَيِّدِنَا مُحَمَّدِ بْنِ عَبْدِاللّٰهِ خَاتِمِ النَّبِيّٖنَ وَسَيِّدِ الْمُرْسَلِيْنَ وَاِمَامِ الْمُتَّقِيْنَ وَرَسُوْلِ رَبِّ الْعٰلَمِيْنَ الشَّاهِدِ الْبَشِيْرِ الدَّاعِىْٓ اِلَيْكَ بِاِذْنِكَ السِّرَاجِ الْمُنِيْرِ عَلَيْهِ السَّلَامُ ۝ **اَللّٰهُمَّ** اجْعَلْ صَلَوَاتِكَ وَبَرَكَاتِكَ وَرَحْمَتَكَ عَلٰى سَيِّدِ الْمُرْسَلِيْنَ وَاِمَامِ الْمُتَّقِيْنَ وَخَاتِمِ النَّبِيّٖنَ سَيِّدِنَا مُحَمَّدٍ عَبْدِكَ وَرَسُوْلِكَ اِمَامِ الْخَيْرِ وَقَآئِدِ الْخَيْرِ وَرَسُوْلِ الرَّحْمَةِ ۝ **اَللّٰهُمَّ** ابْعَثْهُ مَقَامًا مَّحْمُوْدًا يَّغْبِطُهٗ فِيْهِ الْاَوَّلُوْنَ

master **Muḥammad**, Your Servant and Your Messenger, the opener of what was locked and the Seal of what had gone before, the announcer of truth with truth, and the refuter of the forces of falsehood! He who took upon himself the responsibility of Your order in obedience to You, speedily seeking Your Pleasure, earnestly heeding Your Revelation, keeping Your Promise, carrying out and executing Your Command, so that, by kindling a burning brand for the seeker, his followers gain access through him to the blessings of God! Hearts were guided through him after having entered into discord and sin, and he gladdened with evident signs, with enlightening laws and illuminating Islam! And he is Your trustworthy one and safe custodian of Your Secret Knowledge, Your witness on the Day of Judgment and Your envoy, a favor for us, and Your Messenger, in truth, a mercy for us! **O God**, widen for him his place in Your Eden and reward him doubly with the goodness of Your Favor granting him untarnished felicitations from the victory of Your Reward, which is plentiful and fitting, and from Your Lofty Gift!

O God, raise that which he established over all that mankind has established and ennoble his place and his sojourn with You, and complete for him his light and reward him with Your approval so that his testimony is accepted and his word is pleasing to You, making him the one whose utterance is just and whose course is distinct and whose argument is mighty! Verily, God and his angels bless the Prophet! O you who believe, ask (God) to bless him and grant him abundant peace! I am here, O God, at Your service and at Your Command, my Lord! The blessings of God, the Good, the Merciful, and of his closest angels, and of the Prophets and of the sincere ones, and of the martyrs and of the good ones and of whatever else exists which glorifies You, O Lord of the Worlds, are for our master **Muḥammad**, son of ᶜAbd Allāh, the Seal of the Prophets and the master of the Messengers, the leader of the pious and the Messenger of the Lord of the Worlds, the witness, the bringer of good tidings, the caller to You by Your leave, the lamp, the illumined one, on him may there be peace!

O God, grant Your blessings and Your favors and Your Mercy to the master of the Messengers and the leader of the pious and Seal of the Prophets, our master **Muḥammad**, Your Servant and Your Messenger, the pioneer of goodness and guide to the goodness, the Messenger of mercy!

O God, send him to the most praised station, the envy of those who

came first

وَالْاٰخِرُوْنَ ۝ **اَللّٰهُمَّ** صَلِّ عَلٰى سَيِّدِنَا مُحَمَّدٍ وَّعَلٰى اٰلِ سَيِّدِنَا مُحَمَّدٍ كَمَا صَلَّيْتَ عَلٰى سَيِّدِنَآ اِبْرٰهِيْمَ اِنَّكَ حَمِيْدٌ مَّجِيْدٌ ۝ **اَللّٰهُمَّ** بَارِكْ عَلٰى سَيِّدِنَا مُحَمَّدٍ وَّعَلٰى اٰلِ سَيِّدِنَا مُحَمَّدٍ كَمَا بَارَكْتَ عَلٰى سَيِّدِنَآ اِبْرٰهِيْمَ اِنَّكَ حَمِيْدٌ مَّجِيْدٌ ۝ **اَللّٰهُمَّ** صَلِّ عَلٰى سَيِّدِنَا مُحَمَّدٍ وَّعَلٰى اٰلِهٖ وَاَصْحَابِهٖ وَاَوْلَادِهٖ وَاَزْوَاجِهٖ وَذُرِّيَّتِهٖ وَاَهْلِ بَيْتِهٖ وَاَصْهَارِهٖ وَاَنْصَارِهٖ وَاَشْيَاعِهٖ وَمُحِبِّيْهِ وَاُمَّتِهٖ وَعَلَيْنَا مَعَهُمْ اَجْمَعِيْنَ يَا اَرْحَمَ الرَّاحِمِيْنَ ۝ **اَللّٰهُمَّ** صَلِّ عَلٰى سَيِّدِنَا مُحَمَّدٍ عَدَدَ مَنْ صَلّٰى عَلَيْهِ وَصَلِّ عَلٰى سَيِّدِنَا مُحَمَّدٍ عَدَدَ مَنْ لَّمْ يُصَلِّ عَلَيْهِ وَصَلِّ عَلٰى سَيِّدِنَا مُحَمَّدٍ كَمَآ اَمَرْتَنَا بِالصَّلٰوةِ عَلَيْهِ وَصَلِّ عَلَيْهِ كَمَا يُحِبُّ اَنْ يُّصَلّٰى عَلَيْهِ ۝ **اَللّٰهُمَّ** صَلِّ عَلٰى سَيِّدِنَا مُحَمَّدٍ وَّعَلٰى اٰلِ سَيِّدِنَا مُحَمَّدٍ كَمَآ اَمَرْتَنَآ اَنْ نُّصَلِّيَ عَلَيْهِ ۝ **اَللّٰهُمَّ** صَلِّ عَلٰى سَيِّدِنَا مُحَمَّدٍ وَّعَلٰى اٰلِ سَيِّدِنَا مُحَمَّدٍ كَمَا هُوَ اَهْلُهٗ ۝ **اَللّٰهُمَّ** صَلِّ عَلٰى سَيِّدِنَا مُحَمَّدٍ وَّعَلٰى اٰلِ سَيِّدِنَا مُحَمَّدٍ كَمَا تُحِبُّ وَتَرْضَاهُ لَهٗ ۝ **اَللّٰهُمَّ** يَا رَبَّ سَيِّدِنَا مُحَمَّدٍ وَّاٰلِ سَيِّدِنَا مُحَمَّدٍ صَلِّ عَلٰى سَيِّدِنَا مُحَمَّدٍ وَّاٰلِ سَيِّدِنَا مُحَمَّدٍ وَّاَعْطِ سَيِّدِنَا مُحَمَّدَنِ الدَّرَجَةَ وَالْوَسِيْلَةَ فِى الْجَنَّةِ ۝ **اَللّٰهُمَّ** يَا رَبَّ سَيِّدِنَا مُحَمَّدٍ وَاٰلِ سَيِّدِنَا مُحَمَّدِنِ اجْزِ سَيِّدِنَا مُحَمَّدًا صَلَّى اللّٰهُ عَلَيْهِ وَسَلَّمَ مَا هُوَ اَهْلُهٗ ۝ **اَللّٰهُمَّ** صَلِّ عَلٰى سَيِّدِنَا مُحَمَّدٍ وَّعَلٰى اٰلِ سَيِّدِنَا مُحَمَّدٍ وَّعَلٰى اَهْلِ بَيْتِهٖ ۝ **اَللّٰهُمَّ** صَلِّ عَلٰى سَيِّدِنَا مُحَمَّدٍ وَّعَلٰى اٰلِ سَيِّدِنَا مُحَمَّدٍ حَتّٰى لَا يَبْقٰى مِنَ الصَّلٰوةِ شَيْءٌ ۝ وَّارْحَمْ سَيِّدِنَا مُحَمَّدًا وَّاٰلَ سَيِّدِنَا مُحَمَّدٍ حَتّٰى لَا يَبْقٰى مِنَ الرَّحْمَةِ شَيْءٌ ۝ وَّبَارِكْ عَلٰى سَيِّدِنَا مُحَمَّدٍ وَّعَلٰى اٰلِ سَيِّدِنَا مُحَمَّدٍ حَتّٰى لَا يَبْقٰى مِنَ الْبَرَكَةِ شَيْءٌ ۝ وَّسَلِّمْ عَلٰى سَيِّدِنَا مُحَمَّدٍ وَّعَلٰى اٰلِ سَيِّدِنَا مُحَمَّدٍ حَتّٰى لَا يَبْقٰى مِنَ

and those who came last!

O God, bless our master Muḥammad and the family of our master Muḥammad just as You blessed our master Abraham, for You are the Praiseworthy, the Mighty! **O God**, sanctify our master Muḥammad and the family of our master Muḥammad just as You sanctified our master Abraham, for You are the Praiseworthy, the Mighty!

O God, bless our master Muḥammad, his family, his Companions, his children, his wives, his descendants, the People of his House, his relations by marriage, his Helpers, his adherents, his lovers, his nation and all of us along with them, O Most Merciful of the Merciful!

O God, bless our master Muḥammad as many times as those who have asked for blessings upon him and bless our master Muḥammad as many times as those who have not asked for blessings upon him! And bless him as we have been ordered to ask You to bless him and bless him just as You like him to be blessed!

O God, bless our master Muḥammad and the family of our master Muḥammad as we have been ordered to ask for blessings upon him!

O God, bless our master Muḥammad and the family of our master Muḥammad as he deserves!

O God, bless our master Muḥammad and the family of our master Muḥammad just as You like and just as You are pleased with him!

O God, O Lord of our master Muḥammad and family of our master Muḥammad, bless our master Muḥammad and the family of our master Muḥammad and grant to our master Muḥammad the rank of the closest access in the Garden!

O God, O Lord of our master Muḥammad and the family of our master Muḥammad, reward our master Muḥammad, may God bless him and give him peace, just as he is deserving!

O God, bless our master Muḥammad and the family of our master Muḥammad and the People of his House!

O God, bless our master Muḥammad and the family of our master Muḥammad until there remains not a single drop of blessings!

O God, Favor our master Muḥammad and the family of our master Muḥammad until there remains not a single drop of Favor!

Have mercy on our master Muḥammad and the family of our master Muhammad until there remains not a single drop of mercy!

Bless our master Muḥammad and the family of our master Muhammad until nothing remains of blessings.

Grant peace to our master Muḥammad and the family of our master Muḥammad until there remains not

السَّلَامِ شَىْءٌ ۝ **اَللّٰهُمَّ** صَلِّ عَلٰى سَيِّدِنَا مُحَمَّدٍ فِى الْاَوَّلِيْنَ ۝ وَصَلِّ عَلٰى سَيِّدِنَا مُحَمَّدٍ فِى الْاٰخِرِيْنَ ۝ وَصَلِّ عَلٰى سَيِّدِنَا مُحَمَّدٍ فِى النَّبِيِّيْنَ ۝ وَصَلِّ عَلٰى سَيِّدِنَا مُحَمَّدٍ فِى الْمُرْسَلِيْنَ ۝ وَصَلِّ عَلٰى سَيِّدِنَا مُحَمَّدٍ فِى الْمَلَاِ الْاَعْلٰٓى اِلٰى يَوْمِ الدِّيْنِ ۝ **اَللّٰهُمَّ** اَعْطِ سَيِّدِنَا مُحَمَّدَ ࣙالْوَسِيْلَةَ وَالْفَضِيْلَةَ وَالشَّرَفَ وَالدَّرَجَةَ الْكَبِيْرَةَ ۝ **اَللّٰهُمَّ** اِنِّىٓ اٰمَنْتُ بِسَيِّدِنَا مُحَمَّدٍ وَّلَمْ اَرَهُ فَلَا تَحْرِمْنِى فِى الْجِنَانِ رُؤْيَتَهٗ وَارْزُقْنِى صُحْبَتَهٗ وَتَوَفَّنِى عَلٰى مِلَّتِهٖ وَاسْقِنِى مِنْ حَوْضِهٖ مَشْرَبًا رَّوِيًّا سَآئِغًا هَنِيْٓئًا لَّا نَظْمَأُ بَعْدَهٗ اَبَدًا اِنَّكَ عَلٰى كُلِّ شَىْءٍ قَدِيْرٌ ۝ **اَللّٰهُمَّ** اَبْلِغْ رُوْحَ سَيِّدِنَا مُحَمَّدٍ مِّنِّىْ تَحِيَّةً وَّسَلَامًا ۝ **اَللّٰهُمَّ** وَكَمَآ اٰمَنْتُ بِسَيِّدِنَا مُحَمَّدٍ وَّلَمْ اَرَهُ فَلَا تَحْرِمْنِىْ فِى الْجِنَانِ رُؤْيَتَهٗ ۝ **اَللّٰهُمَّ** تَقَبَّلْ شَفَاعَةَ سَيِّدِنَا مُحَمَّدِ ࣙالْكُبْرٰى وَارْفَعْ دَرَجَتَهُ الْعُلْيَا وَآتِهٖ سُؤْلَهٗ فِى الْاٰخِرَةِ وَالْاُوْلٰى كَمَآ اٰتَيْتَ سَيِّدَنَآ اِبْرٰهِيْمَ وَسَيِّدَنَا مُوْسٰى ۝ **اَللّٰهُمَّ** صَلِّ عَلٰى سَيِّدِنَا مُحَمَّدٍ وَّعَلٰٓى اٰلِ سَيِّدِنَا مُحَمَّدٍ كَمَا صَلَّيْتَ عَلٰى سَيِّدِنَآ اِبْرٰهِيْمَ وَعَلٰٓى اٰلِ سَيِّدِنَآ اِبْرٰهِيْمَ وَبَارِكْ عَلٰى سَيِّدِنَا مُحَمَّدٍ وَّعَلٰٓى اٰلِ سَيِّدِنَا مُحَمَّدٍ كَمَا بَارَكْتَ عَلٰى سَيِّدِنَآ اِبْرٰهِيْمَ وَعَلٰٓى اٰلِ سَيِّدِنَآ اِبْرٰهِيْمَ اِنَّكَ حَمِيْدٌ مَّجِيْدٌ ۝ **اَللّٰهُمَّ** صَلِّ وَسَلِّمْ وَ بَارِكْ عَلٰى سَيِّدِنَا مُحَمَّدٍ نَّبِيِّكَ وَرَسُوْلِكَ ۝ وَ سَيِّدِنَآ اِبْرٰهِيْمَ خَلِيْلِكَ وَصَفِيِّكَ وَ سَيِّدِنَا مُوْسٰى كَلِيْمِكَ وَنَجِيِّكَ ۝ وَسَيِّدِنَا عِيْسٰى رُوْحِكَ وَ كَلِمَتِكَ وَعَلٰى جَمِيْعِ مَلٰٓئِكَتِكَ وَ رُسُلِكَ وَ اَنْبِيَآئِكَ وَخِيَرَتِكَ مِنْ خَلْقِكَ وَ اَصْفِيَآئِكَ وَ خَآصَّتِكَ وَ اَوْلِيَآئِكَ مِنْ اَهْلِ اَرْضِكَ وَسَمَآئِكَ ۝ وَصَلَّى اللّٰهُ عَلٰى سَيِّدِنَا مُحَمَّدٍ عَدَدَ خَلْقِهٖ وَرِضٰى نَفْسِهٖ وَزِنَةَ عَرْشِهٖ وَمِدَادَ كَلِمَاتِهٖ وَكَمَا هُوَ اَهْلُهٗ وَكُلَّمَا ذَكَرَهُ الذّٰكِرُوْنَ وَغَفَلَ عَنْ

a single drop of blessing!

O God, bless our master Muḥammad among the first!

O God, bless our master Muḥammad among the last!

O God, bless our master Muḥammad among the Prophets!

O God, bless our master Muḥammad among the Messengers!

O God, bless our master Muḥammad in the heavenly assembly until the Day of Reckoning!

O God, grant our master Muḥammad the position of the closest access, the pre-eminence and the noblest and greatest rank!

O God, I have believed in our master Muḥammad and I have not seen him so do not deprive my heart of a vision of him and provide me with his companionship and have me die on his way and lead me to drink from his pool plentifully, blissfully, heartily, a drink after which we will never feel thirst, for You are the Power of all things!

O God, send to the soul of our master Muḥammad my greetings and my salutations!

O God, just as I have believed in our master Muḥammad without seeing him, so do not deprive my heart of a vision of him!

O God, accept the great intercession of our master Muḥammad, raise his rank high and give him that which he asks for in the Hereafter and in this present life, just as You gave to our master Abraham and our master Moses!

O God, bless our master Muḥammad and the family of our master Muḥammad just as You blessed our master Abraham and the family of Abraham and sanctify our master Muḥammad and the family of our master Muḥammad just as You sanctified our master Abraham and the family of our master Abraham, for You are the Praiseworthy, the Mighty!

O God, bless, sanctify and grant peace to our master Muḥammad, Your Prophet, Your Messenger! And also our master Abraham, Your friend and pure one and our master Moses, Your interlocutor and intimate! And also our master Jesus, Your spirit and Word, all the angels, Messengers and Prophets, the righteous ones from Your creation, the pure ones, the elected ones and Your saints from the folk of Your earth and Your heaven! And may God's blessings be for our master Muḥammad in all of His creation, to the extent of His pleasure, in the decoration of the Throne, in the ink of His words, to the measure that he deserves, and whenever those who remember him do so and whenever

they neglect

ذِكْرِهِ الْغَافِلُوْنَ وَعَلٰى اَهْلِ بَيْتِهٖ وَعِتْرَتِهِ الطَّاهِرِيْنَ وَسَلِّمْ تَسْلِيْمًا ○ **اَللّٰهُمَّ** صَلِّ عَلٰى سَيِّدِنَا مُحَمَّدٍ وَّعَلٰى اَزْوَاجِهٖ وَذُرِّيَّتِهٖ وَعَلٰى جَمِيْعِ النَّبِيِّيْنَ وَالْمُرْسَلِيْنَ وَالْمَلٰٓئِكَةِ وَالْمُقَرَّبِيْنَ وَجَمِيْعِ عِبَادِ اللّٰهِ الصّٰلِحِيْنَ عَدَدَ مَآ اَمْطَرَتِ السَّمَآءُ مُنْذُ بَنَيْتَهَا وَصَلِّ عَلٰى سَيِّدِنَا مُحَمَّدٍ عَدَدَ مَا اَنْبَتَتِ الْاَرْضُ مُنْذُ دَحَوْتَهَا ○ وَصَلِّ عَلٰى سَيِّدِنَا مُحَمَّدٍ عَدَدَ النُّجُوْمِ فِى السَّمَآءِ فَاِنَّكَ اَحْصَيْتَهَا ○ وَصَلِّ عَلٰى سَيِّدِنَا مُحَمَّدٍ عَدَدَ مَا تَنَفَّسَتِ الْاَرْوَاحُ مُنْذُ خَلَقْتَهَا ○ وَصَلِّ عَلٰى سَيِّدِنَا مُحَمَّدٍ عَدَدَ مَا خَلَقْتَ وَمَا تَخْلُقُ وَ مَآ اَحَاطَ بِهٖ عِلْمُكَ وَاَضْعَافَ ذٰلِكَ ○ **اَللّٰهُمَّ** صَلِّ عَلَيْهِمْ عَدَدَ خَلْقِكَ وَرِضَا نَفْسِكَ وَزِنَةَ عَرْشِكَ وَمِدَادَ كَلِمَاتِكَ وَمَبْلَغَ عِلْمِكَ وَ آيَاتِكَ ○ **اَللّٰهُمَّ** صَلِّ عَلَيْهِ صَلٰوةً تَفُوْقُ وَتَفْضُلُ صَلٰوةَ الْمُصَلِّيْنَ عَلَيْهِمْ مِّنَ الْخَلْقِ اَجْمَعِيْنَ كَفَضْلِكَ عَلٰى جَمِيْعِ خَلْقِكَ ○ **اَللّٰهُمَّ** صَلِّ عَلَيْهِمْ صَلٰوةً دَآئِمَةً مُّسْتَمِرَّةَ الدَّوَامِ عَلٰى مَرِّ اللَّيَالِيْ وَالْاَيَّامِ مُتَّصِلَةَ الدَّوَامِ لَا نْقِضَآءَ لَهَا وَالَا انْصِرَامَ عَلٰى مَرِّ اللَّيَالِيْ وَالْاَيَّامِ عَدَدَ كُلِّ وَابِلٍ وَّطَلٍّ ○ **اَللّٰهُمَّ** صَلِّ عَلٰى سَيِّدِنَا مُحَمَّدٍ نَّبِيِّكَ وَ سَيِّدِنَآ اِبْرٰهِيْمَ خَلِيْلِكَ وَعَلٰى جَمِيْعِ اَنْبِيَآئِكَ وَ اَصْفِيَآئِكَ مِنْ اَهْلِ اَرْضِكَ وَسَمَآئِكَ عَدَدَ خَلْقِكَ وَ رِضَا نَفْسِكَ وَزِنَةَ عَرْشِكَ وَ مِدَادَ كَلِمَاتِكَ وَ مُنْتَهٰى عِلْمِكَ وَزِنَةَ جَمِيْعِ مَخْلُوْقَاتِكَ صَلٰوةً مُّكَرَّرَةً اَبَدًا عَدَدَ مَآ اَحْصٰى عِلْمُكَ وَمِلْءَ مَآ اَحْصٰى عِلْمُكَ وَاَضْعَافَ مَآ اَحْصٰى عِلْمُكَ صَلٰوةً تَزِيْدُ وَتَفُوْقُ وَتَفْضُلُ صَلٰوةَ الْمُصَلِّيْنَ عَلَيْهِمْ مِّنَ الْخَلْقِ اَجْمَعِيْنَ كَفَضْلِكَ عَلٰى جَمِيْعِ خَلْقِكَ ○ ثُمَّ تَدْعُوْ بِهٰذَا الدُّعَآءِ فَاِنَّهٗ مَرْجُوُّ الْاِجَابَةِ اِنْ شَآءَ اللّٰهُ تَعَالٰى بَعْدَ الصَّلٰوةِ عَلَى النَّبِيِّ صَلَّى اللّٰهُ عَلَيْهِ وَسَلَّمَ ○ **اَللّٰهُمَّ** اجْعَلْنِىْ

to remember him, and may these blessings be also for the People of his House and the pure perfumed descendants, on whom may there be peace, over and over again! **O God**, bless our master Muḥammad and his wives and progeny and all the Prophets and Messengers and closest angels and all the righteous servants of God in all the rain that has fallen since the sky was formed and bless our master Muḥammad in everything the Earth has produced since it was spread out!

And bless our master **Muḥammad** as many times as there are stars in the sky and You alone are their counter!And bless our master Muḥammad in every breath of every soul from the moment You created them!

And bless our master Muḥammad in everything You have already created and in what You will create and in whatever is encompassed by Your knowledge and then double all of that!

O God, bless them in all of Your Creation and as much as it pleases Yourself, in the decoration of Your Throne, in the ink of Your Words and to the extent of Your Knowledge and Signs!

O God, bless them, with blessings excellent, and more gracious, with blessings equal to all the requests for blessings ever uttered by the whole of creation just as, in like measure, the whole of creation enjoys Your Favor!

O God, bless them, with eternal and permanent blessings, for as long as the duration of all future nights and days, never ending and perpetual, with blessings equal to the duration of all the days and nights which have already passed, with blessings as copious as the rain contained in every downpour and in every shower which have ever fallen!

O God, bless our master Muḥammad, Your Prophet, and our master Abraham, Your Friend, and all the Prophets and pure ones from the folk of Your earth and Your heaven, in all of Your creation and as it pleases Yourself, in the decoration of Your Throne, in the ink of Your words, to the extent of Your Knowledge and Adornment of Your created beings, with blessings repeated eternally as much as Your knowledge and to the depth of Your knowledge and then double this! With blessings, abundant and excellent and gracious, blessings equal to all the requests for blessings ever uttered by all of creation just as, in like measure, the whole of creation enjoys Your Favor!

(Then make this supplication, for it is to be hoped it will be answered, God willing, after asking for blessings upon the Prophet, may God grant him peace!)

O God, grant me

مِمَّنْ لَزِمَ مِلَّةَ نَبِيِّكَ سَيِّدِنَا مُحَمَّدٍ صَلَّى اللّٰهُ عَلَيْهِ وَسَلَّمَ وَعَظَّمَ حُرْمَتَهُ وَاَعَزَّ كَلِمَتَهُ وَحَفِظَ عَهْدَهُ وَذِمَّتَهُ وَنَصَرَ حِزْبَهُ وَدَعْوَتَهُ وَكَثَّرَ تَابِعِيْهِ وَفِرْقَتَهُ وَوَافَىٰ زُمْرَتَهُ وَلَمْ يُخَالِفْ سَبِيْلَهُ وَسُنَّتَهُ ○ **اَللّٰهُمَّ** اِنِّىٓ اَسْئَلُكَ الْاِسْتِمْسَاكَ بِسُنَّتِهٖ وَاَعُوْذُبِكَ مِنَ الْاِنْحِرَافِ عَمَّا جَآءَ بِهٖ ○ **اَللّٰهُمَّ** اِنِّىٓ اَسْئَلُكَ مِنْ خَيْرِ مَا سَئَلَكَ مِنْهُ سَيِّدُنَا مُحَمَّدٌ نَّبِيُّكَ وَرَسُوْلُكَ صَلَّى اللّٰهُ عَلَيْهِ وَسَلَّمَ وَ اَعُوْذُبِكَ مِنْ شَرِّ مَاسْتَعَاذَكَ مِنْهُ سَيِّدُنَا مُحَمَّدٌ نَّبِيُّكَ وَ رَسُوْلُكَ صَلَّى اللّٰهُ عَلَيْهِ وَسَلَّمَ ○ **اَللّٰهُمَّ** اَعْصِمْنِىْ مِنْ شَرِّ الْفِتَنِ وَعَافِنِىْ مِنْ جَمِيْعِ الْمِحَنِ وَاَصْلِحْ مِنِّىْ مَا ظَهَرَ وَمَا بَطَنَ وَنَقِّ قَلْبِىْ مِنَ الْحِقْدِ وَالْحَسَدِ وَلَا تَجْعَلْ عَلَىَّ تِبَاعَةً لِّاَحَدٍ ○ **اَللّٰهُمَّ** اِنِّىٓ اَسْئَلُكَ الْاَخْذَ بِاَحْسَنِ مَا تَعْلَمُ وَالتَّرْكَ لِسَيِّئِ مَا تَعْلَمُ وَ اَسْئَلُكَ التَّكَفُّلَ بِالرِّزْقِ وَالزُّهْدَ فِى الْكَفَافِ وَالْمَخْرَجَ بِالْبَيَانِ مِنْ كُلِّ شُبْهَةٍ وَّالْفَلْجَ بِالصَّوَابِ فِىْ كُلِّ حُجَّةٍ وَّ الْعَدْلَ فِى الْغَضَبِ وَالرِّضَا وَالتَّسْلِيْمَ لِمَا يَجْرِىْ بِهِ الْقَضَآءُ وَالْاِقْتِصَادَ فِى الْفَقْرِ وَالْغِنٰى وَالتَّوَاضُعَ فِى الْقَوْلِ وَالْفِعْلِ وَالصِّدْقَ فِى الْجِدِّ وَالْهَزْلِ ○ **اَللّٰهُمَّ** اِنَّ لِىْ ذُنُوْبًا فِيْمَا بَيْنِىْ وَ بَيْنَكَ وَ ذُنُوْبًا فِيْمَا بَيْنِىْ وَبَيْنَ خَلْقِكَ ○ **اَللّٰهُمَّ** مَا كَانَ لَكَ مِنْهَا فَاغْفِرْهُ وَمَا كَانَ مِنْهَا لِخَلْقِكَ فَتَحَمَّلْهُ عَنِّىْ وَاَغْنِنِىْ بِفَضْلِكَ اِنَّكَ وَاسِعُ الْمَغْفِرَةِ ○ اَللّٰهُمَّ نَوِّرْ بِالْعِلْمِ قَلْبِىْ ○ وَاسْتَعْمِلْ بِطَاعَتِكَ بَدَنِىْ ○ وَخَلِّصْ مِنَ الْفِتَنِ سِرِّىْ ○ وَاشْغَلْ بِالْاِعْتِبَارِ فِكْرِىْ ○ وَقِنِىْ شَرَّ وَسَاوِسِ الشَّيْطَانِ ○ وَاَجِرْنِىْ مِنْهُ يَا رَحْمٰنُ حَتّٰى لَا يَكُوْنَ لَهٗ عَلَىَّ سُلْطَانٌ ○

to be from among those who stick close to the way of Your Prophet, our master Muḥammad, the blessings of God be always upon him!

Strengthen his holiness, empower his words, protect his promise and security, and give victory to his party and calling and increase those who pledge him and his company allegiance!

And grant that we may die in his company and do not allow us to stray from his path and way!

O God, I ask You for loyalty to his way and seek refuge in You from all deviation from it!

O God, I ask of You the good that our master Muḥammad, Your Prophet and Your Messenger, asked of You.

And I seek refuge in You from the evil from which our master Muḥammad, Your Prophet and Your Messenger, sought refuge, may God grant him peace and bless him!

O God, protect me from the evil of discord and absolve me from all tests and purify me from within and without and cleanse my heart from hatred and envy and do not allow anyone to oppress me!

O God, I ask You for the good that You know and to let me pass by the evil that You know.

And I ask You to provide me with provision, for indifference to being physically satisfied, a clear way out from every uncertainty, a proper stance in every argument, justice in anger and pleasure, peace whatever fate ordains, providence in thought and wealth, humility in my words and actions and sincerity in my seriousness and in my jesting!

O God, indeed there are sins between me and You and there are sins between me and Your creation!

O God, what is this for You?

So forgive me my sins and whatever arises from them, bear them for me and enrich me with Your Favor, for Your forgiveness spreads wide!

O God, enlighten the knowledge of my heart and render my body obedient to You and purify me from inner discord and occupy me with contemplation.

And protect me from the whisperings of Satan and save me from
him, O Compassionate One,
until he no longer has any power over me!

اَلْحِزْبُ الثَّانِىْ فِىْ يَوْمِ الثَّلاَثَآءِ

اَللّٰهُمَّ اِنِّىٓ اَسْئَلُكَ مِنْ خَيرِ مَا تَعْلَمُ وَ اَعُوْذُبِكَ مِنْ شَرِّ مَا تَعْلَمُ وَاَسْتَغْفِرُكَ مِنْ كُلِّ مَا تَعْلَمُ اِنَّكَ تَعْلَمُ وَلاَ نَعْلَمُ وَ اَنْتَ عَلاَّمُ الْغُيُوْبِ ۝ **اَللّٰهُمَّ** ارْحَمْنِىْ مِنْ زَمَانِىْ هٰذَا وَاِحْدَاقِ الْفِتَنِ وَ تَطَاوُلِ اَهْلِ الْجُرْاَةِ عَلَىَّ وَاسْتِضْعَافِهِمْ اِيَّاىَ ۝ **اَللّٰهُمَّ** اجْعَلْنِىْ مِنْكَ فِىْ عِيَاذٍ مَّنِيْعٍ وَّحِرْزٍ حَصِيْنٍ مِّنْ جَمِيْعِ خَلْقِكَ حَتّٰى تُبَلِّغَنِىْ اَجلِىْ مُعَافًى ۝ **اَللّٰهُمَّ** صَلِّ عَلٰى سَيِّدِنَا مُحَمَّدٍ وَّعَلٰى اٰلِ سَيِّدِنَا مُحَمَّدٍ عَدَدَ مَنْ صَلّٰى عَلَيْهِ ۝ وَصَلِّ عَلٰى سَيِّدِنَا مُحَمَّدٍ وَّعَلٰى اٰلِ سَيِّدِنَا مُحَمَّدٍ عَدَدَ مَنْ لَّمْ يُصَلِّ عَلَيْهِ وَصَلِّ عَلٰى سَيِّدِنَا مُحَمَّدٍ وَّعَلٰى اٰلِ سَيِّدِنَا مُحَمَّدٍ كَمَا تَنْبَغِى الصَّلٰوةُ عَلَيْهِ وَصَلِّ عَلٰى سَيِّدِنَا مُحَمَّدٍ وَّعَلٰى اٰلِ سَيِّدِنَا مُحَمَّدٍ كَمَا تَجِبُ الصَّلٰوةُ عَلَيْهِ ۝ وَصَلِّ عَلٰى سَيِّدِنَا مُحَمَّدٍ وَّعَلٰى اٰلِ سَيِّدِنَا مُحَمَّدٍ كَمَآ اَمَرْتَ اَنْ يُّصَلّٰى عَلَيْهِ ۝ وَصَلِّ عَلٰى سَيِّدِنَا مُحَمَّدٍ وَّعَلٰى اٰلِ سَيِّدِنَا مُحَمَّدٍ ۝ اِلَّذِىْ نُوْرُهٗ مِنْ نُّوْرِ الْاَنْوَارِ وَاَشْرَقَ بِشُعَاعِ سِرِّهِ الْاَسْرَارُ ۝ **اَللّٰهُمَّ** صَلِّ عَلٰى سَيِّدِنَا مُحَمَّدٍ وَّعَلٰى اٰلِ سَيِّدِنَا مُحَمَّدٍ وَعَلٰى اَهْلِ بَيْتِهِ الْاَبْرَارِ اَجْمَعِيْنَ ۝ **اَللّٰهُمَّ** صَلِّ عَلٰى سَيِّدِنَا مُحَمَّدٍ وَّعَلٰى اٰلِهٖ بَحْرِ اَنْوَارِكَ وَمَعْدِنِ اَسْرَارِكَ وَلِسَانِ حُجَّتِكَ وَعُرُوْسِ مَمْلَكَتِكَ وَ اِمَامِ حَضْرَتِكَ وَخَاتِمِ اَنْبِيَآئِكَ صَلٰوةً تَدُوْمُ بِدَوَامِكَ وَتَبْقٰى بِبَقَآئِكَ صَلٰوةً تُرْضِيْكَ وَتُرْضِيْهِ وَتَرْضٰى بِهَا عَنَّا يَا رَبَّ الْعٰلَمِيْنَ ۝ **اَللّٰهُمَّ** رَبَّ الْحِلِّ وَالْحَرَامِ وَرَبَّ الْمَشْعَرِ الْحَرَامِ وَرَبَّ الْبَيْتِ الْحَرَامِ وَرَبَّ الرُّكْنِ وَالْمَقَامِ اَبْلِغْ لِسَيِّدِنَا وَمَوْلٰنَا مُحَمَّدٍ مِّنَّا السَّلاَمَ ۝ **اَللّٰهُمَّ** صَلِّ عَلٰى سَيِّدِنَا وَمَوْلٰنَا مُحَمَّدٍ سَيِّدِ الْاَوَّلِيْنَ وَالْاٰخِرِيْنَ ۝ **اَللّٰهُمَّ** صَلِّ عَلٰى سَيِّدِنَا وَمَوْلٰنَا مُحَمَّدٍ فِىْ كُلِّ وَقْتٍ

The Second Part to be Read on Tuesday

O God, I ask You the good of what You know and I seek refuge in You from the evil of what You know and I seek Your forgiveness for everything You know, for You indeed know and we do not know and indeed You are the Knower of the Unseen!

O God, have mercy on me in this time from the encirclement of discord, from the oppression of the insolent and their deficiencies and all such ills! **O God**, give me an unassailable refuge in You, an impenetrable protection with You from all of Your creation until I come to a virtuous end!

O God, bless our master Muḥammad and the family of our master Muḥammad as many times as those who have asked for blessings upon him!

O God, bless our master Muḥammad and the family of our master Muḥammad as many times as those who have not asked for blessings upon him and bless our master Muḥammad and the family of our master Muḥammad with as many blessings as are fitting for him and bless our master Muḥammad and the family of our master Muḥammad with as many blessings as are his due! And bless our master Muḥammad and the family of our master Muḥammad as You have ordered him to be blessed! And bless our master Muḥammad and the family of our master Muḥammad whose light is from the light of lights and who with a ray from his secret illuminated all secrets!

O God, bless our master Muḥammad and the family of our master Muḥammad and all the chosen people of his House!

O God, bless our master Muḥammad and his family, the sea of Your Lights, the mine of Your Secrets, the tongue of Your Proof, the bridegroom of Your Kingdom, the leader of Your Presence and the Seal of Your Prophets, with blessings which last as long as You last and remain as long as You remain, blessings which please You, which please him, and which make You pleased with us, O Lord of the Worlds!

O God, Lord of the Lawful and the Prohibited, Lord of the Sanctuary, Lord of the Sacred House, and Lord of the Corner and the Station of Abraham (all places connected with pilgrimage to Mecca), send peace from us to our lord and master Muḥammad!

O God, bless our liege and master Muḥammad the master of the first and the last!

O God, bless our liege and master Muḥammad at every

moment

وَّحِيْنٍ ۝ **اَللّٰهُمَّ** صَلِّ عَلٰى سَيِّدِنَا وَمَوْلٰنَا مُحَمَّدٍ فِى الْمَلَاِ الْاَعْلٰٓى اِلٰى يَوْمِ الدِّيْنِ ۝ **اَللّٰهُمَّ** صَلِّ عَلٰى سَيِّدِنَا وَمَوْلٰنَا مُحَمَّدٍ حَتّٰى تَرِثُ الْاَرْضَ وَمَنْ عَلَيْهَا وَ اَنْتَ خَيْرُ الْوَارِثِيْنَ ۝ **اَللّٰهُمَّ** صَلِّ عَلٰى سَيِّدِنَا مُحَمَّدِ نِ النَّبِيِّ الْاُمِّيِّ وَعَلٰٓى اٰلِ سَيِّدِنَا مُحَمَّدٍ كَمَا صَلَّيْتَ عَلٰى سَيِّدِنَآ اِبْرٰهِيْمَ اِنَّكَ حَمِيْدٌ مَّجِيْدٌ ۝ وَبَارِكْ عَلٰى سَيِّدِنَا مُحَمَّدِ نِ النَّبِيِّ الْاُمِّيِّ كَمَا بَارَكْتَ عَلٰى سَيِّدِنَآ اِبْرٰهِيْمَ اِنَّكَ حَمِيْدٌ مَّجِيْدٌ ۝ **اَللّٰهُمَّ** صَلِّ عَلٰى سَيِّدِنَا مُحَمَّدٍ وَّعَلٰٓى اٰلِ سَيِّدِنَا مُحَمَّدٍ عَدَدَ مَآ اَحَاطَ بِهٖ عِلْمُكَ وَجَرٰى بِهٖ قَلَمُكَ وَسَبَقَتْ بِهٖ مَشِيْئَتُكَ وَ صَلَّتْ عَلَيْهِ مَلٰٓئِكَتُكَ صَلٰوةً دَآئِمَةً بِدَوَامِكَ بَاقِيَةً بِفَضْلِكَ وَاِحْسَانِكَ اِلٰٓى اَبَدِ الْاَبَدِ اَبَدًا لَّا نِهَايَةَ لِاَبَدِيَّتِهٖ وَلَا فَنَآءَ لِدَيْمُوْمَتِهٖ ۝ **اَللّٰهُمَّ** صَلِّ عَلٰى سَيِّدِنَا مُحَمَّدٍ وَّعَلٰٓى اٰلِ سَيِّدِنَا مُحَمَّدٍ عَدَدَ مَآ اَحَاطَ بِهٖ عِلْمُكَ وَاَحْصَاهُ كِتَابُكَ وَشَهِدَتْ بِهٖ مَلٰٓئِكَتُكَ وَارْضَ عَنْ اَصْحَابِهٖ وَارْحَمْ اُمَّتَهٗ اِنَّكَ حَمِيْدٌ مَّجِيْدٌ ۝ **اَللّٰهُمَّ** صَلِّ عَلٰى سَيِّدِنَا مُحَمَّدٍ وَّعَلٰٓى اٰلِ سَيِّدِنَا مُحَمَّدٍ وَّعَلٰى جَمِيْعِ اَصْحَابِ سَيِّدِنَا مُحَمَّدٍ ۝ **اَللّٰهُمَّ** صَلِّ عَلٰى سَيِّدِنَا مُحَمَّدٍ وَّعَلٰٓى اٰلِ سَيِّدِنَا مُحَمَّدٍ كَمَا صَلَّيْتَ عَلٰى سَيِّدِنَآ اِبْرٰهِيْمَ وَبَارِكْ عَلٰى سَيِّدِنَا مُحَمَّدٍ وَّعَلٰٓى اٰلِ سَيِّدِنَا مُحَمَّدٍ كَمَا بَارَكْتَ عَلٰى سَيِّدِنَآ اِبْرٰهِيْمَ وَعَلٰٓى اٰلِ سَيِّدِنَآ اِبْرٰهِيْمَ فِى الْعَالَمِيْنَ اِنَّكَ حَمِيْدٌ مَّجِيْدٌ ۝ **اَللّٰهُمَّ** بِخُشُوْعِ الْقَلْبِ عِنْدَ السُّجُوْدِ لَكَ يَا سَيِّدِىْ بِغَيْرِ جُحُوْدٍ وَّبِكَ يَآ اَللّٰهُ يَا جَلِيْلُ فَلَا شَىْءَ يُدَانِيْكَ فِىْ غَلِيْظِ الْعُهُوْدِ وَبِكُرْسِيِّكَ الْمُكَلَّلِ بِالنُّوْرِ اِلٰى عَرْشِكَ الْعَظِيْمِ الْمَجِيْدِ ۝ وَبِمَا كَانَ تَحْتَ عَرْشِكَ حَقًّا قَبْلَ اَنْ تَخْلُقَ السَّمٰوٰتِ وَصَوْتِ الرُّعُوْدِ لَكَ اِذْ كُنْتَ مِثْلَ مَا لَمْ تَزَلْ قَطُّ اِلٰهًا عُرِفْتَ بِالتَّوْحِيْدِ فَاجْعَلْنِىْ مِنَ

and in every instant!

O God, bless our liege and master Muḥammad in the heavenly assembly until the Day of Judgment!

O God, bless our liege and master Muḥammad until the earth bequeaths itself and what is on it to You and You are the best of those who inherit!

O God, bless our liege and master Muḥammad, the unlettered Prophet, and the family of Muḥammad just as You blessed our master Abraham, for You are Praiseworthy, the Mighty! And bless our liege and master Muḥammad, the unlettered Prophet, and the family of Muḥammad just as You blessed our master Abraham, for You are Praiseworthy, the Mighty!

O God, bless our master Muḥammad and the family of our master Muḥammad in all that Your Knowledge encompasses, in everything that Your Pen writes, in all that Your Will preordains, and as often as Your angels have blessed him, with eternal blessings, lasting as long as You last, remaining, by Your Grace and Your Generosity, until the end of eternity, never ending, with no beginning to them, and no disappearing of them, for ever and ever!

O God, bless our master Muḥammad and the family of our master Muḥammad as much as You know him, as much as Your Book and as much as the witnessing of Your angels and be pleased with his Companions and be merciful on his nation for You are Praiseworthy, the Mighty!

O God, bless our master Muḥammad and the family of the liege Muḥammad, and all the Companions of our master Muḥammad!

O God, bless our master Muḥammad and the family of the liege Muḥammad just as You blessed our master Abraham and bless our master Muḥammad and the family of the liege Muḥammad just as You blessed our master Abraham in all the worlds, for You are the Praiseworthy, the Mighty!

O God, with heart humbled in prostration before You, O my Lord, with no unbelief, and for Your sake,

O God, O Sublime! Nothing can match You in inviolable promises! And for the sake of Your Footstool adorned with light as far as Your Mighty and Powerful Throne! And for the sake of that which lay beneath Your Throne truly before You created the heavens and the sound of Your thunder! And since You are infinite, a deity to be known only through Unity, then count me among

الْمُحِبِّيْنَ الْمَحْبُوْبِيْنَ الْمُقَرَّبِيْنَ الْعَارِفِيْنَ الْعَاشِقِيْنَ لَكَ يَآ اَللّٰهُ يَآ اَللّٰهُ يَآ اَللّٰهُ يَآ
اَللّٰهُ يَآ اَللّٰهُ يَآ اَللّٰهُ يَآ اَللّٰهُ يَآ اَللّٰهُ يَا وَدُوْدُ ۝ **اَللّٰهُمَّ** صَلِّ عَلٰى سَيِّدِنَا وَمَوْلٰنَا مُحَمَّدٍ
عَدَدَ مَآ اَحَاطَ بِهٖ عِلْمُكَ ۝ **اَللّٰهُمَّ** صَلِّ عَلٰى سَيِّدِنَا وَمَوْلٰنَا مُحَمَّدٍ عَدَدَ مَآ
اَحْصَاهُ كِتَابُكَ ۝ **اَللّٰهُمَّ** صَلِّ عَلٰى سَيِّدِنَا وَمَوْلٰنَا مُحَمَّدٍ عَدَدَ مَا نَفَذَتْ بِهٖ
قُدْرَتُكَ ۝ **اَللّٰهُمَّ** صَلِّ عَلٰى سَيِّدِنَا وَمَوْلٰنَا مُحَمَّدٍ عَدَدَ مَا خَصَّصَتْهُ اِرَادَتُكَ ۝
اَللّٰهُمَّ صَلِّ عَلٰى سَيِّدِنَا وَمَوْلٰنَا مُحَمَّدٍ عَدَدَ مَا تَوَجَّهَ اِلَيْهِ اَمْرُكَ وَنَهْيُكَ ۝ **اَللّٰهُمَّ**
صَلِّ عَلٰى سَيِّدِنَا وَمَوْلٰنَا مُحَمَّدٍ عَدَدَ مَا وَسِعَهٗ سَمْعُكَ ۝ **اَللّٰهُمَّ** صَلِّ عَلٰى
سَيِّدِنَا وَمَوْلٰنَا مُحَمَّدٍ عَدَدَ مَآ اَحَاطَ بِهٖ بَصَرُكَ ۝ **اَللّٰهُمَّ** صَلِّ عَلٰى سَيِّدِنَا وَمَوْلٰنَا
مُحَمَّدٍ عَدَدَ مَا ذَكَرَهُ الذَّاكِرُوْنَ ۝ **اَللّٰهُمَّ** صَلِّ عَلٰى سَيِّدِنَا وَمَوْلٰنَا مُحَمَّدٍ عَدَدَ
مَا غَفَلَ عَنْ ذِكْرِهِ الْغٰفِلُوْنَ ۝ **اَللّٰهُمَّ** صَلِّ عَلٰى سَيِّدِنَا وَمَوْلٰنَا مُحَمَّدٍ عَدَدَ قَطْرِ
الْاَمْطَارِ ۝ **اَللّٰهُمَّ** صَلِّ عَلٰى سَيِّدِنَا وَمَوْلٰنَا مُحَمَّدٍ عَدَدَ اَوْرَاقِ الْاَشْجَارِ ۝ **اَللّٰهُمَّ**
صَلِّ عَلٰى سَيِّدِنَا وَمَوْلٰنَا مُحَمَّدٍ عَدَدَ دَوَآبِّ الْقِفَارِ ۝ **اَللّٰهُمَّ** صَلِّ عَلٰى سَيِّدِنَا
وَمَوْلٰنَا مُحَمَّدٍ عَدَدَ دَوَآبِّ الْبِحَارِ ۝ **اَللّٰهُمَّ** صَلِّ عَلٰى سَيِّدِنَا وَمَوْلٰنَا مُحَمَّدٍ عَدَدَ
مِيَاهِ الْبِحَارِ ۝ **اَللّٰهُمَّ** صَلِّ عَلٰى سَيِّدِنَا وَمَوْلٰنَا مُحَمَّدٍ عَدَدَ مَآ اَظْلَمَ عَلَيْهِ الَّيْلُ
وَاَضَاءَ عَلَيْهِ النَّهَارُ ۝ **اَللّٰهُمَّ** صَلِّ عَلٰى سَيِّدِنَا وَمَوْلٰنَا مُحَمَّدٍ بِالْغُدُوِّ وَالْاٰصَالِ ۝
اَللّٰهُمَّ صَلِّ عَلٰى سَيِّدِنَا وَمَوْلٰنَا مُحَمَّدٍ عَدَدَ الرِّمَالِ ۝ **اَللّٰهُمَّ** صَلِّ عَلٰى سَيِّدِنَا
وَمَوْلٰنَا مُحَمَّدٍ عَدَدَ النِّسَآءِ وَالرِّجَالِ ۝ **اَللّٰهُمَّ** صَلِّ عَلٰى سَيِّدِنَا وَمَوْلٰنَا مُحَمَّدٍ
رِضَا نَفْسِكَ ۝ **اَللّٰهُمَّ** صَلِّ عَلٰى سَيِّدِنَا وَمَوْلٰنَا مُحَمَّدٍ مِّدَادَ كَلِمَاتِكَ ۝ **اَللّٰهُمَّ**
صَلِّ عَلٰى سَيِّدِنَا وَمَوْلٰنَا مُحَمَّدٍ مِّلْءَ سَمٰوَاتِكَ وَاَرْضِكَ ۝ **اَللّٰهُمَّ** صَلِّ عَلٰى

Your lovers, Your beloved ones, Your near ones, Your knowers and Your desirers,

O God, O God, O God, O God, O God, O God, O God, O God, O Bestower of Love!

O God, bless our liege and master Muḥammad as much as You know of him!

O God, bless our liege and master Muḥammad as much as Your Book!

O God, bless our liege and master Muḥammad as much that would exhaust Your powers by doing so!

O God, bless our liege and master Muḥammad as much as he is distinguished by Your Will!

O God, bless our liege and master Muḥammad as much as he is crowned by Your command and Your prohibition!

O God, bless our liege and master Muḥammad as much as all that is within range of Your Hearing!

O God, bless our liege and master Muḥammad as much as all that is encompassed by Your Vision!

O God, bless our liege and master Muḥammad as many times as those who remember him do so!

O God, bless our liege and master Muḥammad as many times as those who neglect to remember him do so! **O God**, bless our liege and master Muḥammad as many times as there are drops of rain! **O God**, bless our liege and master Muḥammad as many times as there are leaves on the trees!

O God, bless our liege and master Muḥammad as many times as there are beasts of the desert! **O God**, bless our liege and master Muhammad as many times as there are creatures in the sea! **O God**, bless our liege and master Muḥammad as much as there is water in the sea! **O God**, bless our liege and master Muḥammad as much as all that the night has covered and the day has illuminated! **O God**, bless our liege and master Muḥammad by morn and by eve! **O God**, bless our liege and master Muḥammad as many times as there are grains of sand! **O God**, bless our liege and master Muḥammad as many times as there are men and women! **O God**, bless our liege and master Muḥammad as much as pleases You! **O God**, bless our liege and master Muḥammad as much as the ink of Your words!

O God, bless our liege and master Muḥammad to the fullness of Your heavens and Your earth!

O God, bless

سَيِّدِنَا وَمَوْلَنَا مُحَمَّدٍ زِنَةَ عَرْشِكَ ○ **اَللّٰهُمَّ** صَلِّ عَلٰى سَيِّدِنَا وَمَوْلَنَا مُحَمَّدٍ عَدَدَ مَخْلُوْقَاتِكَ ○ **اَللّٰهُمَّ** صَلِّ عَلٰى سَيِّدِنَا وَمَوْلَنَا مُحَمَّدٍ اَفْضَلَ صَلَوَاتِكَ ○ **اَللّٰهُمَّ** صَلِّ عَلٰى نَبِيِّ الرَّحْمَةِ ○ **اَللّٰهُمَّ** صَلِّ عَلٰى شَفِيْعِ الْاُمَّةِ ○ **اَللّٰهُمَّ** صَلِّ عَلٰى كَاشِفِ الْغُمَّةِ ○ **اَللّٰهُمَّ** صَلِّ عَلٰى مُجْلِي الظُّلْمَةِ ○ **اَللّٰهُمَّ** صَلِّ عَلٰى مَوْلَى النِّعْمَةِ ○ **اَللّٰهُمَّ** صَلِّ عَلٰى مُوْلِي الرَّحْمَةِ ○ **اَللّٰهُمَّ** صَلِّ عَلٰى صَاحِبِ الْحَوْضِ الْمَوْرُوْدِ ○ **اَللّٰهُمَّ** صَلِّ عَلٰى صَاحِبِ الْمَقَامِ الْمَحْمُوْدِ ○ **اَللّٰهُمَّ** صَلِّ عَلٰى صَاحِبِ اللِّوَآءِ الْمَعْقُوْدِ ○ **اَللّٰهُمَّ** صَلِّ عَلٰى صَاحِبِ الْمَكَانِ الْمَشْهُوْدِ ○ **اَللّٰهُمَّ** صَلِّ عَلٰى الْمَوْصُوْفِ بِالْكَرَمِ وَالْجُوْدِ ○ **اَللّٰهُمَّ** صَلِّ عَلٰى مَنْ هُوَ فِي السَّمَآءِ سَيِّدُنَا مَحْمُوْدٌ وَّفِي الْاَرْضِ سَيِّدُنَا مُحَمَّدٌ ○ **اَللّٰهُمَّ** صَلِّ عَلٰى صَاحِبِ الشَّامَةِ ○ **اَللّٰهُمَّ** صَلِّ عَلٰى صَاحِبِ الْعَلَامَةِ ○ **اَللّٰهُمَّ** صَلِّ عَلٰى الْمَوْصُوْفِ بِالْكَرَامَةِ ○ **اَللّٰهُمَّ** صَلِّ عَلَى الْمَخْصُوْصِ بِالزَّعَامَةِ ○ **اَللّٰهُمَّ** صَلِّ عَلٰى مَنْ كَانَ تُظِلُّهُ الْغَمَامَةُ ○ **اَللّٰهُمَّ** صَلِّ عَلٰى مَنْ كَانَ يَرٰى مَنْ خَلْفَهٗ كَمَا يَرٰى مَنْ اَمَامَهٗ ○ **اَللّٰهُمَّ** صَلِّ عَلٰى الشَّفِيْعِ الْمُشَفَّعِ يَوْمَ الْقِيٰمَةِ ○ **اَللّٰهُمَّ** صَلِّ عَلٰى صَاحِبِ الضَّرَاعَةِ ○ **اَللّٰهُمَّ** صَلِّ عَلٰى صَاحِبِ الشَّفَاعَةِ ○ **اَللّٰهُمَّ** صَلِّ عَلٰى صَاحِبِ الْوَسِيْلَةِ ○ **اَللّٰهُمَّ** صَلِّ عَلٰى صَاحِبِ الْفَضِيْلَةِ ○ **اَللّٰهُمَّ** صَلِّ عَلٰى صَاحِبِ الدَّرَجَةِ الرَّفِيْعَةِ ○ **اَللّٰهُمَّ** صَلِّ عَلٰى صَاحِبِ الْهِرَاوَةِ ○ **اَللّٰهُمَّ** صَلِّ عَلٰى صَاحِبِ النَّعْلَيْنِ ○ **اَللّٰهُمَّ** صَلِّ عَلٰى صَاحِبِ الْحُجَّةِ ○ **اَللّٰهُمَّ** صَلِّ عَلٰى صَاحِبِ الْبُرْهَانِ ○ **اَللّٰهُمَّ** صَلِّ عَلٰى صَاحِبِ السُّلْطَانِ ○ **اَللّٰهُمَّ** صَلِّ عَلٰى صَاحِبِ التَّاجِ ○ **اَللّٰهُمَّ** صَلِّ عَلٰى صَاحِبِ الْمِعْرَاجِ ○ **اَللّٰهُمَّ** صَلِّ عَلٰى صَاحِبِ

our liege and master Muḥammad in the decoration of Your Throne!

O God, bless our liege and master Muḥammad as many times as there are created beings!

O God, bless our liege and master Muḥammad with the very best of Your blessings! **O God**, bless the Prophet of mercy!

O God, bless the intercessor of his nation!

O God, bless the remover of grief!

O God, bless the clarifier of darkness!

O God, bless the master of happiness! O God, bless the granter of mercy!

O God, bless the owner of the visited pool!

O God, bless the owner of the most praised station!

O God, bless the owner of the flag!

O God, bless the owner of the site of witnessing!

O God, bless the one dressed in nobility and generosity!

O God, bless the one called Maḥmūd in heaven and Muḥammad on the earth!

O God, bless the possessor of the mole!

O God, bless the possessor of the distinguishing mark!

O God, bless the one dressed in miracles!

O God, bless the one with special leadership!

O God, bless the one shaded by clouds!

O God, bless the one who can see equally from behind him as before him!

O God, bless the one whose intercession is accepted on the Day of Resurrection!

O God, bless the possessor of humility!

O God, bless the possessor of Intercession!

O God, bless the possessor of the closest access!

O God, bless the possessor of pre-eminence!

O God, bless the possessor of the lofty rank!

O God, bless the owner of the stalwart staff!

O God, bless the owner of the sandals!

O God, bless the possessor of sound argument!

O God, bless the possessor of convincing reason!

O God, bless the possessor of authority! **O God**, bless the owner of the turban!

O God, bless the master of the night journey!

O God, bless

الْقَضِيْبِ ۝ **اَللّٰهُمَّ** صَلِّ عَلٰى رَاكِبِ النَّجِيْبِ ۝ **اَللّٰهُمَّ** صَلِّ عَلٰى رَاكِبِ الْبُرَاقِ ۝ **اَللّٰهُمَّ** صَلِّ عَلٰى مُخْتَرِقِ السَّبْعِ الطِّبَاقِ ۝ **اَللّٰهُمَّ** صَلِّ عَلٰى الشَّفِيْعِ فِيْ جَمِيْعِ الْاَنَامِ ۝ **اَللّٰهُمَّ** صَلِّ عَلٰى مَنْ سَبَّحَ فِيْ كَفِّهِ الطَّعَامُ ۝ **اَللّٰهُمَّ** صَلِّ عَلٰى مَنْ بَكٰى اِلَيْهِ الْجِذْعُ وَحَنَّ لِفِرَاقِهٖ ۝ **اَللّٰهُمَّ** صَلِّ عَلٰى مَنْ تَوَسَّلَ بِهٖ طَيْرُ الْفَلَاةِ ۝ **اَللّٰهُمَّ** صَلِّ عَلٰى مَنْ سَبَّحَتْ فِيْ كَفِّهِ الْحِصَاةُ ۝ **اَللّٰهُمَّ** صَلِّ عَلٰى مَنْ تَشَفَّعَ اِلَيْهِ الظَّبْيُ بِاَفْصَحِ كَلَامٍ ۝ **اَللّٰهُمَّ** صَلِّ عَلٰى مَنْ كَلَّمَهُ الضَّبُّ فِيْ مَجْلِسِهٖ مَعَ اَصْحَابِهِ الْاَعْلَامِ ۝ **اَللّٰهُمَّ** صَلِّ عَلَى الْبَشِيْرِ النَّذِيْرِ ۝ **اَللّٰهُمَّ** صَلِّ عَلَى السِّرَاجِ الْمُنِيْرِ ۝ **اَللّٰهُمَّ** صَلِّ عَلٰى مَنْ شَكٰى اِلَيْهِ الْبَعِيْرُ ۝ **اَللّٰهُمَّ** صَلِّ عَلٰى مَنْ تَفَجَّرَ مِنْ بَيْنِ اَصَابِعِهِ الْمَآءُ النَّمِيْرُ ۝ **اَللّٰهُمَّ** صَلِّ عَلَى الطَّاهِرِ الْمُطَهَّرِ ۝ **اَللّٰهُمَّ** صَلِّ عَلٰى نُوْرِ الْاَنْوَارِ ۝ **اَللّٰهُمَّ** صَلِّ عَلٰى مَنِ انْشَقَّ لَهُ الْقَمَرُ ۝ **اَللّٰهُمَّ** صَلِّ عَلَى الطَّيِّبِ الْمُطَيِّبِ ۝ **اَللّٰهُمَّ** صَلِّ عَلَى الرَّسُوْلِ الْمُقَرَّبِ ۝ **اَللّٰهُمَّ** صَلِّ عَلَى الْفَجْرِ السَّاطِعِ ۝ **اَللّٰهُمَّ** صَلِّ عَلَى النَّجْمِ الثَّاقِبِ ۝ **اَللّٰهُمَّ** صَلِّ عَلَى الْعُرْوَةِ الْوُثْقٰى ۝ **اَللّٰهُمَّ** صَلِّ عَلٰى نَذِيْرِ اَهْلِ الْاَرْضِ ۝ **اَللّٰهُمَّ** صَلِّ عَلَى الشَّفِيْعِ يَوْمَ الْعَرْضِ ۝ **اَللّٰهُمَّ** صَلِّ عَلَى السَّاقِيْ لِلنَّاسِ مِنَ الْحَوْضِ ۝ **اَللّٰهُمَّ** صَلِّ عَلٰى صَاحِبِ لِوَآءِ الْحَمْدِ ۝ **اَللّٰهُمَّ** صَلِّ عَلَى الْمُشَمِّرِ عَنْ سَاعِدِ الْجِدِّ ۝ **اَللّٰهُمَّ** صَلِّ عَلَى الْمُسْتَعْمِلِ فِيْ مَرْضَاتِكَ غَايَةَ الْجَهْدِ ۝ **اَللّٰهُمَّ** صَلِّ عَلَى النَّبِيِّ الْخَاتِمِ ۝ **اَللّٰهُمَّ** صَلِّ عَلَى الرَّسُوْلِ الْخَاتِمِ ۝ **اَللّٰهُمَّ** صَلِّ عَلَى الْمُصْطَفَى الْقَآئِمِ ۝ **اَللّٰهُمَّ** صَلِّ عَلٰى رَسُوْلِكَ اَبِى الْقَاسِمِ ۝ **اَللّٰهُمَّ** صَلِّ عَلٰى صَاحِبِ الْاٰيَاتِ ۝ **اَللّٰهُمَّ** صَلِّ عَلٰى صَاحِبِ الدَّلَالَاتِ ۝ **اَللّٰهُمَّ** صَلِّ عَلٰى صَاحِبِ الْاِشَارَاتِ ۝ **اَللّٰهُمَّ** صَلِّ

the owner of the scepter!

O God, bless the noble rider!

O God, bless the rider of Buraq! **O God**, bless the one who traversed the seven heavens!

O God, bless the intercessor for all creatures!

O God, bless the one who held food in his hand which glorified God!

O God, bless the one for whom a palm trunk wept and sighed at its separation from him!

O God, bless the one whose mediation was sought by the birds of the desert!

O God, bless the one who held stones in his hand which glorified God!

O God, bless the one whose intercession was sought by the gazelles and whose request was made in human speech!

O God, bless the one to whom a lizard spoke at an open gathering of the most learned Companions!

O God, bless the bearer of glad tidings and the warner! **O God**, bless the brilliant lamp!

O God, bless the one to whom a camel made its complaint!

O God, bless the one for whom sparkling water burst forth from his fingertips for his Companions!

O God, bless the pure one, the purifier!

O God, bless the light of lights!

O God, bless the one for whom the moon was split open! **O God**, bless the one who was good and did good! **O God**, bless the Messenger close to God! **O God**, bless the breaking dawn! **O God**, bless the shining star! **O God**, bless the trusty handhold!

O God, bless the warner of the folk of the earth! **O God**, bless the intercessor of the Day of Petition! **O God**, bless the one who will give people to drink from the pool!

O God, bless the owner of the flag of happiness! **O God**, bless the one who was ever ready for Your service!

O God, bless the one who strived his utmost for Your pleasure! **O God**, bless the Prophet, the Seal!

O God, bless the Messenger, the seal! **O God**, bless the chosen one, the upright one! **O God**, bless Your Messenger, father of Qasim! **O God**, bless the possessor of signs! **O God**, bless the possessor of portents! **O God**, bless the possessor of indicators!

O God, bless

عَـلٰى صَاحِبِ الْكَرَامَاتِ ○ **اَللّٰهُمَّ** صَـلِّ عَلٰى صَاحِبِ الْعَلَامَاتِ ○ **اَللّٰهُمَّ** صَلِّ عَـلٰى صَاحِبِ الْبَيِّنَاتِ ○ **اَللّٰهُمَّ** صَـلِّ عَـلٰى صَاحِبِ الْمُعْجِزَاتِ ○ **اَللّٰهُمَّ** صَلِّ عَـلٰى صَـاحِـبِ الْـخَوَارِقِ الْعَادَاتِ ○ **اَلـلّٰهُمَّ** صَلِّ عَـلٰى مَـنْ سَلَّمَتْ عَلَيْـهِ الْاَحْجَارُ○ **اَللّٰهُمَّ** صَلِّ عَلٰى مَنْ سَجَدَتْ بَيْنَ يَدَيْهِ الْاَشْجَارُ○ **اَللّٰهُمَّ** صَلِّ عَلٰى مَـنْ تَفَتَّقَتْ مِنْ نُّوْرِهِ الْاَزْهَارُ○ **اَللّٰهُمَّ** صَـلِّ عَـلٰى مَنْ طَابَتْ بِبَرْكَتِهِ الثِّمَارُ ○ **اَللّٰهُمَّ** صَلِّ عَلٰى مَنِ اخْضَرَّتْ مِنْۢ بَقِيَّةِ وُضُوْئِهِ الْاَشْجَارُ○ **اَللّٰهُمَّ** صَلِّ عَلٰى مَنْ فَـاضَـتْ مِنْ نُّوْرِهٖ جَمِيْعُ الْاَنْوَارِ○ **اَللّٰهُمَّ** صَـلِّ عَلٰى مَنْۢ بِـالـصَّـلٰوةِ عَلَيْهِ تُحَطُّ الْاَوْزَارُ○ **اَللّٰهُمَّ** صَلِّ عَلٰى مَنْۢ بِـالـصَّلٰوةِ عَلَيْهِ تُنَالُ مَنَازِلُ الْاَبْرَارِ○ **اَللّٰهُمَّ** صَلِّ عَلٰى مَنْۢ بِـالصَّلٰوةِ عَلَيْهِ يُرْحَمُ الْكِبَارُ وَالصِّغَارُ ○ **اَللّٰهُمَّ** صَلِّ عَلٰى مَنْۢ بِالصَّلٰوةِ عَـلَيْهِ نَتَنَعَّمُ فِىْ هٰذِهِ الدَّارِ وَفِىْ تِلْكَ الدَّارِ ○ **اَللّٰهُمَّ** صَلِّ عَلٰى مَنْۢ بِالصَّلٰوةِ عَلَيْهِ تُنَالُ رَحْمَةُ الْعَزِيْزِ الْغَفَّارِ○ **اَللّٰهُمَّ** صَلِّ عَلَى الْمَنْصُوْرِ الْمُؤَيَّدِ○ **اَللّٰهُمَّ** صَلِّ عَلَى الْـمُخْتَارِ الْمُمَجَّدِ○ **اَللّٰهُمَّ** صَـلِّ عَلٰى سَيِّدِنَا وَمَوْلٰنَا مُحَمَّدٍ ○ **اَللّٰهُمَّ** صَلِّ عَلٰى مَـنْ كَانَ اِذَا مَشٰى فِى الْبَرِّ الْاَقْـفَـرِ تَعَلَّقَتِ الْوُحُوْشُ بِاَذْيَالِهٖ○ **اَللّٰهُمَّ** صَلِّ عَلَيْهِ وَعَلٰى اٰلِهٖ وَصَحْبِهٖ وَسَلِّمْ تَسْلِيْمًا وَّالْحَمْدُ لِلّٰهِ رَبِّ الْعٰلَمِيْنَ○

اِبْتِدَآءُ الرُّبْعِ الثَّانِىْ

اَلْـحَمْدُ لِلّٰهِ عَلٰى حِلْمِهٖ بَعْدَ عِلْمِهٖ وَعَلٰى عَفْوِهٖ بَعْدَ قُدْرَتِهٖ ○ **اَللّٰهُمَّ** اِنِّىْۤ اَعُوْذُبِكَ مِنَ الْفَقْرِ اِلَّآ اِلَيْكَ○ وَمِنَ الذُّلِّ اِلَّا لَكَ وَمِنَ الْخَوْفِ اِلَّا مِنْكَ ○ وَاَعُوْذُ بِكَ اَنْ اَقُوْلَ زُوْرًا○ اَوْ اَغْشٰى فُجُوْرًا ○ اَوْ اَكُوْنَ بِكَ مَغْرُوْرًا ○ وَاَعُـوْذُبِكَ مِنْ شَمَاتَةِ الْاَعْـدَآءِ وَعُـضَـالِ الـدَّآءِ وَخَيْبَةِ الـرَّجَآءِ وَزَوَالِ النِّعْمَةِ وَفَجَاْةِ النِّقْمَةِ○ **اَللّٰهُمَّ**

the possessor or miracles!

O God, bless the possessor of marks!

O God, bless the possessor of proofs!

O God, bless the possessor of marvels!

O God, bless the possessor of wondrous events!

O God, bless the one who was greeted by rocks!

O God, bless the one before whom trees prostrated!

O God, bless the one from whose light blossom unfolds!

O God, bless the one from whose blessing fruit ripens!

O God, bless the one from whose leftover ablution water trees become green!

O God, bless the one whose light engulfs all other lights!

O God, bless the one, the request for blessings upon whom lightens our every load!

O God, bless the one, the request for blessings upon whom grants mercy to the young and old!

O God, bless the one, the request for blessings upon whom brings Favor to this house and that house!

O God, bless the one, the request for blessings upon whom brings mercy from the Almighty, the Forgiving!

O God, bless the victorious one, the confirmer!

O God, bless the chosen one, the extolled!

O God, bless the one who when he walked in the desert wild creatures would cling to the hem of his cloak!

O God, bless and grant abundant peace to him and his family and companions, and praise be to God, Lord of all the worlds!

(beginning of the second quarter)

Praise be to God for His forbearance in spite of His knowledge and His clemency in spite of His power!

O God, I seek refuge in You from all thought which is not directed towards You! And from all humility which is not for You and from all fear which is not fear of You!

And I seek refuge in You from telling lies! Or from being dishonest and immoral!

Or that I be proud in front of You! And I seek refuge in You from gloating over my enemies, from disease, malady and despair, from the waning of Favor and from sudden catastrophes!

O God,

صَلِّ عَلٰى سَيِّدِنَا مُحَمَّدٍ وَّسَلِّمْ عَلَيْهِ وَاجْزِهٖ عَنَّا مَا هُوَ اَهْلُهٗ حَبِيْبُكَ ثَلٰثًا ۝ **اَللّٰهُمَّ** صَلِّ عَلٰى سَيِّدِنَآ اِبْرٰهِيْمَ وَسَلِّمْ عَلَيْهِ وَاجْزِهٖ عَنَّا مَا هُوَ اَهْلُهٗ خَلِيْلُكَ ثَلٰثًا ۝ **اَللّٰهُمَّ** صَلِّ عَلٰى سَيِّدِنَا مُحَمَّدٍ وَّعَلٰٓى اٰلِ سَيِّدِنَا مُحَمَّدٍ كَمَا صَلَّيْتَ وَرَحِمْتَ وَبَارَكْتَ عَلٰى سَيِّدِنَآ اِبْرٰهِيْمَ فِى الْعَالَمِيْنَ اِنَّكَ حَمِيْدٌ مَّجِيْدٌ ۝ عَدَدَ خَلْقِكَ وَرِضٰى نَفْسِكَ وَزِنَةَ عَرْشِكَ وَمِدَادَ كَلِمَاتِكَ ۝ **اَللّٰهُمَّ** صَلِّ عَلٰى سَيِّدِنَا مُحَمَّدٍ عَدَدَ مَنْ صَلّٰى عَلَيْهِ ۝ **اَللّٰهُمَّ** صَلِّ عَلٰى سَيِّدِنَا مُحَمَّدٍ عَدَدَ مَنْ لَّمْ يُصَلِّ عَلَيْهِ ۝ **اَللّٰهُمَّ** صَلِّ عَلٰى سَيِّدِنَا مُحَمَّدٍ عَدَدَ مَا صُلِّيَ عَلَيْهِ ۝ **اَللّٰهُمَّ** صَلِّ عَلٰى سَيِّدِنَا مُحَمَّدٍ اَضْعَافَ مَا صُلِّيَ عَلَيْهِ ۝ **اَللّٰهُمَّ** صَلِّ عَلٰى سَيِّدِنَا مُحَمَّدٍ كَمَا هُوَ اَهْلُهٗ ۝ **اَللّٰهُمَّ** صَلِّ عَلٰى سَيِّدِنَا مُحَمَّدٍ كَمَا تُحِبُّ وَتَرْضٰى لَهٗ ۝

اَلْحِزْبُ الثَّالِثُ فِىْ يَوْمِ الْاَرْبِعَآءِ

اَللّٰهُمَّ صَلِّ عَلٰى رُوْحِ سَيِّدِنَا مُحَمَّدٍ فِى الْاَرْوَاحِ وَعَلٰى جَسَدِهٖ فِى الْاَجْسَادِ وَعَلٰى قَبْرِهٖ فِى الْقُبُوْرِ وَعَلٰٓى اٰلِهٖ وَصَحْبِهٖ وَسَلِّمْ ۝ **اَللّٰهُمَّ** صَلِّ عَلٰى سَيِّدِنَا مُحَمَّدٍ كُلَّمَا ذَكَرَهُ الذَّاكِرُوْنَ ۝ **اَللّٰهُمَّ** صَلِّ عَلٰى سَيِّدِنَا مُحَمَّدٍ كُلَّمَا غَفَلَ عَنْ ذِكْرِهِ الْغَافِلُوْنَ ۝ **اَللّٰهُمَّ** صَلِّ وَسَلِّمْ وَبَارِكْ عَلٰى سَيِّدِنَا مُحَمَّدِ ۨالنَّبِيِّ الْاُمِّيِّ وَاَزْوَاجِهٖ اُمَّهَاتِ الْمُؤْمِنِيْنَ وَذُرِّيَّتِهٖ وَاَهْلِ بَيْتِهٖ صَلٰوةً وَّسَلَامًا لَّا يُحْصٰى عَدَدُهُمَا وَلَا يُقْطَعُ مَدَدُهُمَا ۝ **اَللّٰهُمَّ** صَلِّ عَلٰى سَيِّدِنَا مُحَمَّدٍ عَدَدَ مَآ اَحَاطَ بِهٖ عِلْمُكَ وَاَحْصَاهُ كِتَابُكَ صَلٰوةً تَكُوْنُ لَكَ رِضًى وَّلِحَقِّهٖ اَدَآءً وَّ اَعْطِهِ الْوَسِيْلَةَ وَالْفَضِيْلَةَ وَالدَّرَجَةَ الرَّفِيْعَةَ وَابْعَثْهُ اللّٰهُمَّ الْمَقَامَ الْمَحْمُوْدَ الَّذِىْ وَعَدْتَّهٗ وَاجْزِهٖ عَنَّا مَا هُوَ اَهْلُهٗ وَعَلٰى جَمِيْعِ اِخْوَانِهٖ مِنَ النَّبِيّٖنَ وَالصِّدِّيْقِيْنَ وَالشُّهَدَآءِ

bless our master **Muḥammad** and grant him peace and reward him as much as he deserves, and he is Your beloved! (**three times**)

O God, bless our master Abraham and grant him peace and reward him as much as he deserves, and he is Your friend! (**three times**)

O God, bless our master **Muḥammad** and the family of our master Muḥammad just as You blessed and were merciful to and blessed our master Abraham in all the worlds, for You are the Praiseworthy, the Mighty! As much as all of Your Creation, to the extent of Your Pleasure, in the decoration of Your throne and in the ink of Your Words! **O God**, bless our master **Muḥammad** as many times as those who have asked for blessings upon him! **O God**, bless our master Muḥammad as many times as those who have not asked for blessings upon him! **O God**, bless our master **Muḥammad** as many times as he has been blessed! **O God**, bless our master Muḥammad twice as many times as he has been blessed! **O God**, bless our master Muḥammad just as he deserves! **O God**, bless our master Muḥammad just as You love and You desire for him!

The Third Part to be Read on Wednesday

O God, more than other soul in existence, bless the soul of our master Muḥammad! And more than other body in existence, bless the body of our master Muḥammad! And more than other grave in existence, bless the grave of our master Muḥammad! And bless and grant abundant peace to him, his family and his Companions!

O God, bless our master Muḥammad whenever those who remember him do so! **O God**, bless our master Muḥammad whenever those who neglect to remember him do so!

O God, bless, grant peace to and sanctify our master Muḥammad, the unlettered Prophet, and also his wives, the Mothers of the Believers, his descendants and the People of his House, such blessings and peace which are measureless and the grant of which is incessant!

O God, bless our master Muḥammad in all that is encompassed by Your Knowledge, in all that is contained in Your Book, with blessings which are a pleasure for You and which befit his legitimate right, and grant him the closest access, the pre-eminence and the lofty rank, and send him, O God, to the most praised station which You promised him, and reward him on our behalf as he deserves and likewise reward his

brother Prophets, and the truthful, the martyrs

وَالصَّالِحِيْنَ ۝ **اَللّٰهُمَّ** صَلِّ عَلٰى سَيِّدِنَا مُحَمَّدٍ وَّاَنْزِلْهُ الْمُنْزَلَ الْمُقَرَّبَ يَوْمَ
الْقِيٰمَةِ ۝ **اَللّٰهُمَّ** صَلِّ عَلٰى سَيِّدِنَا مُحَمَّدٍ ۝ **اَللّٰهُمَّ** تَوِّجْهُ بِتَاجِ الْعِزِّ وَالرِّضَا
وَالْكَرَامَةِ ۝ **اَللّٰهُمَّ** اَعْطِ لِسَيِّدِنَا مُحَمَّدٍ اَفْضَلَ مَا سَاَلَكَ لِنَفْسِهٖ وَاَعْطِ لِسَيِّدِنَا
مُحَمَّدٍ اَفْضَلَ مَا سَاَلَكَ لَهٗ اَحَدٌ مِّنْ خَلْقِكَ وَاَعْطِ لِسَيِّدِنَا مُحَمَّدٍ اَفْضَلَ مَآ اَنْتَ
مَسْئُوْلٌ لَهٗ اِلٰى يَوْمِ الْقِيٰمَةِ ۝ **اَللّٰهُمَّ** صَلِّ عَلٰى سَيِّدِنَا مُحَمَّدٍ وَّ وَسَيِّدِنَآ اٰدَمَ
وَسَيِّدِنَا نُوْحٍ وَّ وَسَيِّدِنَآ اِبْرٰهِيْمَ وَسَيِّدِنَا مُوْسٰى وَسَيِّدِنَا عِيْسٰى وَمَا بَيْنَهُمْ مِّنَ
النَّبِيِّيْنَ وَالْمُرْسَلِيْنَ صَلَوَاتُ اللّٰهِ وَسَلَامُهٗ عَلَيْهِمْ اَجْمَعِيْنَ ثَلٰثًا ۝ **اَللّٰهُمَّ** صَلِّ عَلٰى
اَبِيْنَا سَيِّدِنَآ اٰدَمَ وَاُمِّنَا سَيِّدَتِنَا حَوَّآءَ صَلٰوةَ مَلٰٓئِكَتِكَ وَاَعْطِهِمَا مِنَ الرِّضْوَانِ
حَتّٰى تُرْضِيَهُمَا وَاجْزِهِمَا **اَللّٰهُمَّ** اَفْضَلَ مَا جَازَيْتَ بِهٖٓ اَبًا وَّ اُمًّا عَنْ وَّلَدَيْهِمَا ۝
اَللّٰهُمَّ صَلِّ عَلٰى سَيِّدِنَا جِبْرِيْلَ وَسَيِّدِنَا مِيْكَآئِيْلَ وَسَيِّدِنَآ اِسْرَافِيْلَ وَسَيِّدِنَا
عِزْرَآئِيْلَ وَحَمَلَةِ الْعَرْشِ وَعَلَى الْمَلٰٓئِكَةِ وَالْمُقَرَّبِيْنَ وَعَلٰى جَمِيْعِ الْاَنْبِيَآءِ
وَالْمُرْسَلِيْنَ صَلَوَاتُ اللّٰهِ وَسَلَامُهٗ عَلَيْهِمْ اَجْمَعِيْنَ ثَلٰثًا ۝ **اَللّٰهُمَّ** صَلِّ عَلٰى سَيِّدِنَا
مُحَمَّدٍ عَدَدَ مَا عَلِمْتَ وَمِلْءَ مَا عَلِمْتَ وَزِنَةَ مَا عَلِمْتَ وَمِدَادَ كَلِمَاتِكَ ۝
اَللّٰهُمَّ صَلِّ عَلٰى سَيِّدِنَا مُحَمَّدٍ صَلٰوةً مَّوْصُوْلَةً بِالْمَزِيْدِ ۝ **اَللّٰهُمَّ** صَلِّ عَلٰى
سَيِّدِنَا مُحَمَّدٍ صَلٰوةً لَّا تَنْقَطِعُ اَبَدَ الْاٰبَدِ وَلَا تَبِيْدُ ۝ **اَللّٰهُمَّ** صَلِّ عَلٰى سَيِّدِنَا
مُحَمَّدٍ صَلَاتَكَ الَّتِيْ صَلَّيْتَ عَلَيْهِ وَسَلِّمْ عَلٰى سَيِّدِنَا مُحَمَّدٍ سَلَامَكَ الَّذِيْ
سَلَّمْتَ عَلَيْهِ وَاجْزِهٖ عَنَّا مَا هُوَ اَهْلُهٗ ۝ **اَللّٰهُمَّ** صَلِّ عَلٰى سَيِّدِنَا مُحَمَّدٍ صَلٰوةً
تُرْضِيْكَ وَتُرْضِيْهِ وَتَرْضٰى بِهَا عَنَّا وَ اجْزِهٖ عَنَّا مَا هُوَ اَهْلُهٗ ۝ **اَللّٰهُمَّ** صَلِّ عَلٰى
سَيِّدِنَا مُحَمَّدٍ بَحْرِ اَنْوَارِكَ وَمَعْدِنِ اَسْرَارِكَ وَلِسَانِ حُجَّتِكَ وَعَرُوْسِ مَمْلَكَتِكَ

and the righteous ones!

O God, bless our master Muḥammad and bestow upon him the nearest position on the Day of Resurrection!

O God, bless our master Muḥammad! **O God**, crown him with the crown of might, satisfaction and honor!

O God, grant our master Muḥammad better than anyone of Your Creation has ever asked for himself, and grant our master Muḥammad better than anyone of Your Creation has ever asked for him, and grant our master Muḥammad better than You can be asked to grant him until the Day of Resurrection!

O God, bless our master Muḥammad, and Adam, and Abraham, and Moses, and Jesus, and all the Prophets and Messengers between them, and the blessings and peace of God be upon all of them! (**three times**)

O God, bless our father Adam and our mother Eve, with the blessings of Your angels, and grant them Your Pleasure until it pleases them and reward them,

O God, better than You have rewarded any father and mother on behalf of their children!

O God, bless our master Gabriel, and Michael, and Israfil, and Azrail, and the bearers of the Throne, and the Angels of Intimacy, and all the Prophets and Messengers, and the blessings and peace of God be upon all of them! (**three times**)

O God, bless our master Muḥammad as much as Your Knowledge, as much as the depths of Your Knowledge, as much as the weight of Your Knowledge and as much as the ink of Your Words!

O God, bless our master Muḥammad, with blessings which are continuously abundant!

O God, bless our master Muḥammad, with blessings never-ending and unceasing!

O God, bless our master Muḥammad with as much blessings as all the blessings You have so far bestowed upon him and grant as much peace to our master Muḥammad with as much peace as You have so far granted him and reward him on our behalf as he deserves!

O God, bless our master Muḥammad with blessings which please You, which please him and by which You are pleased with us and reward him on our behalf as he deserves!

O God, bless our master Muḥammad, the ocean of Your Lights, the mine of Your secrets, the tongue of Your proof, the bridegroom of Your

kingdoms,

وَ اِمَامِ حَضْرَتِكَ وَطِرَازِ مُلْكِكَ وَخَزَآئِنِ رَحْمَتِكَ وَطَرِيْقِ شَرِيْعَتِكَ الْمُتَلَذِّذِ بِتَوْحِيْدِكَ اِنْسَانِ عَيْنِ الْوُجُوْدِ وَالسَّبَبِ فِىْ كُلِّ مَوْجُوْدٍ عَيْنِ اَعْيَانِ خَلْقِكَ الْمُتَقَدِّمِ مِنْ نُّوْرِ ضِيَآئِكَ صَلٰوةً تَدُوْمُ بِدَوَامِكَ وَتَبْقٰى بِبَقَآئِكَ لَا مُنْتَهٰى لَهَا دُوْنَ عِلْمِكَ صَلٰوةً تُرْضِيْكَ وَتُرْضِيْهِ وَ تَرْضٰى بِهَا عَنَّا يَا رَبَّ الْعٰلَمِيْنَ ○ **اَللّٰهُمَّ** صَلِّ عَلٰى سَيِّدِنَا مُحَمَّدٍ عَدَدَ مَا فِىْ عِلْمِ اللّٰهِ صَلٰوةً دَآئِمَةً ۢ بِدَوَامِ مُلْكِ اللّٰهِ ○ **اَللّٰهُمَّ** صَلِّ عَلٰى سَيِّدِنَا مُحَمَّدٍ كَمَا صَلَّيْتَ عَلٰى سَيِّدِنَآ اِبْرٰهِيْمَ وَ بَارِكْ عَلٰى سَيِّدِنَا مُحَمَّدٍ وَعَلٰٓى اٰلِ سَيِّدِنَا مُحَمَّدٍ كَمَا بَارَكْتَ عَلٰى اٰل سَيِّدِنَآ اِبْرٰهِيْمَ فِى الْعٰلَمِيْنَ اِنَّكَ حَمِيْدٌ مَّجِيْدٌ ○ عَدَدَ خَلْقِكَ وَرِضٰى نَفْسِكَ وَزِنَةَ عَرْشِكَ وَمِدَادَ كَلِمَاتِكَ وَعَدَدَ مَا ذَكَرَكَ بِهٖ خَلْقُكَ فِيْمَا مَضٰى وَعَدَدَ مَا هُمْ ذَاكِرُوْنَكَ بِهٖ فِيْمَا بَقِىَ فِىْ كُلِّ سَنَةٍ وَّشَهْرٍ وَّجُمُعَةٍ وَّيَوْمٍ وَّلَيْلَةٍ وَّسَاعَةٍ مِّنَ السَّاعَاتِ وَشَمٍّ وَّنَفَسٍ وَّطَرْفَةٍ وَّلَمْحَةٍ مِّنَ الْاَبَدِ اِلَى الْاَبَدِ وَاٰبَادِ الدُّنْيَا وَاٰبَادِ الْاٰخِرَةِ وَاَكْثَرَ مِنْ ذٰلِكَ لَا يَنْقَطِعُ اَوَّلُهٗ وَلَا يَنْفَدُ اٰخِرُهٗ ○ **اَللّٰهُمَّ** صَلِّ عَلٰى سَيِّدِنَا مُحَمَّدٍ عَلٰى قَدْرِ حُبِّكَ فِيْهِ ○ **اَللّٰهُمَّ** صَلِّ عَلٰى سَيِّدِنَا مُحَمَّدٍ عَلٰى قَدْرِ عِنَايَتِكَ بِهٖ ○ **اَللّٰهُمَّ** صَلِّ عَلٰى سَيِّدِنَا مُحَمَّدٍ حَقَّ قَدْرِهٖ وَمِقْدَارِهٖ ○ **اَللّٰهُمَّ** صَلِّ عَلٰى سَيِّدِنَا مُحَمَّدٍ صَلٰوةً تُنَجِّيْنَا بِهَا مِنْ جَمِيْعِ الْاَهْوَالِ وَالْاٰفَاتِ وَتَقْضِىْ لَنَا بِهَا جَمِيْعَ الْحَاجَاتِ وَتُطَهِّرُنَا بِهَا مِنْ جَمِيْعِ السَّيِّاٰتِ وَتَرْفَعُنَا بِهَآ اَعْلَى الدَّرَجَاتِ وَتُبَلِّغُنَا بِهَآ اَقْصَى الْغَايَاتِ مِنْ جَمِيْعِ الْخَيْرَاتِ فِى الْحَيٰوةِ وَبَعْدَ الْمَمَاتِ ○ **اَللّٰهُمَّ** صَلِّ عَلٰى سَيِّدِنَا مُحَمَّدٍ صَلٰوةَ الرِّضٰى وَارْضَ عَنْ اَصْحَابِهٖ رِضَا الرِّضٰى ○ **اَللّٰهُمَّ** صَلِّ عَلٰى سَيِّدِنَا مُحَمَّدِنِ السَّابِقِ لِلْخَلْقِ نُوْرُهٗ وَرَحْمَةٌ لِّلْعٰلَمِيْنَ ظُهُوْرُهٗ عَدَدَ مَنْ

the leader of Your Presence, the embroidery of Your Dominion, the vault of Your Mercy, the way of Your Law, the delight of Your Unity, the pupil of the eye of existence, the cause of all existence, the most eminent of Your Creation, the representative of the light of Your Resplendence, with blessings which last for as long as You last and remain for as long as You remain, blessings which are limitless apart from Your knowledge thereof, blessings which please You, which please him and by which You are pleased with us, O Lord of the Worlds!

O God, bless our master **Muḥammad** as much as all that which is within the knowledge of God, blessings which are eternal and which last as long as the duration of the Kingdom of God!

O God, bless our master **Muḥammad** just as You blessed our master Abraham and sanctify our master **Muḥammad** and the family of our master **Muḥammad** just as You sanctified the family of our master Abraham, in all the worlds, for You are the Praiseworthy, the Mighty! (And bless him) As much as all of Your Creation, to the extent of Your Pleasure, in the decoration of Your Throne and in the ink of Your Words, and as often as Your Creation has remembered You in the past and as often as they will remember You throughout the rest of time, and bless him in every year, in every month, in every week, in every day, in every night, in every hour, in every sniff, in every breath, in every blink and in every glance, for ever and ever, for the duration of this world and the duration of the next world, and for longer than this, with a beginning that never ends and an end which never finishes!

O God, bless our master **Muḥammad** as much as Your love for him!

O God, bless our master **Muḥammad** as befits his legitimate rank!

O God, bless our master **Muḥammad**, with blessings which serve as a sanctuary for us from all terrors and oppression, which settle all our affairs, which purify us from all sins, which raise our ranks in Your Presence, and which allow us to attain ultimate goodness in this life and after death!

O God, bless our master **Muḥammad**, a blessing of contentment, and be pleased with his Companions, a pleasure of contentment!

O God, bless our master **Muḥammad**, whose light preceded all creation, whose appearance is a mercy to all the worlds, as much as

مَّضٰى مِنْ خَلْقِكَ وَمَنْ بَقِىَ وَمَنْ سَعِدَ مِنْهُمْ وَمَنْ شَقِىَ صَلٰوةً تَسْتَغْرِقُ الْعَدَّ وَتُحِيْطُ بِالْحَدِّ صَلٰوةً لَّا غَايَةَ لَهَا وَلَا مُنْتَهٰى وَلَا انْقِضَآءَ صَلٰوةً دَآئِمَةً بِدَوَامِكَ وَعَلٰى اٰلِهٖ وَصَحْبِهٖ وَسَلِّمْ تَسْلِيْمًا مِّثْلَ ذٰلِكَ ۝ اَللّٰهُمَّ صَلِّ عَلٰى سَيِّدِنَا مُحَمَّدِ نِ الَّذِىْ مَلَاْتَ قَلْبَهٗ مِنْ جَلَالِكَ وَعَيْنَهٗ مِنْ جَمَالِكَ فَاَصْبَحَ فَرِحًا مُّؤَيَّدًا مَّنْصُوْرًا وَّعَلٰى اٰلِهٖ وَصَحْبِهٖ وَسَلِّمْ تَسْلِيْمًا وَّالْحَمْدُ لِلّٰهِ عَلٰى ذٰلِكَ ۝ اَللّٰهُمَّ صَلِّ عَلٰى سَيِّدِنَا وَمَوْلٰنَا مُحَمَّدٍ عَدَدَ اَوْرَاقِ الزَّيْتُوْنِ وَجَمِيْعِ الثِّمَارِ ۝ اَللّٰهُمَّ صَلِّ عَلٰى سَيِّدِنَا وَمَوْلٰنَا مُحَمَّدٍ عَدَدَ مَا كَانَ وَمَا يَكُوْنُ وَعَدَدَ مَآ اَظْلَمَ عَلَيْهِ الَّيْلُ وَاَضَآءَ عَلَيْهِ النَّهَارُ ۝ اَللّٰهُمَّ صَلِّ عَلٰى سَيِّدِنَا وَمَوْلٰنَا مُحَمَّدٍ وَّعَلٰى اٰلِهٖ وَاَزْوَاجِهٖ وَذُرِّيَّتِهٖ عَدَدَ اَنْفَاسِ اُمَّتِهٖ ۝ اَللّٰهُمَّ بِبَرَكَةِ الصَّلٰوةِ عَلَيْهِ اجْعَلْنَا بِالصَّلٰوةِ عَلَيْهِ مِنَ الْفَآئِزِيْنَ وَعَلٰى حَوْضِهٖ مِنَ الْوَارِدِيْنَ الشَّارِبِيْنَ ۝ وَبِسُنَّتِهٖ وَطَاعَتِهٖ مِنَ الْعَامِلِيْنَ ۝ وَلَا تَحُلْ بَيْنَنَا وَبَيْنَهٗ يَوْمَ الْقِيٰمَةِ يَا رَبَّ الْعٰلَمِيْنَ ۝ وَاغْفِرْلَنَا وَلِوَالِدَيْنَا وَلِجَمِيْعِ الْمُسْلِمِيْنَ اَلْحَمْدُ لِلّٰهِ رَبِّ الْعٰلَمِيْنَ ۝

اِبْتِدَآءُ الثُّلُثِ الثَّانِىْ

اَللّٰهُمَّ صَلِّ وَسَلِّمْ وَبَارِكْ عَلٰى سَيِّدِنَا مُحَمَّدٍ وَّعَلٰى اٰلِ سَيِّدِنَا مُحَمَّدٍ اَكْرَمِ خَلْقِكَ وَسِرَاجِ اُفُقِكَ وَاَفْضَلِ قَآئِمٍ بِحَقِّكَ الْمَبْعُوْثِ بِتَيْسِيْرِكَ وَرِفْقِكَ صَلٰوةً يَّتَوَالٰى تَكْرَارُهَا وَتَلُوْحُ عَلَى الْاَكْوَانِ اَنْوَارُهَا ۝ اَللّٰهُمَّ صَلِّ وَسَلِّمْ وَبَارِكْ عَلٰى سَيِّدِنَا مُحَمَّدٍ وَّعَلٰى اٰلِ سَيِّدِنَا مُحَمَّدٍ اَفْضَلِ مَمْدُوْحٍ بِقَوْلِكَ وَاَشْرَفِ دَاعٍ لِّلْاِعْتِصَامِ بِحَبْلِكَ وَخَاتِمِ اَنْبِيَآئِكَ وَرُسُلِكَ صَلٰوةً تُبَلِّغُنَا فِى الدَّارَيْنِ عَمِيْمَ فَضْلِكَ وَكَرَامَةَ رِضْوَانِكَ وَوَصْلِكَ ۝ اَللّٰهُمَّ صَلِّ وَسَلِّمْ وَبَارِكْ عَلٰى سَيِّدِنَا

all Your Creation which has passed and as much as that which remains, as much as those of Your Creation who are fortunate and those who are not, blessings which exceed all enumeration and which encompass all limits, blessings with no utmost limit, boundless and ceaseless, blessings which are eternal, as long as Your duration, and likewise bless his family, his Companions and grant him and them abundant peace in like measure! **O God**, bless our master **Muḥammad**, whose heart is so full with Your Glory, and whose eyes are so full of Your Beauty that he came to be overjoyed, supported and victorious, and bless likewise his family and Companions and grant him and them abundant peace, and praise be to God for all of that!

O God, bless our master **Muḥammad** as many times as the leaves of the olive tree and all of its fruit!

O God, bless our master **Muḥammad** as much as all that has been and all that will be, and as much as all that the night has enshrouded in darkness and the day has enlightened with its radiance!

O God, bless our master and master **Muḥammad** and his family, his wives and his descendants as many times as all the breaths of his nation!

O God, through the grace of this asking for blessings upon him, make us be numbered because of it among the victorious ones and at the Pool among the drinkers and waterers! And make us observe his way and obey him! And do not untie the knot which binds us together on the Day of Resurrection, O Lord of the Worlds! And forgive us and our parents and all those who have submitted themselves (ie. Muslims) and praise be to God, the Lord of the worlds!

(beginning of the second third)

O God, bless, grant peace to and sanctify our master Muḥammad and the family of our master Muḥammad, the noblest of Your Creation, the shining lamp of the horizons, the best upholder of Your Reality, the envoy of Your Relief and Kindness, with blessings which continue and repeat and permeate their light all over the universes!

O God, bless, grant peace to and sanctify our master Muḥammad and the family of our master Muḥammad, the one praised most by Your Words, the noblest one calling to adherence to Your Bond, and Seal of Your Prophets and Messengers, with blessings which permit us to attain both here and hereafter Your general favor and the honor of Your Pleasure and Union!

O God, bless, grant peace to and sanctify our master

مُحَمَّدٍ وَّعَلَى اٰلِ سَيِّدِنَا مُحَمَّدٍ اَكْرَمِ الْكُرَمَآءِ مِنْ عِبَادِكَ وَاَشْرَفِ الْمُنَادِيْنَ
لِطُرُقِ رَشَادِكَ وَسِرَاجِ اَقْطَارِكَ وَبِلَادِكَ صَلٰوةً لَّا تَفْنٰى وَلَا تَبِيْدُ تُبَلِّغُنَا بِهَا كَرَامَةَ
الْمَزِيْدِ ○ **اَللّٰهُمَّ** صَلِّ وَسَلِّمْ وَبَارِكْ عَلٰى سَيِّدِنَا مُحَمَّدٍ وَّعَلٰى اٰلِ سَيِّدِنَا مُحَمَّدِنِ
الرَّفِيْعِ مَقَامُهٗ الْوَاجِبِ تَعْظِيْمُهٗ وَاحْتِرَامُهٗ صَلٰوةً لَّا تَنْقَطِعُ اَبَدًا وَّلَا تَفْنٰى سَرْمَدًا
وَّلَا تَنْحَصِرُ عَدَدًا ○ **اَللّٰهُمَّ** صَلِّ عَلٰى سَيِّدِنَا مُحَمَّدٍ وَّعَلٰى اٰلِ سَيِّدِنَا مُحَمَّدٍ
كَمَا صَلَّيْتَ عَلٰى سَيِّدِنَآ اِبْرٰهِيْمَ وَعَلٰى اٰلِ سَيِّدِنَآ اِبْرٰهِيْمَ فِى الْعٰلَمِيْنَ اِنَّكَ
حَمِيْدٌ مَّجِيْدٌ ○ وَصَلِّ اللّٰهُمَّ عَلٰى سَيِّدِنَا مُحَمَّدٍ وَّعَلٰى اٰلِ سَيِّدِنَا مُحَمَّدٍ كُلَّمَا
ذَكَرَهُ الذَّاكِرُوْنَ وَغَفَلَ عَنْ ذِكْرِهِ الْغٰفِلُوْنَ ○ **اَللّٰهُمَّ** صَلِّ عَلٰى سَيِّدِنَا مُحَمَّدٍ
وَّعَلٰى اٰلِ سَيِّدِنَا مُحَمَّدٍ وَّارْحَمْ سَيِّدِنَا مُحَمَّدًا وَّاٰلَ سَيِّدِنَا مُحَمَّدٍ وَّبَارِكْ عَلٰى
سَيِّدِنَا مُحَمَّدٍ وَّعَلٰى اٰلِ سَيِّدِنَا مُحَمَّدٍ كَمَا صَلَّيْتَ وَرَحِمْتَ وَبَارَكْتَ عَلٰى
سَيِّدِنَآ اِبْرٰهِيْمَ وَعَلٰى اٰلِ سَيِّدِنَآ اِبْرٰهِيْمَ اِنَّكَ حَمِيْدٌ مَّجِيْدٌ ○ **اَللّٰهُمَّ** صَلِّ عَلٰى
سَيِّدِنَا مُحَمَّدِنِ النَّبِيِّ الْاُمِّيِّ الطَّاهِرِ الْمُطَهَّرِ وَعَلٰى اٰلِهٖ وَسَلِّمْ ○ **اَللّٰهُمَّ** صَلِّ عَلٰى
مَنْ خَتَمْتَ بِهِ الرِّسَالَةَ وَاَيَّدْتَّهٗ بِالنَّصْرِ وَالْكَوْثَرِ وَالشَّفَاعَةِ ○ **اَللّٰهُمَّ** صَلِّ عَلٰى
سَيِّدِنَا وَمَوْلٰنَا مُحَمَّدٍ نَّبِيِّ الْحُكْمِ وَالْحِكْمَةِ السِّرَاجِ الْوَهَّاجِ الْمَخْصُوْصِ
بِالْخُلُقِ الْعَظِيْمِ وَخَتْمِ الرُّسُلِ ذِى الْمِعْرَاجِ وَعَلٰى اٰلِهٖ وَاَصْحَابِهٖ وَاَتْبَاعِهٖ
السَّالِكِيْنَ عَلٰى مَنْهَجِهِ الْقَوِيْمِ ○ فَاَعْظِمِ اللّٰهُمَّ بِهٖ مِنْهَاجَ نُجُوْمِ الْاِسْلَامِ
وَمَصَابِيْحِ الظَّلَامِ الْمُهْتَدٰى بِهِمْ فِىْ ظُلْمَةِ لَيْلِ الشَّكِّ الدَّاجِّ صَلٰوةً دَآئِمَةً
مُّسْتَمِرَّةً مَّا تَلَاطَمَتْ فِى الْاَبْحُرِ الْاَمْوَاجُ وَطَافَ بِالْبَيْتِ الْعَتِيْقِ مِنْ كُلِّ فَجٍّ
عَمِيْقِنِ الْحُجَّاجُ وَاَفْضَلُ الصَّلٰوةِ وَالتَّسْلِيْمِ عَلٰى سَيِّدِنَا مُحَمَّدٍ رَّسُوْلِهٖ

Muḥammad and the family of our master Muḥammad, the noblest of Your noble servants, the most distinguished of the callers to the paths of Your Guidance and the shining lamp of all regions and countries, with blessings which have no end and no beginning and which, through them, bring us great favors! **O God**, bless, grant peace to and sanctify our master Muḥammad and the family of our master Muḥammad, whose rank is high, whose exaltation and admiration are incumbent upon us, with blessings which are never curtailed and never finish, endless blessings which are immeasurable!

O God, bless our master Muḥammad and the family of our master Muḥammad just as You blessed Abraham and the family of Abraham in all the worlds, for You are the Praiseworthy, the Mighty! And bless,

O God, our master Muḥammad and the family of our master Muḥammad whenever those who remember him do so and whenever those who neglect to remember him do so!

O God, bless our master Muḥammad and the family of our master Muḥammad, and have mercy upon our master Muḥammad and the family of our master Muḥammad, and sanctify our master Muḥammad and the family of our master Muḥammad just as You blessed, had mercy upon and sanctified Abraham and the family of Abraham, for You are the Praiseworthy, the Mighty! **O God**, bless and grant peace to our master Muḥammad, the unlettered Prophet, the pure, the immaculate, and his family! **O God**, bless the one with whom You sealed the message, and the one to whom You granted victory, the pool known as *kawthar* and the intercession!

O God, bless our liege and master Muḥammad, the Prophet of judiciousness and wisdom, the brilliant lamp, the one destined for the greatest character, the Seal of the Messengers, the master of the night journey, and likewise bless his family, his Companions, his Followers, the sincere travelers on the true path! Magnify, **O God**, through him, the path of the stars of Islam (i.e. the Companions) and the lamps (i.e. the Followers), the path sign posted by them, the path that dispels the darkness in the murky gloom of the night of doubt! And send blessings which are eternal and continuous and which last for as long as the waves crash in the oceans and the Ancient House (the Holy Kabah) is circumambulated from all sides by throngs of pilgrims! The best of all blessings and peace be

upon our master Muḥammad,

الْكَرِيْمِ وَصَفْوَتِهِ مِنَ الْعِبَادِ وَشَفِيْعِ الْخَلاَئِقِ فِى الْمِيْعَادِ صَاحِبِ الْمَقَامِ الْمَحْمُوْدِ وَ الْحَوْضِ الْمَوْرُوْدِ النَّاهِضِ بِاَعْبَآءِ الرِّسَالَةِ وَالتَّبْلِيْغِ الْاَعَمِّ وَالْمَخْصُوْصِ بِشَرَفِ السِّعَايَةِ فِى الصَّلاَحِ الْاَعْظَمِ ٥ صَلَّى اللّٰهُ عَلَيْهِ وَعَلٰى اٰلِهٖ صَلٰوةً دَآئِمَةً مُّسْتَمِرَّةَ الدَّوَامِ عَلٰى مَرِّ اللَّيَالِىْ وَالْاَيَّامِ ٥ فَهُوَ سَيِّدُ الْاَوَّلِيْنَ وَالْاٰخِرِيْنَ وَاَفْضَلُ الْاَوَّلِيْنَ وَالْاٰخِرِيْنَ ٥ عَلَيْهِ اَفْضَلُ صَلٰوةِ الْمُصَلِّيْنَ ٥ وَاَزْكٰى سَلاَمِ الْمُسْلِمِيْنَ ٥ وَاَطْيَبُ ذِكْرِ الذَّاكِرِيْنَ ٥ وَاَفْضَلُ صَلَوَاتِ اللّٰهِ ٥ وَاَحْسَنُ صَلَوَاتِ اللّٰهِ ٥ وَاَجَلُّ صَلَوَاتِ اللّٰهِ ٥ وَاَجْمَلُ صَلَوَاتِ اللّٰهِ ٥ وَاَكْمَلُ صَلَوَاتِ اللّٰهِ ٥ وَاَسْبَغُ صَلَوَاتِ اللّٰهِ ٥ وَاَتَمُّ صَلَوَاتِ اللّٰهِ ٥ وَاَظْهَرُ صَلَوَاتِ اللّٰهِ ٥ وَاَعْظَمُ صَلَوَاتِ اللّٰهِ ٥ وَاَذْكٰى صَلَوَاتِ اللّٰهِ ٥ وَاَطْيَبُ صَلَوَاتِ اللّٰهِ ٥ وَاَبْرَكُ صَلَوَاتِ اللّٰهِ ٥ وَاَزْكٰى صَلَوَاتِ اللّٰهِ ٥ وَاَنْمٰى صَلَوَاتِ اللّٰهِ ٥ وَاَوْفٰى صَلَوَاتِ اللّٰهِ ٥ وَاَسْنٰى صَلَوَاتِ اللّٰهِ ٥ وَاَعْلٰى صَلَوَاتِ اللّٰهِ ٥ وَاَكْثَرُ صَلَوَاتِ اللّٰهِ ٥ وَاَجْمَعُ صَلَوَاتِ اللّٰهِ ٥ وَاَعَمُّ صَلَوَاتِ اللّٰهِ ٥ وَاَدْوَمُ صَلَوَاتِ اللّٰهِ ٥ وَاَبْقٰى صَلَوَاتِ اللّٰهِ ٥ وَاَعَزُّ صَلَوَاتِ اللّٰهِ ٥ وَاَرْفَعُ صَلَوَاتِ اللّٰهِ ٥ وَاَعْظَمُ صَلَوَاتِ اللّٰهِ ٥ عَلٰى اَفْضَلِ خَلْقِ اللّٰهِ ٥ وَاَحْسَنِ خَلْقِ اللّٰهِ ٥ وَاَجَلِّ خَلْقِ اللّٰهِ ٥ وَاَكْرَمِ خَلْقِ اللّٰهِ ٥ وَاَجْمَلِ خَلْقِ اللّٰهِ ٥ وَاَكْمَلِ خَلْقِ اللّٰهِ ٥ وَاَتَمِّ خَلْقِ اللّٰهِ ٥ وَاَعْظَمِ خَلْقِ اللّٰهِ عِنْدَاللّٰهِ ٥ رَسُوْلِ اللّٰهِ ٥ وَنَبِيِّ اللّٰهِ ٥ وَحَبِيْبِ اللّٰهِ ٥ وَصَفِيِّ اللّٰهِ ٥ وَنَجِيِّ اللّٰهِ ٥ وَخَلِيْلِ اللّٰهِ ٥ وَوَلِيِّ اللّٰهِ ٥ وَاَمِيْنِ اللّٰهِ ٥ وَخِيْرَةِ اللّٰهِ مِنْ خَلْقِ اللّٰهِ ٥ وَنُخْبَةِ اللّٰهِ مِنْ بَرِيَّةِ اللّٰهِ ٥ وَصَفْوَةِ اللّٰهِ مِنْ اَنْبِيَآءِ اللّٰهِ ٥ وَعُرْوَةِ اللّٰهِ ٥ وَعِصْمَةِ اللّٰهِ ٥ وَنِعْمَةِ اللّٰهِ ٥ وَ مِفْتَاحِ رَحْمَةِ اللّٰهِ ٥ الْمُخْتَارِ مِنْ رُّسُلِ اللّٰهِ ٥ الْمُنْتَخَبِ مِنْ خَلْقِ اللّٰهِ

the generous Messenger, His friend among all the servants, the intercessor for all created beings at the appointed time, owner of the most praised station and the oft-visited pool, the one who took on the burden of the Message and the responsibility of spreading it far and wide, the one destined for honor and one who strove for the greatest righteousness! The blessings of God be upon him and upon his family, eternal and continuous blessings, lasting as long as the passing of all nights and all days! For he is the master of the first and the last and the best of the first and the last! The best blessings of those who ask for blessings upon him are for him! The purest peace of those who seek peace for him is for him! As well as the finest thoughts of those who remember him! As well as the finest blessings of God! As well as the choicest blessings of God! As well as the greatest blessings of God! As well as the fairest blessings of God! As well as the fullest blessings of God! As well as the most abundant blessings of God! As well as the utmost blessings of God! As well as the clearest blessings of God! As well as the mightiest blessings of God! As well as the sweetest blessings of God! As well as the freshest blessings of God! As well as the holiest blessings of God! As well as the purest blessings of God! As well as the richest blessings of God! As well as the most sincere blessings of God! As well as the matchless blessings of God! As well as the highest blessings of God! As well as the most lavish blessings of God! As well as the myriad blessings of God! As well as the universal blessings of God! As well as the longest lasting blessings of God! As well as the longest remaining blessings of God! As well as the strongest blessings of God! As well as the loftiest blessings of God! As well as the mightiest blessings of God! Upon the best of God's creation! The finest of God's creation! The greatest of God's creation! The noblest of God's creation! The fairest of God's creation! The most perfect of God's creation! The most complete of God's creation! The mightiest of God's creation in the sight of God! The Messenger of God! The Prophet of God! The beloved of God! The intimate of God! The confidant of God! The friend of God! The loved one of God! The trustee of God! The gift of God from the creation of God! The choice of God from the innocent of God! The confidant of God from the Prophets of God! The handhold of God! The modesty of God! The favor of God! The key to the mercy of God! The chosen one from the

Messengers of God! The elected one from the creation of God

الْفَآئِزِ بِالْمَطْلَبِ فِى الْمَرْهَبِ وَالْمَرْغَبِ ۝ الْمُخْلَصِ فِيْمَا وُهِبَ ۝ اَكْرَمِ مَبْعُوْثٍ ۝ اَصْدَقِ قَآئِلٍ ۝ اَنْجَحِ شَافِعٍ ۝ اَفْضَلِ مُشَفَّعٍ ۝ الْاَمِيْنِ فِىْ مَا اسْتُوْدِعَ الصَّادِقِ فِىْ مَا بَلَّغَ الصَّادِعِ بِاَمْرِ رَبِّهِ الْمُضْطَلِعِ بِمَا حُمِّلَ ۝ اَقْرَبِ رُسُلِ اللّٰهِ اِلَى اللّٰهِ وَسِيْلَةً وَّاَعْظَمِهِمْ غَدًا عِنْدَ اللّٰهِ مَنْزِلَةً وَّفَضِيْلَةً ۝ وَاَكْرَمِ اَنْبِيَآءِ اللّٰهِ الْكِرَامِ الصَّفْوَةِ عَلَى اللّٰهِ ۝ وَاَحَبِّهِمْ اِلَى اللّٰهِ وَ اَقْرَبِهِمْ زُلْفٰى لَدَى اللّٰهِ ۝ وَاَكْرَمِ الْخَلْقِ عَلَى اللّٰهِ ۝ وَ اَحْظَاهُمْ وَاَرْضَاهُمْ لَدَى اللّٰهِ ۝ وَاَعْلَى النَّاسِ قَدْرًا ۝ وَاَعْظَمِهِمْ مَّحَلًّا وَّاَكْمَلِهِمْ مَّحَاسِنًا وَّ فَضْلًا وَّ اَفْضَلِ الْاَنْبِيَآءِ دَرَجَةً ۝ وَ اَكْمَلِهِمْ شَرِيْعَةً وَّ اَشْرَفِ الْاَنْبِيَآءِ نِصَابًا وَّ اَبْيَنِهِمْ بَيَانًا وَّخِطَابًا وَّ اَفْضَلِهِمْ مَّوْلِدًا وَّ مُهَاجَرًا وَّ عِتْرَةً وَّ اَصْحَابًا وَّ اَكْرَمِ النَّاسِ اَرُوْمَةً وَّ اَشْرَفِهِمْ جُرْثُوْمَةً وَّ خَيْرِهِمْ نَفْسًا وَّ اَطْهَرِهِمْ قَلْبًا وَّاَصْدَقِهِمْ قَوْلًا وَّاَزْكٰهُمْ فِعْلًا وَّاَثْبَتِهِمْ اَصْلًا وَّ اَوْفٰهُمْ عَهْدًا وَّ اَمْكَنِهِمْ مَّجْدًا وَّاَكْرَمِهِمْ طَبْعًا وَّاَحْسَنِهِمْ صُنْعًا وَّاَطْيَبِهِمْ فَرْعًا وَّ اَكْثَرِهِمْ طَاعَةً وَّ سَمْعًا وَّ اَعْلٰهُمْ مَّقَامًا وَّ اَحْلٰهُمْ كَلَامًا وَّ اَزْكٰهُمْ سَلَامًا وَّ اَجَلِّهِمْ قَدْرًا وَّ اَعْظَمِهِمْ فَخْرًا وَّاَسْنٰهُمْ فَخْرًا وَّ اَرْفَعِهِمْ فِى الْمَلَاِ الْاَعْلٰى ذِكْرًا وَّ اَصْدَقِهِمْ وَعْدًا وَّ اَكْثَرِهِمْ شُكْرًا وَّ اَعْلٰهُمْ اَمْرًا وَّ اَجْمَلِهِمْ صَبْرًا وَّ اَحْسَنِهِمْ خَيْرًا وَّ اَقْرَبِهِمْ يُسْرًا وَّ اَبْعَدِهِمْ مَّكَانًا وَّ اَعْظَمِهِمْ شَاْنًا وَّاَثْبَتِهِمْ بُرْهَانًا وَّ اَرْجَحِهِمْ مِّيْزَانًا وَّ اَوَّلِهِمْ اِيْمَانًا وَّ اَوْضَحِهِمْ بَيَانًا وَّ اَفْصَحِهِمْ لِسَانًا وَّاَظْهَرِهِمْ سُلْطَانًا ۝

اَلْحِزْبُ الرَّابِعُ فِىْ يَوْمِ الْخَمِيْسِ

اَللّٰهُمَّ صَلِّ عَلٰى سَيِّدِنَا مُحَمَّدٍ عَبْدِكَ وَرَسُوْلِكَ النَّبِيِّ الْاُمِّيِّ وَّعَلٰى اٰلِ سَيِّدِنَا مُحَمَّدٍ ۝ **اَللّٰهُمَّ** صَلِّ عَلٰى سَيِّدِنَا مُحَمَّدٍ وَّعَلٰى اٰلِ سَيِّدِنَا مُحَمَّدٍ صَلٰوةً تَكُوْنُ

and the one who succeeds with his requests at times of fear and dread! The sincere one in what he is granted! Most honored envoy! Truest speaker! Most successful intercessor! The best intercessor, the one faithful to his pledge, the one true to his mission, the one who complied with the order of his Lord, and the one who bore his responsibility! The Messenger of God with the closest access to God and the one whose position and pre-eminence in the sight of God is greater than that of all Prophets and Messengers! The most honored of God's honored Prophets and the loved one of God! More in love with God than them and closer to God than them! The most honored creation in the sight of God! More fortunate and more satisfied than them in the presence of God! The highest ranking human being! With a position greater than theirs and a kindness and favor more perfect than theirs, and a rank better than all the Prophets! With a law greater than theirs and whose origin is more noble than all Prophets! Whose evidence and preaching were clearer than theirs and whose birth, migration, perfumed descendants and companions were more gracious than theirs! The most tender human being! Whose origin was nobler than theirs, whose soul was better than theirs, whose heart was purer than theirs, whose word was truer than theirs, whose act was purer than theirs, whose descent was more solid than theirs, who was more faithful to his pledge than them, whose distinction was more weighty than theirs, whose disposition was more honored than theirs, whose design was finer than theirs, whose branch was better than theirs, whose obedience and dutifulness were more than theirs, whose station was higher than theirs, whose speech was more beautiful than theirs, whose peace was purer than theirs, whose rank was more splendid than theirs, whose glory was greater than theirs, whose glory was more resplendent than theirs, whose mention in the celestial realm was loftier than theirs, whose promise was more sincere than theirs, whose gratitude was more profuse than theirs, whose authority was higher than theirs, whose patience was more beautiful than theirs, whose goodness was finer than theirs, whose ease was more accessible than theirs, whose position was loftier than theirs, whose value was greater than theirs, whose argument was sounder than theirs, whose judgment was more balanced than theirs, whose faith was more advanced than theirs, whose evidence was clearer than theirs, whose tongue was more eloquent than theirs and whose authority was more obvious than theirs!

The Fourth Part to be Read on Thursday

O God, bless our master Muḥammad, Your servant and Your Messenger, the unlettered Prophet, and the family of our master Muḥammad! **O God**, bless our master Muḥammad and the family of our master Muḥammad blessings which

لَكَ رِضًى وَّلَهٗ جَزَآءً وَّلِحَقِّهٖ اَدَآءً وَّ اَعْطِهِ الْوَسِيْلَةَ وَالْفَضِيْلَةَ وَالْمَقَامَ الْمَحْمُوْدَ ن الَّذِيْ وَعَدْتَّهٗ وَاجْزِهٖ عَنَّا مَا هُوَ اَهْلُهٗ وَ اجْزِهٖ اَفْضَلَ مَا جَازَيْتَ نَبِيًّا عَنْ قَوْمِهٖ وَ رَسُوْلًا عَنْ اُمَّتِهٖ وَصَلِّ عَلٰى جَمِيْعِ اِخْوَانِهٖ مِنَ النَّبِيّٖنَ وَالصّٰلِحِيْنَ يَا اَرْحَمَ الرَّاحِمِيْنَ ۝ **اَللّٰهُمَّ** اجْعَلْ فَضَآئِلَ صَلَوَاتِكَ وَشَرَآئِفَ زَكَوَاتِكَ وَنَوَامِيَ بَرَكَاتِكَ وَعَوَاطِفَ رَاْفَتِكَ وَرَحْمَتِكَ وَتَحِيَّتِكَ وَفَضَآئِلَ اٰلَآئِكَ عَلٰى سَيِّدِنَا مُحَمَّدٍ سَيِّدِ الْمُرْسَلِيْنَ وَ رَسُوْلِ رَبِّ الْعٰلَمِيْنَ قَآئِدِ الْخَيْرِ وَفَاتِحِ الْبِرِّ وَنَبِيِّ الرَّحْمَةِ وَ سَيِّدِ الْاُمَّةِ ۝ **اَللّٰهُمَّ** ابْعَثْهُ مَقَامًا مَّحْمُوْدًا تُزْلِفُ بِهٖ قُرْبَهٗ وَتُقِرُّ بِهٖ عَيْنَهٗ يَغْبِطُهٗ بِهِ الْاَوَّلُوْنَ وَالْاٰخِرُوْنَ ۝ **اَللّٰهُمَّ** اَعْطِهِ الْفَضْلَ وَالْفَضِيْلَةَ وَالشَّرَفَ وَالْوَسِيْلَةَ وَالدَّرَجَةَ الرَّفِيْعَةَ وَالْمَنْزِلَةَ الشَّامِخَةَ ۝ **اَللّٰهُمَّ** اَعْطِ سَيِّدِنَا مُحَمَّدَنِ الْوَسِيْلَةَ وَبَلِّغْهُ مَاْمُوْلَهٗ وَاجْعَلْهُ اَوَّلَ شَافِعٍ وَّ اَوَّلَ مُشَفَّعٍ ۝ **اَللّٰهُمَّ** عَظِّمْ بُرْهَانَهٗ وَثَقِّلْ مِيْزَانَهٗ وَاَبْلِجْ حُجَّتَهٗ وَارْفَعْ فِيْٓ اَهْلِ عِلِّيِّيْنَ دَرَجَتَهٗ ۝ وَ فِيْٓ اَعْلَى الْمُقَرَّبِيْنَ مَنْزِلَتَهٗ ۝ **اَللّٰهُمَّ** اَحْيِنَا عَلٰى سُنَّتِهٖ ۝ وَتَوَفَّنَا عَلٰى مِلَّتِهٖ ۝ وَاجْعَلْنَا مِنْ اَهْلِ شَفَاعَتِهٖ ۝ وَاحْشُرْنَا فِيْ زُمْرَتِهٖ وَاَوْرِدْنَا حَوْضَهٗ ۝ وَاسْقِنَا مِنْ كَاْسِهٖ غَيْرَ خَزَايَا وَلَا نَادِمِيْنَ وَلَا شَآكِّيْنَ وَلَا مُبَدِّلِيْنَ وَلَا مُغَيِّرِيْنَ وَلَا فَاتِنِيْنَ وَلَا مَفْتُوْنِيْنَ اٰمِيْنَ يَا رَبَّ الْعٰلَمِيْنَ ۝ **اَللّٰهُمَّ** صَلِّ عَلٰى سَيِّدِنَا مُحَمَّدٍ وَّعَلٰى اٰلِ سَيِّدِنَا مُحَمَّدٍ وَّاَعْطِهِ الْوَسِيْلَةَ وَالْفَضِيْلَةَ وَالدَّرَجَةَ الرَّفِيْعَةَ وَابْعَثْهُ الْمَقَامَ الْمَحْمُوْدَ الَّذِيْ وَعَدْتَّهٗ مَعَ اِخْوَانِهِ النَّبِيّٖنَ ۝ صَلَّى اللّٰهُ عَلٰى سَيِّدِنَا مُحَمَّدٍ نَّبِيِّ الرَّحْمَةِ وَسَيِّدِ الْاُمَّةِ وَعَلٰٓى اَبِيْنَا سَيِّدِنَآ اٰدَمَ وَاُمِّنَا سَيِّدَتِنَا حَوَّآءَ وَمَنْ وَّلَدَا مِنَ النَّبِيّٖنَ وَالصِّدِّيْقِيْنَ وَالشُّهَدَآءِ وَالصَّالِحِيْنَ وَصَلِّ عَلٰى مَلٰٓئِكَتِكَ اَجْمَعِيْنَ مِنْ اَهْلِ

are pleasing to You, a reward for him, and which are his dutiful right, and grant him the closest access, the pre-eminence and the most praised station which You promised him, and reward him on our behalf as he deserves and reward him better than You have rewarded on behalf of his people any other Prophet or on behalf of his nation any other Messenger, and bless all his brothers, the Prophets and righteous ones, O Most Merciful of the Merciful! **O God**, bestow the favors of Your noble blessings and virtues, and the increase of Your benedictions, and the benevolence of Your Compassion, and Your Mercy, and Your Salutations, and the favors of Your bounties, upon our master Muḥammad, the master of the Messengers, the Messenger of the Lord of the Worlds, the guide to goodness, the opener of piety, the Prophet of mercy and the master of the nation!

O God, send him to the most praised station, thereby advancing his nearness, comforting his eyes, and making him the envy of those who came first and those who came last!

O God, grant him divine favor, divine grace, divine honor, the closest access, the lofty rank and the high standing! **O God**, grant our master Muḥammad the closest access and send him what he hopes for and make him the first intercessor and the first whose intercession is accepted! **O God**, strengthen his proof, make his judgment sound, make his argument shine and raise his rank among the dwellers of the uppermost heaven! And raise his standing among the heights of those who are closest!

O God, cause us to live according to his way! And pass away following his religion! And make us among the people of his intercession! And resurrect us in his company and make us to be watered from his pool! And to drink from his drinking bowl with no disgrace, no regrets, no doubts, and no temptations, amen, O Lord of the Worlds!

O God, bless our master Muḥammad and the family of our master Muḥammad and grant him the closest access, the pre-eminence and lofty rank and send him to the most praised station which You promised him with his brother Prophets! The blessings of God be upon our master Muḥammad, the Prophet of mercy and the master of his nation, and upon our father, our master Adam, and upon our mother, our lady Eve, and upon all the offspring of the Prophets, the truthful ones, the martyrs and the righteous ones, and bless all Your angels among the folk

السَّمٰوٰتِ وَالْاَرَضِيْنَ وَعَلَيْنَا مَعَهُمْ يَا اَرْحَمَ الرَّاحِمِيْنَ۝ **اَللّٰهُمَّ** اغْفِرْلِىْ ذُنُوْبِىْ وَلِوَالِدَىَّ وَارْحَمْهُمَا كَمَا رَبَّيَانِىْ صَغِيْرًا وَّلِجَمِيْعِ الْمُؤْمِنِيْنَ وَالْمُؤْمِنَاتِ وَالْمُسْلِمِيْنَ وَالْمُسْلِمَاتِ الْاَحْيَآءِ مِنْهُمْ وَالْاَمْوَاتِ وَتَابِعْ بَيْنَنَا وَبَيْنَهُمْ بِالْخَيْرَاتِ رَبِّ اغْفِرْ وَارْحَمْ وَاَنْتَ خَيْرُ الرَّاحِمِيْنَ وَلَا حَوْلَ وَلَا قُوَّةَ اِلَّا بِاللّٰهِ الْعَلِيِّ الْعَظِيْمِ۝

اَللّٰهُمَّ صَلِّ عَلٰى سَيِّدِنَا مُحَمَّدٍ نُّوْرِ الْاَنْوَارِ وَسِرِّ الْاَسْرَارِ وَسَيِّدِ الْاَبْرَارِ وَزَيْنِ الْمُرْسَلِيْنَ الْاَخْيَارِ وَاَكْرَمِ مَنْ اَظْلَمَ عَلَيْهِ اللَّيْلُ وَاَشْرَقَ عَلَيْهِ النَّهَارُ عَدَدَ مَا نَزَلَ مِنْ اَوَّلِ الدُّنْيَآ اِلٰٓى اٰخِرِهَا مِنْ قَطْرِ الْاَمْطَارِ وَعَدَدَ مَا نَبَتَ مِنْ اَوَّلِ الدُّنْيَآ اِلٰٓى اٰخِرِهَا مِنَ النَّبَاتِ وَالْاَشْجَارِ صَلٰوةً دَآئِمَةً ۢ بِدَوَامِ مُلْكِ اللّٰهِ الْوَاحِدِ الْقَهَّارِ ۝ **اَللّٰهُمَّ** صَلِّ عَلٰى سَيِّدِنَا مُحَمَّدٍ صَلٰوةً تُكْرِمُ بِهَا مَثْوَاهُ وَ تُشَرِّفُ بِهَا عُقْبَاهُ وَ تُبَلِّغُ بِهَا يَوْمَ الْقِيٰمَةِ مُنَاهُ وَرِضَاهُ۝ هٰذِهِ الصَّلٰوةُ تَعْظِيْمًا لِّحَقِّكَ يَا سَيِّدَنَا مُحَمَّدٍ ۝ثَلٰثًا۝ **اَللّٰهُمَّ** صَلِّ عَلٰى سَيِّدِنَا مُحَمَّدٍ حَآءِ الرَّحْمَةِ وَمِيْمَيِ الْمُلْكِ وَ دَالِ الدَّوَامِ السَّيِّدِ الْكَامِلِ الْفَاتِحِ الْخَاتِمِ عَدَدَ مَا فِىْ عِلْمِكَ كَآئِنٌ اَوْ قَدْ كَانَ كُلَّمَا ذَكَرَكَ وَذَكَرَهُ الذَّاكِرُوْنَ وَكُلَّمَا غَفَلَ عَنْ ذِكْرِكَ وَذِكْرِهِ الْغَافِلُوْنَ۝ صَلٰوةً دَآئِمَةً ۢ بِدَوَامِكَ بَاقِيَةً ۢ بِبَقَآئِكَ لَا مُنْتَهٰى لَهَا دُوْنَ عِلْمِكَ اِنَّكَ عَلٰى كُلِّ شَىْءٍ قَدِيْرٌ۝ثَلَاثًا۝ **اَللّٰهُمَّ** صَلِّ عَلٰى سَيِّدِنَا مُحَمَّدِ نِ النَّبِيِّ الْاُمِّيِّ وَعَلٰٓى اٰلِ سَيِّدِنَا مُحَمَّدِ نِ الَّذِىْ هُوَ اَبْهٰى شُمُوْسِ الْهُدٰى نُوْرًا وَّ اَبْهَرُهَا ۝ وَاَسْيَرُ الْاَنْبِيَآءِ فَخْرًا وَّ اَشْهَرُهَا ۝ وَ نُوْرُهٗ اَزْهَرُ اَنْوَارِ الْاَنْبِيَآءِ وَاَشْرَقُهَا وَ اَوْضَحُهَا وَاَزْكَى الْخَلِيْقَةِ اَخْلَاقًا وَّ اَطْهَرُهَا وَاَكْرَمُهَا خَلْقًا وَّ اَعْدَلُهَا ۝ **اَللّٰهُمَّ** صَلِّ عَلٰى سَيِّدِنَا

of the heavens and the earths and upon us along with them, O Most Merciful of the Merciful!

O God, forgive me my sins and my parents, and bestow mercy upon them even as they cherished me in childhood, and all the believing men and women, all the surrendering men and women, the living and the dead, and may blessings ensue for us.

O Lord, forgive, bestow mercy, and You are the Best of the Merciful! And there is no help or power save through God, the High, the Great!

O God, bless our master Muḥammad, the light of lights, the secret of secrets, the master of the pious, the adornment of the messengers, the chosen one, the most noble one the night has ever cloaked and the day has ever bathed in light, in every drop of rain which has fallen from the beginning of this world until its end, and in every plant and in every tree which have grown from the beginning of this world to its end, blessings which are eternal, lasting as long as the Dominion of God, the One, the Powerful!

O God, bless our master Muḥammad, blessings which ennoble his place of rest, honor his final destination. And on the Day of Resurrection bring him his heart's desire and contentment! These great blessings are your right, O our master Muḥammad! (**three times**)

O God, bless our master Muḥammad, the *'ha'* (the middle letter of *'Rahmah'*) of mercy, the *'mim'* (the first letter of *'Mulk'*) of sovereignty, and the *'dal'* (the first letter of *'Daʾim'*) of eternity, the perfect master, the opener, the seal, as much as Your Knowledge, now or before, and whenever You are remembered and he is remembered by those who remember and whenever You are forgotten and he is forgotten by those who forget!

Blessings which are eternal, lasting as long as You last, enduring as long as You endure, and with no end without Your Knowledge, for You are the Power over all things! (**three times**)

O God, bless our master Muḥammad, the unlettered Prophet, and the family of our master Muḥammad, him whose light is the most beautiful and most dazzling of all the suns of guidance! And whose conduct and glory are the best and most renowned of all the Prophets! And whose light is more radiant, more noble and more brilliant than the lights of the Prophets, and who has the purest and most immaculate manners in creation, and who is the most just and generous creature! **O God**, bless our master Muḥammad,

the unlettered Prophet, and the family of our master

مُحَمَّدِ ﻨِ النَّبِيِّ الْاُمِّيِّ وَعَلٰى اٰلِ سَيِّدِنَا مُحَمَّدِ ﻨِ الَّذِىْ هُوَ اَبْهٰى مِنَ الْقَمَرِ التَّآمِّ وَاَكْرَمُ مِنَ السَّحَابِ الْمُرْسَلَةِ وَالْبَحْرِ الْخِطَمِ ٥ **اَللّٰهُمَّ** صَلِّ عَلٰى سَيِّدِنَا مُحَمَّدِ ﻨِ النَّبِيِّ الْاُمِّيِّ وَعَلٰى اٰلِ سَيِّدِنَا مُحَمَّدِ ﻨِ الَّذِىْ قُرِنَتِ الْبَرَكَةُ بِذَاتِهٖ وَمُحَيَّاهُ وَتَعَطَّرَتِ الْعَوَالِمُ بِطِيْبِ ذِكْرِهٖ وَرَيَّاهُ ٥ **اَللّٰهُمَّ** صَلِّ عَلٰى سَيِّدِنَا مُحَمَّدٍ وَّعَلٰى اٰلِهٖ وَسَلِّمْ ٥ **اَللّٰهُمَّ** صَلِّ عَلٰى سَيِّدِنَا مُحَمَّدٍ وَّعَلٰى اٰلِ سَيِّدِنَا مُحَمَّدٍ وَّبَارِكْ عَلٰى سَيِّدِنَا مُحَمَّدٍ وَّعَلٰى اٰلِ سَيِّدِنَا مُحَمَّدٍ وَّارْحَمْ سَيِّدِنَا مُحَمَّدًا وَّاٰلَ سَيِّدِنَا مُحَمَّدٍ كَمَا صَلَّيْتَ وَبَارَكْتَ وَتَرَحَّمْتَ عَلٰى سَيِّدِنَآ اِبْرٰهِيْمَ وَعَلٰى اٰلِ سَيِّدِنَآ اِبْرٰهِيْمَ اِنَّكَ حَمِيْدٌ مَّجِيْدٌ ٥ **اَللّٰهُمَّ** صَلِّ عَلٰى سَيِّدِنَا مُحَمَّدٍ عَبْدِكَ وَنَبِيِّكَ وَرَسُوْلِكَ النَّبِيِّ الْاُمِّيِّ وَعَلٰى اٰلِ سَيِّدِنَا مُحَمَّدٍ ٥ **اَللّٰهُمَّ** صَلِّ عَلٰى سَيِّدِنَا مُحَمَّدٍ وَّعَلٰى اٰلِ سَيِّدِنَا مُحَمَّدٍ مِّلْءَ الدُّنْيَا وَمِلْءَ الْاٰخِرَةِ ٥ وَبَارِكْ عَلٰى سَيِّدِنَا مُحَمَّدٍ وَّعَلٰى اٰلِ سَيِّدِنَا مُحَمَّدٍ مِّلْءَ الدُّنْيَا وَمِلْءَ الْاٰخِرَةِ ٥ وَارْحَمْ سَيِّدِنَا مُحَمَّدً وَّاٰلَ سَيِّدِنَا مُحَمَّدٍ مِّلْءَ الدُّنْيَا وَمِلْءَ الْاٰخِرَةِ ٥ وَاجْزِ سَيِّدِنَا مُحَمَّدً وَّاٰلَ سَيِّدِنَا مُحَمَّدٍ مِّلْءَ الدُّنْيَا وَمِلْءَ الْاٰخِرَةِ ٥ وَسَلِّمْ عَلٰى سَيِّدِنَا مُحَمَّدٍ وَّعَلٰى اٰلِ سَيِّدِنَا مُحَمَّدٍ مِّلْءَ الدُّنْيَا وَمِلْءَ الْاٰخِرَةِ ٥ **اَللّٰهُمَّ** صَلِّ عَلٰى سَيِّدِنَا مُحَمَّدٍ كَمَآ اَمَرْتَنَآ اَنْ نُّصَلِّيَ عَلَيْهِ ٥ وَصَلِّ عَلٰى سَيِّدِنَا مُحَمَّدٍ كَمَا يَنْبَغِيْ اَنْ يُّصَلّٰى عَلَيْهِ ٥ **اَللّٰهُمَّ** صَلِّ عَلٰى نَبِيِّكَ الْمُصْطَفٰى وَرَسُوْلِكَ الْمُرْتَضٰى وَوَلِيِّكَ الْمُجْتَبٰى وَاَمِيْنِكَ عَلٰى وَحْيِ السَّمَآءِ ٥ **اَللّٰهُمَّ** صَلِّ عَلٰى سَيِّدِنَا مُحَمَّدٍ اَكْرَمِ الْاَسْلَافِ الْقَآئِمِ بِالْعَدْلِ وَالْاِنْصَافِ الْمَنْعُوْتِ فِيْ سُوْرَةِ الْاَعْرَافِ الْمُنْتَخَبِ مِنْ اَصْلَابِ الشِّرَافِ وَالْبُطُوْنِ الظِّرَافِ الْمُصَفّٰى مِنْ مُّصَاصِ عَبْدِ الْمُطَّلِبِ بْنِ عَبْدِ مَنَافِ ﻨِ الَّذِىْ

Muḥammad, him who is more beautiful than the full moon, more noble than the flowing clouds and the raging sea! **O God**, bless our master Muḥammad, the unlettered Prophet, and the family of our master Muḥammad, him whose face and essence are diffused with benediction, and the remembrance of whom perfumes and sweetens all the worlds! **O God**, bless and grant peace to our master Muḥammad and his family!

O God, bless our master Muḥammad and the family of our master Muḥammad, and bestow grace upon our master Muḥammad and the family of our master Muḥammad, and bestow mercy upon our master Muḥammad and the family of our master Muḥammad, just as You blessed, bestowed grace and bestowed mercy upon our master Abraham and the family of our master Abraham, for You are the Praiseworthy, the Mighty! **O God**, bless our master Muḥammad, Your servant, Your Prophet and Your Messenger, the unlettered Prophet, and the family of our master Muḥammad! **O God**, bless our master Muḥammad and the family of our master Muḥammad to the fullness of this world and to the fullness of the next world!

O God, bestow grace upon our master Muḥammad and the family of our master Muḥammad to the fullness of this world and to the fullness of the next world!

O God, bestow mercy upon our master Muḥammad and the family of our master Muḥammad to the fullness of this world and to the fullness of the next world!

O God, reward our master Muḥammad and the family of our master Muḥammad to the fullness of this world and to the fullness of the next world! **O God**, grant peace to our master Muḥammad and the family of our master Muḥammad to the fullness of this world and to the fullness of the next world! **O God**, bless our master Muḥammad as You ordered us to ask for blessings upon him! And bless our master Muḥammad as he should be blessed!

O God, bless Your Prophet, the chosen one, Your Messenger, the satisfied one, Your friend, the elected one, and Your custodian of the celestial revelation!

O God, bless our master Muḥammad, the most noble ancestor, the upholder of justice and equity, the one described in *Surah al-ᶜAraf*, the one chosen from the noble loins and refined wombs and the one purified by suckling, from ᶜAbd al-Muṭṭalib, son of ᶜAbd al-Manaf, through

هَـدَيْـتَ بِهٖ مِنَ الْخِلَافِ وَبَيَّنْتَ بِهٖ سَبِيْلَ الْعَفَافِ ۝ **اَللّٰهُمَّ** اِنِّيْٓ اَسْئَلُكَ بِاَفْضَلِ مَسْئَـلَتِكَ وَبِـاَحَـبِّ اَسْـمَآئِكَ اِلَيْكَ وَاَكْرَمِهَا عَلَيْكَ وَبِمَا مَنَنْتَ عَلَيْنَا بِسَيِّدِنَا مُـحَـمَّـدٍ نَّبِيِّنَا صَلَّى اللّٰهُ عَلَيْهِ وَسَلَّمَ فَاسْتَنْقَذْتَنَا بِهٖ مِنَ الضَّلَالَةِ وَاَمَرْتَنَا بِالصَّلٰوةِ عَـلَيْـهِ وَجَـعَـلْتَ صَلَاتَنَا عَلَيْهِ دَرَجَةً وَّكَفَّارَةً وَّلُطْفًا وَّمَنًّا مِّنْ اَعْطَآئِكَ فَاَدْعُوْكَ تَعْظِيْمًا لِاَمْـرِكَ وَاتِّبَـاعًـا لِّوَصِيَّتِكَ وَ مُنْتَجِزًالِّمَوْعُوْدِكَ لِمَا يَجِبُ لِنَبِيِّنَا سَيِّدِنَا مُـحَـمَّـدٍ صَـلَّـى اللّٰهُ عَلَيْهِ وَسَلَّمَ فِيْ اَدَآءِ حَقِّهٖ قِبَلَنَآ اِذْ اٰمَنَّا بِهٖ وَصَدَّقْنَاهُ وَاتَّبَعْنَا النُّوْرَ الَّذِيْٓ اُنْـزِلَ مَـعَهٗ وَقُلْتَ وَقَوْلُكَ الْحَقُّ اِنَّ اللّٰهَ وَمَلٰٓئِكَتَهٗ يُصَلُّوْنَ عَلَى النَّبِيِّ يـٰٓاَيُّهَـا الَّذِيْنَ اٰمَنُوْا صَلُّوْا عَلَيْهِ وَسَلِّمُوْا تَسْلِيْمًا ۝ وَاَمَـرْتَ الْعِبَادَ بِالصَّلٰوةِ عَلٰى نَبِيِّهِمْ فَرِيْضَةً ۢ افْتَـرَضْتَهَـا وَاَمَرْتَهُمْ بِهَا فَنَسْأَلُكَ بِجَلَالِ وَجْهِكَ وَنُوْرِ عَظْمَتِكَ وَبِـمَـآ اَوْجَبْـتَ عَلٰى نَفْسِكَ لِلْمُحْسِنِيْنَ اَنْ تُصَلِّيَ اَنْتَ وَمَلٰٓئِكَتُكَ عَلٰى سَيِّدِنَا مُـحَـمَّـدٍ عَبْـدِكَ وَرَسُـوْلِكَ وَنَبِيِّكَ وَصَـفِيِّكَ وَخِيَـرَتِكَ مِـنْ خَلْقِكَ اَفْضَلَ مَا صَـلَّيْـتَ عَـلٰٓى اَحَدٍ مِّنْ خَلْقِكَ اِنَّكَ حَمِيْدٌ مَّجِيْدٌ ۝ **اَللّٰهُمَّ** ارْفَـعْ دَرَجَتَهٗ وَاَكْرِمْ مَّـقَـامَـهٗ وَثَقِّلْ مِيْزَانَهٗ وَابْلِجْ حُجَّتَهٗ وَاَظْهِرْ مِلَّتَهٗ وَ اَجْزِلْ ثَوَابَهٗ وَاَضِئْ نُوْرَهٗ وَادِمْ كَـرَامَتَـهٗ وَاَلْحِقْ بِهٖ مِنْ ذُرِّيَّتِهٖ وَ اَهْلِ بَيْتِهٖ مَا تُقِرُّبِهٖ عَيْنَهٗ وَعَظِّمْهُ فِي النَّبِيِّيْنَ الَّذِيْنَ خَـلَوْا قَبْلَهٗ ۝ **اَللّٰهُمَّ** اجْـعَـلْ سَيِّـدِنَا مُحَمَّدًا اَكْثَرَ النَّبِيِّيْنَ تَبَعًا وَّاَكْثَرَهُمْ وُزَرَآءَ وَ اَفْـضَلَهُمْ كَرَامَةً وَّنُوْرًا ۝ وَّاَعْلَـٰهُمْ دَرَجَةً ۝ وَّاَفْسَـحَهُـمْ فِي الْجَنَّةِ مَنْزِلًا ۝ **اَللّٰهُمَّ** اجْـعَـلْ فِـي السَّـابِقِيْنَ غَايَتَهٗ وَ فِي الْمُنْتَخَبِيْنَ مَنْزِلَهٗ ۝ وَفِـي الْمُقَرَّبِيْنَ دَارَهٗ وَفِي الْمُصْطَفَيْنَ مَنْزِلَهٗ ۝ **اَللّٰهُمَّ** اجْعَلْهُ اَكْرَمَ الْاَكْرَمِيْنَ عِنْدَكَ مَنْزِلًا وَّ اَفْضَلَهُمْ ثَوَابًا وَّ اَقْـرَبَهُـمْ مَّجْلِسًا وَّ اَثْبَتَهُمْ مَّقَامًا وَّ اَصْوَبَهُمْ كَلَامًا وَّاَنْجَحَهُمْ مَّسْئَلَةً وَّ اَفْضَلَهُمْ

whom You guided from deviation and through whom You made clear the path of forgiveness! **O God**, I beseech You by the most superior beseeching, in the most loved of Your Names, in the most noble of Your Names, and for the sake of the fact that You blessed us with our master Muḥammad, the blessings and peace of God be upon him, saving us through him from error! And for the sake of the fact that You ordered us to ask for blessings upon him and for the sake of the fact that You made our asking for blessings upon him a means of raising our rank, an expiation for our sins, and grace and favor for us! Out of obedience to You, I call on You, exalting Your Command, following Your Instruction and fulfilling Your Promise, to render unto our Prophet, our master Muḥammad, the blessings and peace of God be upon him, what is his due from us, for we have faith in him and we believe in him and we follow the light which came down with him and You said, and Your Word is the Truth, 'God and His angels bless the Prophet. O You who believe, ask (God) to bless him and grant him abundant peace.' And for the sake of the fact that You made it obligatory for the servants to ask for blessings upon their Prophet making it an obligation and making it binding on them, I ask You for the sake of the majesty of Your Face and the light of Your Greatness, and for the sake of that which You have made binding on You in respect of the virtuous, that You and Your angels bless our master Muḥammad, Your servant, Your Messenger, Your Prophet, Your pure one and Your treasure from Your Creation, the best blessing ever bestowed upon anyone of Your Creation, for You are the Praiseworthy, the Mighty! **O God**, raise his rank, ennoble his station, make his judgment sound, refine his proof, make his religion triumph, increase his reward, make his light radiant, perpetuate his nobility, join him with his descendants and the People of his House which will be a comfort for his eyes, and exalt him among all the Prophets who lack his power! **O God**, of all the Prophets make our master Muḥammad have the greatest number of followers, increase them in strength, and give them the most perfect nobility and light! And raise their ranks! And widen their abodes in the Garden! **O God**, make their goal be among the foremost in faith and their abode among the elite! And their dwelling place among those who are close and their abode among the chosen ones! **O God**, make their abode the most noble of the noble in Your Presence and Favor them with Your reward, make them sit close to You, strengthen their stations, reward them with Your Word, give their entreaties success, favor their

لَدَيْكَ نَصِيْبًا وَّ اَعْظَمَهُمْ فِيمَا عِنْدَكَ رَغْبَةً وَّ اَنْزِلْهُ فِيْ غُرفَاتِ الْفِرْدَوْسِ مِنَ الدَّرَجَاتِ الْعُلٰى الَّتِيْ لَا دَرَجَةَ فَوْقَهَا ۝ اَللّٰهُمَّ اجْعَلْ سَيِّدِنَا مُحَمَّدًا اَصْدَقَ قَآئِلٍ وَّاَنْجَحَ سَآئِلٍ وَّ اَوَّلَ شَافِعٍ وَّ اَفْضَلَ مُشَفَّعٍ وَّ شَفِّعْهُ فِيْ اُمَّتِهٖ بِشَفَاعَةٍ يَّغْبِطُهٗ بِهَا الْاَوَّلُوْنَ وَالْاٰخِرُوْنَ وَاِذَا مَيَّزْتَ عِبَادَكَ بِفَصْلِ قَضَآئِكَ فَاجْعَلْ سَيِّدِنَا مُحَمَّدًا فِى الْاَصْدَقِيْنَ قِيْلًا وَّفِى الْاَحْسَنِيْنَ عَمَلًا وَّ فِى الْمَهْدِيِّيْنَ سَبِيْلًا ۝ اَللّٰهُمَّ اجْعَلْ نَبِيِّنَا لَنَا فَرَطًا وَّ اجْعَلْ حَوْضَهٗ لَنَا مَوْعِدًا لِاَوَّلِنَا وَاٰخِرِنَا ۝ اَللّٰهُمَّ احْشُرْنَا فِيْ زُمْرَتِهٖ وَاسْتَعْمِلْنَا فِيْ سُنَّتِهٖ وَتَوَفَّنَا عَلٰى مِلَّتِهٖ وَعَرِّفْنَا وَجْهَهٗ وَاجْعَلْنَا فِيْ زُمْرَتِهٖ وَحِزْبِهٖ ۝ اَللّٰهُمَّ اجْمَعْ بَيْنَنَا وَبَيْنَهٗ كَمَآ اٰمَنَّا بِهٖ وَلَمْ نَرَهٗ وَلَا تُفَرِّقْ بَيْنَنَا وَبَيْنَهٗ حَتّٰى تُدْخِلَنَا مُدْخَلَهٗ وَتُوْرِدَنَا حَوْضَهٗ وَتَجْعَلَنَا مِنْ رُّفَقَآئِهٖ مَعَ الْمُنْعَمِ عَلَيْهِمْ مِّنَ النَّبِيِّيْنَ وَالصِّدِّيْقِيْنَ وَالشُّهَدَآءِ وَالصَّالِحِيْنَ وَحَسُنَ اُولٰٓئِكَ رَفِيْقًا ۝ وَالْحَمْدُ لِلّٰهِ رَبِّ الْعٰلَمِيْنَ ۝

اِبْتِدَآءُ الرُّبْعِ الثَّالِثِ

اَللّٰهُمَّ صَلِّ عَلٰى سَيِّدِنَا مُحَمَّدٍ نُّوْرِ الْهُدٰى وَ الْقَآئِدِ اِلَى الْخَيْرِ وَالدَّاعِيْ اِلَى الرُّشْدِ نَبِيِّ الرَّحْمَةِ وَاِمَامِ الْمُتَّقِيْنَ وَرَسُوْلِ رَبِّ الْعٰلَمِيْنَ لَا نَبِيَّ بَعْدَهٗ كَمَا بَلَّغَ رِسَالَتَكَ وَنَصَحَ لِعِبَادِكَ وَتَلَا اٰيَاتِكَ وَاَقَامَ حُدُوْدَكَ وَوَفّٰى بِعَهْدِكَ وَاَنْفَذَ حُكْمَكَ وَ اَمَرَ بِطَاعَتِكَ وَنَهٰى عَنْ مَّعْصِيَتِكَ وَ وَالٰى وَلِيَّكَ الَّذِيْ تُحِبُّ اَنْ تُوَالِيَهٗ وَ عَادٰى عَدُوَّكَ الَّذِيْ تُحِبُّ اَنْ تُعَادِيَهٗ وَصَلَّى اللّٰهُ عَلٰى سَيِّدِنَا مُحَمَّدٍ ۝ اَللّٰهُمَّ صَلِّ عَلٰى جَسَدِهٖ فِى الْاَجْسَادِ وَعَلٰى رُوْحِهٖ فِى الْاَرْوَاحِ وَعَلٰى مَوْقِفِهٖ فِى الْمَوَاقِفِ وَعَلٰى مَشْهَدِهٖ فِى الْمَشَاهِدِ وَعَلٰى ذِكْرِهٖ اِذَا ذُكِرَ صَلٰوةً مِّنَّا عَلٰى

share in Your Presence, strengthen their longing for what is with You and bring them into the chambers of Paradise in high ranks above which there is no other rank!

O God, grant our master Muḥammad the truest word, the most successful petitioning, the first intercession, the most perfect intercession, and intercede on his behalf for his nation, an intercession that will be the envy of those who came first and those who came last, and distinguish Your servant in the discharge of Your Decree, and make our master Muḥammad among the speakers of truth, the doers of good, and the guides to the path!

O God, grant our Prophet to excess and make his pool a promise for the first of us and the last of us!

O God, resurrect us in his company, establish us on his way, cause us to die following his tradition, acquaint us with his face and make us among his company and party!

O God, unite us with him for we have believed in him without seeing him, do not separate us from him until the day you cause us to enter into his entrance hall, water us at his pool, and put us in his company along with those favored from among the Prophets, the truthful ones, the martyrs, and the righteous ones, and what a beautiful company that is! And praise be to God, the Lord of the Worlds!

(beginning of the third quarter)

O God, bless our master Muḥammad, the light of guidance, the guide to goodness, the caller to spiritual direction, the Prophet of mercy, the leader of the pious, the Messenger of the Lord of the Worlds, there being no Prophet after him, just as he conveyed Your message, advised Your servants, recited Your Verses, upheld Your Divine Statutes, faithfully discharged Your Covenant, carried out Your Judgment, enjoined obedience to You, forbid disobedience to You, befriended Your friend whom You chose to befriend, and opposed Your enemy whom You chose to oppose, and the blessings and peace of God be upon him!

O God, of all the bodies in existence, bless his body! Of all the souls in existence, bless his soul! Of all the places in existence, bless his place! Of all tombs in existence bless his tomb, and bless his memory whenever he is remembered, blessings from us on our

نَبِيِّنَا ○ **اَللّٰهُمَّ** اَبْلِغْهُ مِنَّا السَّلَامَ كَمَا ذُكِرَ السَّلَامُ وَالسَّلَامُ عَلٰى النَّبِيِّ وَرَحْمَةُ اللّٰهِ تَعَالٰى وَبَرَكَاتُهٗ ○ **اَللّٰهُمَّ** صَلِّ عَلٰى مَلٰٓئِكَتِكَ الْمُقَرَّبِيْنَ وَ عَلٰى اَنْبِيَآئِكَ الْمُطَهَّرِيْنَ وَعَلٰى رُسُلِكَ الْمُرْسَلِيْنَ وَعَلٰى حَمَلَةِ عَرْشِكَ وَعَلٰى سَيِّدِنَا جِبْرِيْلَ وَ سَيِّدِنَا مِيْكَآئِيْلَ وَ سَيِّدِنَآ اِسْرَافِيْلَ وَ سَيِّدِنَا مَلَكِ الْمَوْتِ وَ سَيِّدِنَا رِضْوَانَ خَازِنِ جَنَّتِكَ وَ سَيِّدِنَا مَالِكٍ وَّصَلِّ عَلَى الْكِرَامِ الْكَاتِبِيْنَ وَصَلِّ عَلٰى اَهْلِ طَاعَتِكَ اَجْمَعِيْنَ مِنْ اَهْلِ السَّمٰوٰتِ وَالْاَرَضِيْنَ ○ **اَللّٰهُمَّ** اٰتِ اَهْلَ بَيْتِ نَبِيِّكَ اَفْضَلَ مَآ اٰتَيْتَ اَحَدًا مِّنْ اَهْلِ بُيُوْتِ الْمُرْسَلِيْنَ وَاجْزِ اَصْحَابَ نَبِيِّكَ اَفْضَلَ مَا جَازَيْتَ اَحَدًا مِّنْ اَصْحَابِ الْمُرْسَلِيْنَ ○ **اَللّٰهُمَّ** اغْفِرْ لِلْمُؤْمِنِيْنَ وَالْمُؤْمِنَاتِ وَ الْمُسْلِمِيْنَ وَالْمُسْلِمَاتِ الْاَحْيَآءِ مِنْهُمْ وَالْاَمْوَاتِ ○ وَاغْفِرْلَنَا وَلِاِخْوَانِنَا الَّذِيْنَ سَبَقُوْنَا بِالْاِيْمَانِ وَلَا تَجْعَلْ فِيْ قُلُوْبِنَا غِلًّا لِّلَّذِيْنَ اٰمَنُوْا رَبَّنَآ اِنَّكَ رَئُوْفٌ رَّحِيْمٌ ○ **اَللّٰهُمَّ** صَلِّ عَلَى النَّبِيِّ الْهَاشِمِيِّ سَيِّدِنَا مُحَمَّدٍ وَّعَلٰى اٰلِهٖ وَصَحْبِهٖ وَسَلِّمْ تَسْلِيْمًا ○ **اَللّٰهُمَّ** صَلِّ عَلٰى سَيِّدِنَا مُحَمَّدٍ خَيْرِ الْبَرِيَّةِ صَلٰوةً تُرْضِيْكَ وَتُرْضِيْهِ وَتَرْضٰى بِهَا عَنَّا يَآ اَرْحَمَ الرَّاحِمِيْنَ ○ **اَللّٰهُمَّ** صَلِّ عَلٰى سَيِّدِنَا مُحَمَّدٍ وَّعَلٰى اٰلِهٖ وَصَحْبِهٖ وَسَلِّمْ تَسْلِيْمًا كَثِيْرًا طَيِّبًا مُّبَارَكًا فِيْهِ جَزِيْلًا جَمِيْلًا دَآئِمًا بِدَوَامِ مُلْكِ اللّٰهِ ○ **اَللّٰهُمَّ** صَلِّ عَلٰى سَيِّدِنَا مُحَمَّدٍ وَّعَلٰى اٰلِهٖ مِلْاَ الْفَضَآءِ وَعَدَدَ النُّجُوْمِ فِي السَّمَآءِ صَلٰوةً تُوَازِنُ السَّمٰوٰتِ وَالْاَرْضَ وَعَدَدَ مَا خَلَقْتَ وَمَآ اَنْتَ خَالِقُهٗٓ اِلٰى يَوْمِ الْقِيٰمَةِ ○ **اَللّٰهُمَّ** صَلِّ عَلٰى سَيِّدِنَا مُحَمَّدٍ وَّعَلٰى اٰلِ سَيِّدِنَا مُحَمَّدٍ كَمَا صَلَّيْتَ عَلٰى سَيِّدِنَآ اِبْرٰهِيْمَ وَبَارِكْ عَلٰى سَيِّدِنَا مُحَمَّدٍ وَّعَلٰى اٰلِ سَيِّدِنَا مُحَمَّدٍ كَمَا بَارَكْتَ عَلٰى سَيِّدِنَآ اِبْرٰهِيْمَ وَعَلٰى اٰلِ سَيِّدِنَآ اِبْرٰهِيْمَ فِي الْعٰلَمِيْنَ اِنَّكَ حَمِيْدٌ

Prophet!

O God, convey to him from us peace just as he invoked peace, and peace, mercy and the benediction of God be upon the Prophet!

O God, bless Your closest angels, Your purest Prophets, Your divine Messengers, the bearers of Your Throne, our master Gabriel, our master Michael, our master Israfil, our master the Angel of Death, our master Ridwan, the guardian of Your Garden, our master Malek, and bless the noble recording angels, and bless all the people obedient to You, those on the earths and those in the heavens!

O God, give the People of the House of Your Prophet the best ever given to any of the People of the Houses of the Messengers, and reward the Companions of Your Prophet the best ever given to any of the Companions of the Messengers!

O God, forgive the believing men and women and the surrendering men and women, the living among them and the dead! And forgive us and our brothers who came before us in faith and leave not in our hearts any rancor against those who believe, our Lord, You are full of Kindness, Most Merciful!

O God, bless and grant abundant peace to the Hashimi Prophet, our master Muḥammad, and to his family and Companions!

O God, bless our master Muḥammad, the best of Creation, blessings which are pleasing to You, pleasing to him and by which You are pleased with us, O Most Merciful of the Merciful!

O God, bless our master Muḥammad and his family and Companions, and grant them peace, abundantly, profusely, agreeably, graciously, generously, beautifully, and eternally for as long as the Sovereignty of God!

O God, bless our master Muḥammad and the family of our master Muḥammad, to the fullness of the cosmic space, and as many times as there are stars in the sky, blessings which outweigh the heavens and the earth, as much as You have created and as much as You will create until the Day of Resurrection!

O God, bless our master Muḥammad and the family of our master Muḥammad just as You blessed our master Abraham, and favor our master Muḥammad and the family of our master Muḥammad just as You favored Abraham and the family of

Abraham in the Worlds, for You are Praiseworthy,

مَّجِيْدٌ ○ **اَللّٰهُمَّ** اِنِّىْٓ اَسْئَلُكَ الْعَفْوَ وَالْعَافِيَةَ فِى الدِّيْنِ وَالدُّنْيَا وَالْاٰخِرَةِ ○ ثَلَاثًا ○ **اَللّٰهُمَّ** اسْتُرْنَا بِسِتْرِكَ الْجَمِيْلِ ○ ثَلَاثًا ○ **اَللّٰهُمَّ** اِنِّىْٓ اَسْئَلُكَ بِحَقِّكَ الْعَظِيْمِ وَبِحَقِّ نُوْرِ وَجْهِكَ الْكَرِيْمِ وَبِحَقِّ عَرْشِكَ الْعَظِيْمِ وَبِمَا حَمَلَ كُرْسِيُّكَ مِنْ عَظْمَتِكَ وَ جَلَالِكَ وَجَمَالِكَ وَبَهَآئِكَ وَقُدْرَتِكَ وَ سُلْطَانِكَ وَبِحَقِّ اَسْمَآئِكَ الْمَخْزُوْنَةِ الْمَكْنُوْنَةِ الَّتِىْ لَمْ يَطَّلِعْ عَلَيْهَآ اَحَدٌ مِّنْ خَلْقِكَ ○ **اَللّٰهُمَّ** وَاَسْئَلُكَ بِالْاِسْمِ الَّذِىْ وَضَعْتَهٗ عَلَى اللَّيْلِ فَاَظْلَمَ وَعَلَى النَّهَارِ فَاسْتَنَارَ وَعَلَى السَّمٰوٰتِ فَاسْتَقَلَّتْ ○ وَعَلَى الْاَرْضِ فَاسْتَقَرَّتْ ○ وَعَلَى الْجِبَالِ فَارْسَتْ وَعَلَى الْبِحَارِ وَالْاَوْدِيَةِ فَجَرَتْ ○ وَعَلَى الْعُيُوْنِ فَنَبَعَتْ ○ وَعَلَى السَّحَابِ فَاَمْطَرَتْ ○ وَاَسْئَلُكَ اَللّٰهُمَّ بِالْاَسْمَآءِ الْمَكْتُوْبَةِ فِىْ جَبْهَةِ سَيِّدِنَآ اِسْرَافِيْلَ عَلَيْهِ السَّلَامُ وَبِالْاَسْمَآءِ الْمَكْتُوْبَةِ فِىْ جَبْهَةِ سَيِّدِنَا جِبْرِيْلَ عَلَيْهِ السَّلَامُ وَعَلَى الْمَلٰٓئِكَةِ الْمُقَرَّبِيْنَ ○ وَاَسْئَلُكَ اَللّٰهُمَّ بِالْاَسْمَآءِ الْمَكْتُوْبَةِ حَوْلَ الْعَرْشِ وَبِالْاَسْمَآءِ الْمَكْتُوْبَةِ حَوْلَ الْكُرْسِىِّ ○ وَاَسْئَلُكَ اَللّٰهُمَّ بِالْاِسْمِ الْمَكْتُوْبِ عَلٰى وَرَقِ الزَّيْتُوْنِ ○ وَاَسْئَلُكَ اَللّٰهُمَّ بِالْاَسْمَآءِ الْعِظَامِ الَّتِىْ سَمَّيْتَ بِهَا نَفْسَكَ مَا عَلِمْتُ مِنْهَا وَمَا لَمْ اَعْلَمْ ○

اَلْحِزْبُ الْخَامِسُ فِىْ يَوْمِ الْجُمُعَةِ

وَاَسْئَلُكَ اَللّٰهُمَّ بِالْاَسْمَآءِ الْعِظَامِ الَّتِىْ سَمَّيْتَ بِهَا نَفْسَكَ مَا عَلِمْتُ مِنْهَا وَمَا لَمْ اَعْلَمْ ○ وَاَسْئَلُكَ اَللّٰهُمَّ بِالْاَسْمَآءِ الَّتِىْ دَعَاكَ بِهَا سَيِّدُنَآ اٰدَمُ عَلَيْهِ السَّلَامُ ○ وَبِالْاَسْمَآءِ الَّتِىْ دَعَاكَ بِهَا سَيِّدُنَا نُوْحٌ عَلَيْهِ السَّلَامُ ○ وَبِالْاَسْمَآءِ الَّتِىْ دَعَاكَ بِهَا سَيِّدُنَا هُوْدٌ عَلَيْهِ السَّلَامُ ○ وَبِالْاَسْمَآءِ الَّتِىْ دَعَاكَ بِهَا سَيِّدُنَآ اِبْرَاهِيْمُ عَلَيْهِ

the Mighty!

O God, I beg You for forgiveness and well-being in my religion, in this life and in the next! (**three times**)

O God, cover my faults with a beautiful covering! (**three times**)

O God, I ask You for the sake of Your Great Truth and for the sake of the Truth of the light of Your Noble Face and for the sake of the truth of Your Great Throne and for the sake of that which bears Your Chair from Your Strength Oceans, Your Glory Oceans, Your Beauty Oceans, Your Light Oceans, Your Might Oceans and Your Power Oceans and for the sake of the Truth of Your Preserved and Hidden Names which no one from Your Creation will ever come to know!

O God, I ask You in the Name which when laid upon the night, darkness falls, and when laid upon the day, light appears, and when laid upon the heavens, they are raised on high! And when laid upon the earth, it becomes firm! And when laid upon the mountains, they become fixed and when laid upon the oceans and the rivers, they begin to flow! And when laid upon the springs, they burst forth! And when laid upon the clouds, they shed their rain! And I ask You, O God, in the Names written upon the forehead of Israfil, peace be upon him, and in the Names written on the forehead on Gabriel, peace be upon him and upon all the Angels of Intimacy! And I ask You, O God, in the Names written around the Holy Throne and in the Names written around the Divine Chair! And I ask You,

O God, in the name written on the olive leaf! And I ask You,

O God, in the Greatest Names which You have named Yourself knowledge of which I have not and which I will never have!

The Fifth Part to be Read on Friday

O God, I ask You in the majestic names with which You have named Yourself, those of which I am aware and those of which I am not aware! And I ask You,

O God, in the names in which our master Adam, peace be upon him, called You! And I ask You,

O God, in the names in which our master Noah, peace be upon him, called You! And I ask You,

O God, in the names in which our master Hud, peace be upon him, called You! And I ask You,

O God, in the names in which our master Abraham, peace

السَّلَامُ ۝ وَبِالْاَسْمَآءِ الَّتِيْ دَعَاكَ بِهَا سَيِّدُنَا صَالِحٌ عَلَيْهِ السَّلَامُ ۝ وَبِالْاَسْمَآءِ الَّتِيْ دَعَاكَ بِهَا سَيِّدُنَا يُوْنُسُ عَلَيْهِ السَّلَامُ ۝ وَبِالْاَسْمَآءِ الَّتِيْ دَعَاكَ بِهَا سَيِّدُنَآ اَيُّوْبُ عَلَيْهِ السَّلَامُ ۝ وَبِالْاَسْمَآءِ الَّتِيْ دَعَاكَ بِهَا سَيِّدُنَا يَعْقُوْبُ عَلَيْهِ السَّلَامُ ۝ وَبِالْاَسْمَآءِ الَّتِيْ دَعَاكَ بِهَا سَيِّدُنَا يُوْسُفُ عَلَيْهِ السَّلَامُ ۝ وَبِالْاَسْمَآءِ الَّتِيْ دَعَاكَ بِهَا سَيِّدُنَا مُوْسٰى عَلَيْهِ السَّلَامُ ۝ وَبِالْاَسْمَآءِ الَّتِيْ دَعَاكَ بِهَا سَيِّدُنَا هَارُوْنُ عَلَيْهِ السَّلَامُ ۝ وَبِالْاَسْمَآءِ الَّتِيْ دَعَاكَ بِهَا سَيِّدُنَا شُعَيْبٌ عَلَيْهِ السَّلَامُ ۝ وَبِالْاَسْمَآءِ الَّتِيْ دَعَاكَ بِهَا سَيِّدُنَآ اِسْمٰعِيْلُ عَلَيْهِ السَّلَامُ ۝ وَبِالْاَسْمَآءِ الَّتِيْ دَعَاكَ بِهَا سَيِّدُنَا دَاوُدُ عَلَيْهِ السَّلَامُ ۝ وَبِالْاَسْمَآءِ الَّتِيْ دَعَاكَ بِهَا سَيِّدُنَا سُلَيْمٰنُ عَلَيْهِ السَّلَامُ ۝ وَبِالْاَسْمَآءِ الَّتِيْ دَعَاكَ بِهَا سَيِّدُنَا زَكَرِيَّا عَلَيْهِ السَّلَامُ ۝ وَبِالْاَسْمَآءِ الَّتِيْ دَعَاكَ بِهَا سَيِّدُنَا يَحْيٰى عَلَيْهِ السَّلَامُ ۝ وَبِالْاَسْمَآءِ الَّتِيْ دَعَاكَ بِهَا سَيِّدُنَآ اَرْمِيَآءُ عَلَيْهِ السَّلَامُ ۝ وَبِالْاَسْمَآءِ الَّتِيْ دَعَاكَ بِهَا سَيِّدُنَا شَعْيَآءُ عَلَيْهِ السَّلَامُ ۝ وَبِالْاَسْمَآءِ الَّتِيْ دَعَاكَ بِهَا سَيِّدُنَآ اِلْيَاسُ عَلَيْهِ السَّلَامُ ۝ وَبِالْاَسْمَآءِ الَّتِيْ دَعَاكَ بِهَا سَيِّدُنَا الْيَسَعُ عَلَيْهِ السَّلَامُ ۝ وَبِالْاَسْمَآءِ الَّتِيْ دَعَاكَ بِهَا سَيِّدُنَا ذُو الْكِفْلِ عَلَيْهِ السَّلَامُ ۝ وَبِالْاَسْمَآءِ الَّتِيْ دَعَاكَ بِهَا سَيِّدُنَا يُوْشَعُ عَلَيْهِ السَّلَامُ ۝ وَبِالْاَسْمَآءِ الَّتِيْ دَعَاكَ بِهَا سَيِّدُنَا عِيْسَى ابْنُ مَرْيَمَ عَلَيْهِ السَّلَامُ ۝ وَبِالْاَسْمَآءِ الَّتِيْ دَعَاكَ بِهَا سَيِّدُنَا مُحَمَّدٌ صَلَّى اللّٰهُ عَلَيْهِ وَسَلَّمَ ۝ وَعَلٰى جَمِيْعِ النَّبِيِّيْنَ وَالْمُرْسَلِيْنَ اَنْ تُصَلِّيَ عَلٰى سَيِّدِنَا مُحَمَّدٍ نَّبِيِّكَ عَدَدَ مَا خَلَقْتَهٗ مِنْ قَبْلِ اَنْ تَكُوْنَ السَّمَآءُ مَبْنِيَّةً وَّالْاَرْضُ مَدْحِيَّةً وَّالْجِبَالُ مُرْسَاةً وَّالْبِحَارُ مُجْرَاةً وَّالْعُيُوْنُ مُنْفَجِرَةً وَّالْاَنْهَارُ مُنْهَمِرَةً وَّالشَّمْسُ مُضْحِيَةً وَّالْقَمَرُ مُضِيْئًا وَّالْكَوَاكِبُ مُسْتَنِيْرَةً كُنْتَ حَيْثُ كُنْتَ لَا

be upon him, called You! And I ask You, **O God**, in the names in which our master Salih, peace be upon him, called You! And I ask You,

O God, in the names in which our master Jonah, peace be upon him, called You! And I ask You, **O God**, in the names in which our master Job, peace be upon him, called You! And I ask You, **O God**, in the names in which our master Jacob, peace be upon him, called You! And I ask You, **O God**, in the names in which our master Joseph, peace be upon him, called You! And I ask You, **O Go** , in the names in which our master Moses, peace be upon him, called You! And I ask You,

O God, in the names in which our master Aaron, peace be upon him, called You! And I ask You, **O God**, in the names in which our master Shuaib, peace be upon him, called You! And I ask You,

O God, in the names in which our master Ishmael, peace be upon him, called You! And I ask You, **O God**, in the names in which our master David, peace be upon him, called You! And I ask You, **O God**, in the names in which our master Solomon, peace be upon him, called You! And I ask You,

O God, in the names in which our master Zechariah, peace be upon him, called You! And I ask You,

O God, in the names in which our master John the Baptist, peace be upon him, called You! And I ask You,

O God, in the names in which our master Jeremiah, peace be upon him, called You! And I ask You, **O God**, in the names in which our master Shuayb, peace be upon him, called You! And I ask You,

O God , in the names in which our master Elias, peace be upon him, called You! And I ask You, **O God**, in the names in which our master Esau, peace be upon him, called You! And I ask You,

O God, in the names in which our master Dhu Kifl, peace be upon him, called You! And I ask You, **O God** , in the names in which our master Joshua, peace be upon him, called You! And I ask You,

O God, in the names in which our master Jesus son of Mary, peace be upon him, called You! And I ask You,

O God, in the names in which our master Muḥammad, the blessings and peace of God be upon him and on all the Prophets and Messengers, called You! That You bless our master Muḥammad, Your Prophet, in all that You created before the sky was built, the earth was spread out, the mountains were made stable, the seas began their flow, the springs burst forth, the rivers streamed out, the sun shone forth, the moon beamed and the planets were lit up and there where You were, You were,

يَعْلَمُ اَحَدٌ حَيْثُ كُنتَ اِلَّآ اَنْتَ وَحْدَكَ لَا شَرِيْكَ لَكَ ۝ **اَللّٰهُمَّ** صَلِّ عَلٰى سَيِّدِنَا مُحَمَّدٍ عَدَدَ حِلْمِكَ ۝ وَصَلِّ عَلٰى سَيِّدِنَا مُحَمَّدٍ عَدَدَ عِلْمِكَ ۝ وَصَلِّ عَلٰى سَيِّدِنَا مُحَمَّدٍ عَدَدَ كَلِمَاتِكَ ۝ وَصَلِّ عَلٰى سَيِّدِنَا مُحَمَّدٍ عَدَدَ نِعْمَتِكَ ۝ وَصَلِّ عَلٰى سَيِّدِنَا مُحَمَّدٍ مِّلْءَ سَمٰوٰتِكَ ۝ وَصَلِّ عَلٰى سَيِّدِنَا مُحَمَّدٍ مِّلْءَ اَرْضِكَ ۝ وَصَلِّ عَلٰى سَيِّدِنَا مُحَمَّدٍ مِلْءَ عَرْشِكَ ۝ وَصَلِّ عَلٰى سَيِّدِنَا مُحَمَّدٍ زِنَةَ عَرْشِكَ ۝ وَصَلِّ عَلٰى سَيِّدِنَا مُحَمَّدٍ عَدَدَ مَا جَرٰى بِهِ الْقَلَمُ فِيْٓ اُمِّ الْكِتَابِ ۝ وَصَلِّ عَلٰى سَيِّدِنَا مُحَمَّدٍ عَدَدَ مَا خَلَقْتَ فِيْ سَبْعِ سَمٰوٰتِكَ ۝ وَصَلِّ عَلٰى سَيِّدِنَا مُحَمَّدٍ عَدَدَ مَآ اَنْتَ خَالِقٌ فِيْهِنَّ اِلٰى يَوْمِ الْقِيٰمَةِ فِيْ كُلِّ يَوْمٍ اَلْفَ مَرَّةٍ ۝ **اَللّٰهُمَّ** صَلِّ عَلٰى سَيِّدِنَا مُحَمَّدٍ عَدَدَ كُلِّ قَطْرَةٍ قَطَرَتْ مِنْ سَمٰوٰتِكَ اِلٰى اَرْضِكَ مِنْ يَّوْمِ خَلَقْتَ الدُّنْيَآ اِلٰى يَوْمِ الْقِيٰمَةِ فِيْ كُلِّ يَوْمٍ اَلْفَ مَرَّةٍ ۝ **اَللّٰهُمَّ** صَلِّ عَلٰى سَيِّدِنَا مُحَمَّدٍ عَدَدَ مَنْ يُّسَبِّحُكَ وَيُهَلِّلُكَ وَيُكَبِّرُكَ وَيُعَظِّمُكَ مِنْ يَّوْمِ خَلَقْتَ الدُّنْيَآ اِلٰى يَوْمِ الْقِيٰمَةِ فِيْ كُلِّ يَوْمٍ اَلْفَ مَرَّةٍ ۝ **اَللّٰهُمَّ** صَلِّ عَلٰى سَيِّدِنَا مُحَمَّدٍ عَدَدَ اَنْفَاسِهِمْ وَاَلْفَاظِهِمْ ۝ وَصَلِّ عَلٰى سَيِّدِنَا مُحَمَّدٍ عَدَدَ كُلِّ نَسَمَةٍ خَلَقْتَهَا فِيْهِمْ مِنْ يَّوْمِ خَلَقْتَ الدُّنْيَآ اِلٰى يَوْمِ الْقِيٰمَةِ فِيْ كُلِّ يَوْمٍ اَلْفَ مَرَّةٍ ۝ **اَللّٰهُمَّ** صَلِّ عَلٰى سَيِّدِنَا مُحَمَّدٍ عَدَدَ السَّحَابِ الْجَارِيَةِ وَصَلِّ عَلٰى سَيِّدِنَا مُحَمَّدٍ عَدَدَ الرِّيَاحِ الذَّارِيَةِ مِنْ يَّوْمِ خَلَقْتَ الدُّنْيَآ اِلٰى يَوْمِ الْقِيٰمَةِ فِيْ كُلِّ يَوْمٍ اَلْفَ مَرَّةٍ ۝ **اَللّٰهُمَّ** صَلِّ عَلٰى سَيِّدِنَا مُحَمَّدٍ عَدَدَ مَا هَبَّتْ عَلَيْهِ الرِّيَاحُ وَحَرَّكَتْهُ مِنَ الْاَغْصَانِ وَ الْاَشْجَارِ وَالْاَوْرَاقِ وَالثِّمَارِ وَجَمِيْعِ مَا خَلَقْتَ عَلٰٓى اَرْضِكَ وَمَا بَيْنَ سَمٰوٰتِكَ مِنْ يَّوْمِ خَلَقْتَ الدُّنْيَآ اِلٰى يَوْمِ الْقِيٰمَةِ فِيْ كُلِّ يَوْمٍ اَلْفَ مَرَّةٍ ۝

and no one knows where You were, except You alone, O You who have no partner!

O God, bless our master Muḥammad to the extent of Your forbearance! **O God**, bless our master Muḥammad to the extent of Your knowledge! **O God**, bless our master Muḥammad as many times as Your words!

O God, bless our master Muḥammad to the extent of Your Favor!

O God, bless our master Muḥammad to the fullness of Your Skies!

O God, bless our master Muḥammad to the fullness of Your Earth!

O God, bless our master Muḥammad to the fullness of Your Throne!

O God, bless our master Muḥammad in the decoration of Your Throne!

O God, bless our master Muḥammad in all that the Pen has written in the Mother of the Book!

O God, bless our master Muḥammad as much as You have created in Your Seven Heavens!

O God, bless our master Muḥammad as much as You will create in them until the Day of Resurrection and every day a thousand times!

O God, bless our master Muḥammad in every drop of rain that has fallen from Your heavens to Your earth from the day You created the world to the Day of Resurrection and every day a thousand times!

O God, bless our master Muḥammad as many times as those who have glorified You, declared Your unity, magnified You and extolled You from the day You created the world to the Day of Resurrection and every day a thousand times!

O God, bless our master Muḥammad in every one of their breaths and their utterances!

O God, bless our master Muḥammad in every one of their fragrant out breathings from the day You created the world to the Day of Resurrection and every day a thousand times!

O God, bless our master Muḥammad in every rolling cloud and bless our master Muḥammad in every sweeping wind from the day You created the world to the Day of Resurrection and every day a thousand times!

O God, bless our master Muḥammad in the movement of every branch, every tree, every leaf and every fruit stirred by the wind and in everything that You have created on Your earth and what is between Your Heavens from the day You created the world to the Day of Resurrection and every day a thousand times!

اَللّٰهُمَّ صَلِّ عَلٰى سَيِّدِنَا مُحَمَّدٍ عَدَدَ نُجُوْمِ السَّمَآءِ مِنْ يَّوْمِ خَلَقْتَ الدُّنْيَآ اِلٰى يَوْمِ الْقِيٰمَةِ فِىْ كُلِّ يَوْمٍ اَلْفَ مَرَّةٍ ○ **اَللّٰهُمَّ** صَلِّ عَلٰى سَيِّدِنَا مُحَمَّدٍ مِّلْءَ اَرْضِكَ مِمَّا حَمَلَتْ وَاَقَلَّتْ مِنْ قُدْرَتِكَ ○ **اَللّٰهُمَّ** صَلِّ عَلٰى سَيِّدِنَا مُحَمَّدٍ عَدَدَ مَا خَلَقْتَ فِىْ سَبْعِ بِحَارِكَ مِمَّا لَا يَعْلَمُ عِلْمَهٗٓ اِلَّآ اَنْتَ وَمَآ اَنْتَ خَالِقُهٗ فِيْهَآ اِلٰى يَوْمِ الْقِيٰمَةِ فِىْ كُلِّ يَوْمٍ اَلْفَ مَرَّةٍ ○ **اَللّٰهُمَّ** صَلِّ عَلٰى سَيِّدِنَا مُحَمَّدٍ عَدَدَ مِلْءِ سَبْعِ بِحَارِكَ ○ وَصَلِّ عَلٰى سَيِّدِنَا مُحَمَّدٍ زِنَةَ سَبْعِ بِحَارِكَ مِمَّا حَمَلَتْ وَاَقَلَّتْ مِنْ قُدْرَتِكَ ○ **اَللّٰهُمَّ** وَصَلِّ عَلٰى سَيِّدِنَا مُحَمَّدٍ عَدَدَ اَمْوَاجِ بِحَارِكَ مِنْ يَّوْمِ خَلَقْتَ الدُّنْيَآ اِلٰى يَوْمِ الْقِيٰمَةِ فِىْ كُلِّ يَوْمٍ اَلْفَ مَرَّةٍ ○ **اَللّٰهُمَّ** وَصَلِّ عَلٰى سَيِّدِنَا مُحَمَّدٍ عَدَدَ الرَّمْلِ وَالْحَصٰى فِىْ مُسْتَقَرِّ الْاَرَضِيْنَ وَسَهْلِهَا وَجِبَالِهَا مِنْ يَّوْمِ خَلَقْتَ الدُّنْيَآ اِلٰى يَوْمِ الْقِيٰمَةِ فِىْ كُلِّ يَوْمٍ اَلْفَ مَرَّةٍ ○ **اَللّٰهُمَّ** صَلِّ عَلٰى سَيِّدِنَا مُحَمَّدٍ عَدَدَ اضْطِرَابِ الْمِيَاهِ الْعَذْبَةِ وَالْمِلْحَةِ مِنْ يَّوْمِ خَلَقْتَ الدُّنْيَآ اِلٰى يَوْمِ الْقِيٰمَةِ فِىْ كُلِّ يَوْمٍ اَلْفَ مَرَّةٍ ○ **وَصَلِّ** عَلٰى سَيِّدِنَا مُحَمَّدٍ عَدَدَ مَا خَلَقْتَهٗ عَلٰى جَدِيْدِ اَرْضِكَ فِىْ مُسْتَقَرِّ الْاَرَضِيْنَ شَرْقِهَا وَغَرْبِهَا سَهْلِهَا وَجِبَالِهَا وَ اَوْدِيَتِهَا وَ طَرِيْقِهَا وَعَامِرِهَا وَغَامِرِهَآ اِلٰى سَآئِرِ مَا خَلَقْتَهٗ عَلَيْهَا وَمَا فِيْهَا مِنْ حَصَاةٍ وَّمَدَرٍ وَّ حَجَرٍ مِّنْ يَّوْمِ خَلَقْتَ الدُّنْيَآ اِلٰى يَوْمِ الْقِيٰمَةِ فِىْ كُلِّ يَوْمٍ اَلْفَ مَرَّةٍ ○ **اَللّٰهُمَّ** صَلِّ عَلٰى سَيِّدِنَا مُحَمَّدِنِ النَّبِيِّ عَدَدَ نَبَاتِ الْاَرْضِ مِنْ قِبْلَتِهَا وَشَرْقِهَا وَغَرْبِهَا وَ سَهْلِهَا وَجِبَالِهَا وَاَوْدِيَتِهَا وَاَشْجَارِهَا وَ ثِمَارِهَا وَ اَوْرَاقِهَا وَزُرُوْعِهَا وَجَمِيْعِ مَا يَخْرُجُ مِنْ نَّبَاتِهَا وَبَرَكَاتِهَا مِنْ يَّوْمِ خَلَقْتَ الدُّنْيَآ اِلٰى يَوْمِ الْقِيٰمَةِ فِىْ كُلِّ يَوْمٍ اَلْفَ مَرَّةٍ ○ **اَللّٰهُمَّ** وَصَلِّ عَلٰى سَيِّدِنَا مُحَمَّدٍ عَدَدَ مَا خَلَقْتَ مِنَ الْجِنِّ وَالْاِنْسِ

O God, bless our master **Muḥammad** in every star in the sky from the day You created the world to the Day of Resurrection and every day a thousand times!

O God, bless our master **Muḥammad** as much as the entire earth and what it holds and what it bears of Your Creation!

O God, bless our master **Muḥammad** in everything You have created in the seven seas, knowledge of which is Yours alone and in everything You will create in them until the Day of Resurrection and every day a thousand times!

O God, bless our master **Muḥammad** to the fullness of Your Seven Seas!

O God, bless our master **Muḥammad** in the adornment of Your Seven Seas in that which they hold and bear of Your Creation!

O God, bless our master **Muḥammad** in every wave on Your seas from the day You created the world to the Day of Resurrection and every day a thousand times!

O God, bless our master **Muḥammad** in every grain of sand and in every pebble on the solid ground of the earth, the soft ground of the earth and the mountains of the earth from the day You created the world to the Day of Resurrection and every day a thousand times!

O God, bless our master **Muḥammad** in the turbulence existing between salt water and fresh water from the day You created the world to the Day of Resurrection and every day a thousand times!

O God, bless our master **Muḥammad** in everything which You have created on the face of Your earth, on solid land, in the West and in the East, on soft ground and on the mountains, in the streets and on the ways, in populated areas and in waste lands, and in what You have created on it and in it elsewhere, in every pebble, in every lump of mud and in every stone, from the day You created the world to the Day of Resurrection and every day a thousand times!

O God, bless our master **Muḥammad**, the Prophet, in every plant on the earth in the direction of the East and the West, on soft ground, on mountains and in the valleys, and may there be blessings in every tree, in every fruit, in every leaf, in every plant, and in any other vegetation or verdure that grows from the day You created the world to the Day of Resurrection and every day a thousand times!

O God, bless our master **Muḥammad** in every jinn, human

وَالشَّيَاطِيْنِ وَمَآ اَنْتَ خَالِقُهٗ مِنْهُمْ اِلٰى يَوْمِ الْقِيٰمَةِ فِىْ كُلِّ يَوْمٍ اَلْفَ مَرَّةٍ ۝ **اَللّٰهُمَّ** وَصَلِّ عَلٰى سَيِّدِنَا مُحَمَّدٍ عَدَدَ كُلِّ شَعْرَةٍ فِىْٓ اَبْدَانِهِمْ وَفِىْ وُجُوْهِهِمْ وَعَلٰى رُءُوْسِهِمْ مُّنْذُ خَلَقْتَ الدُّنْيَآ اِلٰى يَوْمِ الْقِيٰمَةِ فِىْ كُلِّ يَوْمٍ اَلْفَ مَرَّةٍ ۝ **اَللّٰهُمَّ** وَصَلِّ عَلٰى سَيِّدِنَا مُحَمَّدٍ عَدَدَ خَفَقَانِ الطَّيْرِ وَطَيَرَانِ الْجِنِّ وَ الشَّيَاطِيْنِ مِنْ يَّوْمِ خَلَقْتَ الدُّنْيَآ اِلٰى يَوْمِ الْقِيٰمَةِ فِىْ كُلِّ يَوْمٍ اَلْفَ مَرَّةٍ ۝ **اَللّٰهُمَّ** وَصَلِّ عَلٰى سَيِّدِنَا مُحَمَّدٍ عَدَدَ كُلِّ بَهِيْمَةٍ خَلَقْتَهَا عَلٰى جَدِيْدِ اَرْضِكَ مِنْ صَغِيْرٍ اَوْ كَبِيْرٍ فِىْ مَشَارِقِ الْاَرْضِ وَمَغَارِبِهَا مِنْ اِنْسِهَا وَجِنِّهَا مِمَّا لَا يَعْلَمُ عِلْمَهٗٓ اِلَّآ اَنْتَ مِنْ يَّوْمِ خَلَقْتَ الدُّنْيَآ اِلٰى يَوْمِ الْقِيٰمَةِ فِىْ كُلِّ يَوْمٍ اَلْفَ مَرَّةٍ ۝ **اَللّٰهُمَّ** وَصَلِّ عَلٰى سَيِّدِنَا مُحَمَّدٍ عَدَدَ خُطَاهُمْ عَلٰى وَجْهِ الْاَرْضِ مِنْ يَّوْمِ خَلَقْتَ الدُّنْيَآ اِلٰى يَوْمِ الْقِيٰمَةِ فِىْ كُلِّ يَوْمٍ اَلْفَ مَرَّةٍ ۝ **اَللّٰهُمَّ** وَصَلِّ عَلٰى سَيِّدِنَا مُحَمَّدٍ عَدَدَ مَنْ يُّصَلِّىْ عَلَيْهِ ۝ وَصَلِّ عَلٰى سَيِّدِنَا مُحَمَّدٍ عَدَدَ مَنْ لَّمْ يُصَلِّ عَلَيْهِ ۝ وَصَلِّ عَلٰى سَيِّدِنَا مُحَمَّدٍ عَدَدَ الْقَطْرِ وَالْمَطَرِ وَالنَّبَاتِ ۝ وَصَلِّ عَلٰى سَيِّدِنَا مُحَمَّدٍ عَدَدَ كُلِّ شَىْءٍ ۝ **اَللّٰهُمَّ** وَصَلِّ عَلٰى سَيِّدِنَا مُحَمَّدٍ فِى الَّيْلِ اِذَا يَغْشٰى ۝ وَصَلِّ عَلٰى سَيِّدِنَا مُحَمَّدٍ فِي النَّهَارِ اِذَا تَجَلّٰى ۝ وَصَلِّ عَلٰى سَيِّدِنَا مُحَمَّدٍ فِي الْاٰخِرَةِ وَالْاُوْلٰى ۝ وَصَلِّ عَلٰى سَيِّدِنَا مُحَمَّدٍ شَابًّا زَكِيًّا ۝ وَصَلِّ عَلٰى سَيِّدِنَا مُحَمَّدٍ كَهْلًا مَّرْضِيًّا ۝ وَصَلِّ عَلٰى سَيِّدِنَا مُحَمَّدٍ مُّنْذُ كَانَ فِى الْمَهْدِ صَبِيًّا ۝ وَصَلِّ عَلٰى سَيِّدِنَا مُحَمَّدٍ حَتّٰى لَا يَبْقٰى مِنَ الصَّلٰوةِ شَىْءٌ ۝ **اَللّٰهُمَّ** وَاَعْطِ سَيِّدَنَا مُحَمَّدًا نِ الْمَقَامَ الْمَحْمُوْدَ الَّذِىْ وَعَدْتَّهُ الَّذِىْٓ اِذَا قَالَ صَدَّقْتَهٗ وَ اِذَا سَاَلَ اَعْطَيْتَهٗ ۝ **اَللّٰهُمَّ** وَاَعْظِمْ بُرْهَانَهٗ وَ شَرِّفْ بُنْيَانَهٗ وَاَبْلِجْ حُجَّتَهٗ وَبَيِّنْ فَضِيْلَتَهٗ ۝ **اَللّٰهُمَّ** وَتَقَبَّلْ شَفَاعَتَهٗ فِىْٓ

and devil You have created and in every one of them You will create until the Day of Resurrection and every day a thousand times!

O God, bless our master Muḥammad in every follicle of hair on their bodies, on their faces, and on their heads from the moment You created the world to the Day of Resurrection and every day a thousand times!

O God, bless our master Muḥammad in the flapping of birds' wings, in the flying of the jinn and devils from the day You created the world to the Day of Resurrection and every day a thousand times!

O God, bless our master Muḥammad in all the cattle You have created on the surface of Your earth, both big and small, in the East of the earth and in the West, in all the men and the jinn and in all that of which there is no knowledge except Yours from the day You created the world to the Day of Resurrection and every day a thousand times!

O God, bless our master Muḥammad in every ridge on the face of the earth from the day You created the world to the Day of Resurrection and every day a thousand times!

O God, bless our master Muḥammad as many times as those who ask for blessings upon him! And bless our master Muḥammad as many times as those who do not ask for blessings upon him!

And bless our master Muḥammad in every raindrop, in every rainfall and in every plant! And bless our master Muḥammad in everything which exists!

And bless our master Muḥammad at night when it grows dark! And bless our master Muḥammad in the day when it grows light!

And bless our master Muḥammad in the end and at the beginning! And bless our master Muḥammad in his youth, in his purity!

And bless our master Muḥammad in his middle-age! And bless our master Muḥammad even in the cradle! And bless our master Muḥammad until there remains naught from blessings!

O God, grant to our master Muḥammad the Most Praised Station which You promised to him, the place where when he speaks, You vindicate him and when he asks, You give to him!

O God, accept his intercession for

أُمَّتِهِ ○ وَاسْتَعْمِلْنَا بِسُنَّتِهِ وَتَوَفَّنَا عَلٰى مِلَّتِهِ وَاحْشُرْنَا فِىْ زُمْرَتِهِ وَتَحْتَ لِوَآئِهِ وَاجْعَلْنَا مِنْ رُّفَقَآئِهِ وَاَوْرِدْنَا حَوْضَهٗ وَاَسْقِنَا بِكَأْسِهٖ وَانْفَعْنَا بِمَحَبَّتِهٖ ○ اَللّٰهُمَّ اٰمِيْنَ ○ وَاَسْأَلُكَ بِاَسْمَآئِكَ الَّتِىْ دَعَوْتُكَ بِهَآ اَنْ تُصَلِّيَ عَلٰى سَيِّدِنَا مُحَمَّدٍ عَدَدَ مَا وَصَفْتُ وَمِمَّا لَا يَعْلَمُ عِلْمَهٗٓ اِلَّآ اَنْتَ وَاَنْ تَرْحَمَنِىْ وَتَتُوْبَ عَلَيَّ وَتُعَافِيَنِىْ مِنْ جَمِيْعِ الْبَلَآءِ وَالْبَلْوَآءِ وَاَنْ تَغْفِرَلِىْ وَلِوَالِدَيَّ وَتَرْحَمَ الْمُؤْمِنِيْنَ وَالْمُؤْمِنَاتِ وَالْمُسْلِمِيْنَ وَالْمُسْلِمَاتِ الْاَحْيَآءِ مِنْهُمْ وَالْاَمْوَاتِ وَ اَنْ تَغْفِرَ لِعَبْدِكَ فُلَانِ بْنِ فُلَانٍ الْمُذْنِبِ الْخَاطِئِ الضَّعِيْفِ وَاَنْ تَتُوْبَ عَلَيْهِ اِنَّكَ غَفُوْرٌ رَّحِيْمٌ ○ **اَللّٰهُمَّ** اٰمِيْنَ يَا رَبَّ الْعٰلَمِيْنَ ○ قَالَ رَسُوْلُ اللّٰهِ صَلَّى اللّٰهُ عَلَيْهِ وَسَلَّمَ مَنْ قَرَأَ هٰذِهِ الصَّلٰوةَ مَرَّةً وَّاحِدَةً كَتَبَ اللّٰهُ لَهٗ ثَوَابَ حَجَّةٍ مَّقْبُوْلَةٍ وَّثَوَابَ مَنْ اَعْتَقَ رَقَبَةً مِنْ وُّلْدِ اِسْمٰعِيْلَ عَلَيْهِ السَّلَامُ فَيَقُوْلُ اللّٰهُ تَعَالٰى يَا مَلٰٓئِكَتِىْ هٰذَا عَبْدٌ مِّنْ عِبَادِىْٓ اَكْثَرَ الصَّلٰوةَ عَلٰى حَبِيْبِىْ سَيِّدِنَا مُحَمَّدٍ فَوَعِزَّتِىْ وَجَلَالِىْ وَجُوْدِىْ وَمَجْدِىْ وَارْتِفَاعِىْ لَاُعْطِيَنَّهٗ بِكُلِّ حَرْفٍ صَلّٰى بِهٖ قَصْرًا فِى الْجَنَّةِ وَلَيَاْتِيَنِّىْ يَوْمَ الْقِيٰمَةِ تَحْتَ لِوَآءِ الْحَمْدِ نُوْرُ وَجْهِهٖ كَالْقَمَرِ لَيْلَةَ الْبَدْرِ وَ كَفُّهٗ فِىْ كَفِّ حَبِيْبِىْ مُحَمَّدٍ ○ هٰذَا لِمَنْ قَالَهَا فِىْ كُلِّ يَوْمِ جُمُعَةٍ لَّهٗ هٰذَا الْفَضْلُ وَاللّٰهُ ذُو الْفَضْلِ الْعَظِيْمِ ○ وَفِىْ رِوَايَةٍ ○ **اَللّٰهُمَّ** اِنِّىْٓ اَسْئَلُكَ بِحَقِّ مَا حَمَلَ كُرْسِيُّكَ مِنْ عَظْمَتِكَ وَقُدْرَتِكَ وَجَلَالِكَ وَبَهَآئِكَ وَسُلْطَانِكَ وَبِحَقِّ اِسْمِكَ الْمَخْزُوْنِ الْمَكْنُوْنِ الَّذِىْ سَمَّيْتَ بِهٖ نَفْسَكَ وَاَنْزَلْتَهٗ فِىْ كِتَابِكَ وَاسْتَأْثَرْتَ بِهٖ فِىْ عِلْمِ الْغَيْبِ عِنْدَكَ اَنْ تُصَلِّيَ عَلٰى سَيِّدِنَا مُحَمَّدٍ عَبْدِكَ وَرَسُوْلِكَ وَاَسْأَلُكَ بِاسْمِكَ الَّذِىْٓ اِذَا دُعِيْتَ بِهٖٓ اَجَبْتَ وَاِذَا سُئِلْتَ بِهٖٓ اَعْطَيْتَ ○ وَاَسْأَلُكَ بِاسْمِكَ الَّذِىْ وَضَعْتَهٗ عَلٰى

his nation! And establish us on his way, allow us to die in his manner, resurrect us in his company beneath his flag, and make us among his associates, water us at his Pool, allow us to drink from his drinking bowl, and enjoy his love!

O God, Amen! And I ask You, in the names in which I have called on You to bless our master Muḥammad, as much as I have outlined and as much as that of which You alone have knowledge, to have mercy on me and accept my repentance, absolve me of all trials and tribulations, forgive me and my parents and have mercy on the believing men and women, the submitted men and women, the living among them and the dead, and forgive the reader of this book, the sinner, the erroneous one, the weak one, and accept his repentance, for You are the Forgiver, the Merciful!

O God, Amen, O Lord of the worlds! The Messenger of God, God's blessings and peace be upon him, said, "Whoever reads this blessing once, God will write for him the reward of an accepted pilgrimage and the reward of freeing a servant from the descendants of Ishmael, peace be upon him."

And God the Exalted says, "O My angels, this is one of My servants who has asked for abundant blessings upon My beloved Muḥammad, so through My Power, My Glory, My Generosity, My Splendor, and My Sublimity, I grant him for every letter of the words asking for blessings a castle in the Garden.

I will make him come to me on the Day of Resurrection beneath the flag of praise, and the light of his face will be like the full moon and he will be hand in hand with My beloved Muḥammad." And in another relation:

O God, I ask You for the sake of the truth that carries Your Throne from Your Might Oceans, Your Power Oceans, Your Glory Oceans, Your Splendor Oceans and Your Authority Oceans, and for the sake of the truth of Your name, secret and hidden, which You named Yourself and which You sent down in Your Book and which You alone took for Yourself in the unseen world, that You bless our master Muḥammad Your servant and Your Messenger, and I ask You in the name in which were one to call upon You, You would answer, and in which were one to ask You something, You would grant it! And I ask You in Your name

which when laid upon

اللَّيْلِ فَاظْلَمَ ۝ وَعَلَى النَّهَارِ فَاسْتَنَارَ وَعَلَى السَّمٰوٰتِ فَاسْتَقَلَّتْ ۝ وَعَلَى الْاَرْضِ فَاسْتَقَرَّتْ ۝ وَعَلَى الْجِبَالِ فَرَسَتْ ۝ وَعَلَى الصَّعْبَةِ فَذَلَّتْ ۝ وَعَلَى مَآءِ السَّمَآءِ فَسَكَبَتْ ۝ وَعَلَى السَّحَابِ فَامْطَرَتْ ۝ وَاَسْئَلُكَ بِمَا سَاَلَكَ بِهٖ سَيِّدُنَا مُحَمَّدٌ نَّبِيُّكَ ۝ وَاَسْئَلُكَ بِمَا سَاَلَكَ بِهٖ سَيِّدُنَآ اٰدَمُ نَبِيُّكَ ۝ وَاَسْئَلُكَ بِمَا سَاَلَكَ بِهٖ اَنْبِيَآؤُكَ وَرُسُلُكَ وَمَلٰٓئِكَتُكَ الْمُقَرَّبُوْنَ ۝ صَلَّى اللّٰهُ عَلَيْهِمْ اَجْمَعِيْنَ ۝ وَاَسْئَلُكَ بِمَا سَاَلَكَ بِهٖٓ اَهْلُ طَاعَتِكَ اَجْمَعِيْنَ لا اَنْ تُصَلِّيَ عَلٰى سَيِّدِنَا مُحَمَّدٍ وَّعَلٰٓى اٰلِ سَيِّدِنَا مُحَمَّدٍ عَدَدَ مَا خَلَقْتَ مِنْ قَبْلِ اَنْ تَكُوْنَ السَّمَآءُ مَبْنِيَّةً وَّ الْاَرْضُ مَطْحِيَّةً وَّ الْجِبَالُ مُرْسِيَّةً وَّالْعُيُوْنُ مُنْفَجِرَةً وَّ الْاَنْهَارُ مُنْهَمِرَةً وَّالشَّمْسُ مُضْحِيَةً وَّ الْقَمَرُ مُضِيئًا وَّ الْكَوَاكِبُ مُنِيْرَةً ۝ **اَللّٰهُمَّ** صَلِّ عَلٰى سَيِّدِنَا مُحَمَّدٍ وَّعَلٰٓى اٰلِ سَيِّدِنَا مُحَمَّدٍ عَدَدَ عِلْمِكَ ۝ وَصَلِّ عَلٰى سَيِّدِنَا مُحَمَّدٍ وَّعَلٰٓى اٰلِ سَيِّدِنَا مُحَمَّدٍ عَدَدَ حِلْمِكَ ۝ وَصَلِّ عَلٰى سَيِّدِنَا مُحَمَّدٍ وَّعَلٰٓى اٰلِ سَيِّدِنَا مُحَمَّدٍ عَدَدَ مَآ اَحْصَاهُ اللَّوْحُ الْمَحْفُوْظُ مِنْ عِلْمِكَ ۝ **اَللّٰهُمَّ** صَلِّ عَلٰى سَيِّدِنَا مُحَمَّدٍ وَّعَلٰٓى اٰلِ سَيِّدِنَا مُحَمَّدٍ عَدَدَ مَا جَرٰى بِهِ الْقَلَمُ فِيْٓ اُمِّ الْكِتٰبِ عِنْدَكَ ۝ وَصَلِّ عَلٰى سَيِّدِنَا مُحَمَّدٍ وَّعَلٰٓى اٰلِ سَيِّدِنَا مُحَمَّدٍ مِّلْءَ سَمٰوٰتِكَ ۝ وَصَلِّ عَلٰى سَيِّدِنَا مُحَمَّدٍ وَّعَلٰٓى اٰلِ سَيِّدِنَا مُحَمَّدٍ مِّلْءَ اَرْضِكَ ۝ وَصَلِّ عَلٰى سَيِّدِنَا مُحَمَّدٍ وَّعَلٰٓى اٰلِ سَيِّدِنَا مُحَمَّدٍ مِّلْءَ مَآ اَنْتَ خَالِقُهٗ مِنْ يَّوْمِ خَلَقْتَ الدُّنْيَآ اِلٰى يَوْمِ الْقِيٰمَةِ ۝ **اَللّٰهُمَّ** صَلِّ عَلٰى سَيِّدِنَا مُحَمَّدٍ وَّعَلٰٓى اٰلِ سَيِّدِنَا مُحَمَّدٍ عَدَدَ صُفُوْفِ الْمَلٰٓئِكَةِ وَتَسْبِيْحِهِمْ وَتَقْدِيْسِهِمْ وَتَحْمِيْدِهِمْ وَتَمْجِيْدِهِمْ وَتَكْبِيْرِهِمْ وَ تَهْلِيْلِهِمْ مِّنْ يَّوْمِ خَلَقْتَ الدُّنْيَآ اِلٰى يَوْمِ الْقِيٰمَةِ ۝ **اَللّٰهُمَّ** صَلِّ عَلٰى سَيِّدِنَا مُحَمَّدٍ وَّعَلٰٓى اٰلِ سَيِّدِنَا

the night darkness falls! And when laid upon the day light arises and when laid upon the heavens they are raised up! And when laid upon the earth it becomes solid and firm! And when laid upon the mountains they form summits! And when laid upon difficulties they are overcome! And when laid upon the water of the sky it pours forth! And when laid upon the clouds they rain! And I ask You, for the sake of what our master Muḥammad, Your Prophet, asked You for the sake of! And I ask You, for the sake of what our master Adam, Your Prophet, asked You for the sake of! And I ask You, for the sake of what Your Prophets and Your Messengers and Your Closest Angels asked You for the sake of! God's blessings upon them all! And I ask You, for the sake of what all the Folk of Your Obedience asked You for, that You bless our master Muḥammad and the family of our master Muḥammad in all that You created before the sky was built, the earth was spread out, the mountains were made stable, the seas began to flow, the springs burst open, the rivers poured forth, the sun shone forth, the moon beamed and the planets were illuminated!

O God, bless our master Muḥammad and the family of our master Muḥammad as much as Your knowledge!

O God, bless our master Muḥammad and the family of our master Muḥammad as much as Your forbearance!

O God, bless our master Muḥammad and the family of our master Muḥammad as much as Your knowledge is registered on the Preserved Tablet!

O God, bless our master Muḥammad and the family of our master Muḥammad as much as the Pen has flowed in the mother of the book lodged with You! And bless our master Muḥammad and the family of our master Muḥammad to the fullness of Your heavens! And bless our master Muḥammad and the family of our master Muḥammad to the fullness of Your earth! And bless our master Muḥammad and the family of our master Muḥammad in all that You have created from the day You created this world until the Day of Resurrection!

O God, bless our master Muḥammad and the family of our master Muḥammad as many times as the ranks of angels, their glorifications, their sanctifications, their praises, their magnifications, their declarations of Your greatness and Your unity from the day You created this world until the Day of Resurrection!

O God, bless our master Muḥammad and the family of our master

مُحَمَّدٍ عَدَدَ السَّحَابِ الْجَارِيَةِ وَالرِّيَاحِ الذَّارِيَةِ مِنْ يَّوْمِ خَلَقْتَ الدُّنْيَآ اِلٰى يَوْمِ الْقِيٰمَةِ ۝ **اَللّٰهُمَّ** صَلِّ عَلٰى سَيِّدِنَا مُحَمَّدٍ وَّعَلٰٓى اٰلِ سَيِّدِنَا مُحَمَّدٍ عَدَدَ كُلِّ قَطْرَةٍ تَقْطُرُ مِنْ سَمٰوٰتِكَ اِلٰٓى اَرْضِكَ وَمَا تَقْطُرُ اِلٰى يَوْمِ الْقِيٰمَةِ ۝ **اَللّٰهُمَّ** صَلِّ عَلٰى سَيِّدِنَا مُحَمَّدٍ وَّعَلٰٓى اٰلِ سَيِّدِنَا مُحَمَّدٍ عَدَدَ مَا هَبَّتِ الرِّيَاحُ وَعَدَدَ مَا تَحَرَّكَتِ الْاَشْجَارُ وَالْاَوْرَاقُ وَالزَّرْعُ وَ جَمِيْعِ مَا خَلَقْتَ فِيْ قَرَارِ الْحِفْظِ مِنْ يَّوْمِ خَلَقْتَ الدُّنْيَآ اِلٰى يَوْمِ الْقِيٰمَةِ ۝ **اَللّٰهُمَّ** صَلِّ عَلٰى سَيِّدِنَا مُحَمَّدٍ وَّعَلٰٓى اٰلِ سَيِّدِنَا مُحَمَّدٍ عَدَدَ الْقَطْرِ وَالْمَطَرِ وَالنَّبَاتِ مِنْ يَّوْمِ خَلَقْتَ الدُّنْيَآ اِلٰى يَوْمِ الْقِيٰمَةِ ۝ **اَللّٰهُمَّ** صَلِّ عَلٰى سَيِّدِنَا مُحَمَّدٍ وَّعَلٰٓى اٰلِ سَيِّدِنَا مُحَمَّدٍ عَدَدَ النُّجُوْمِ فِي السَّمَآءِ مِنْ يَّوْمِ خَلَقْتَ الدُّنْيَآ اِلٰى يَوْمِ الْقِيٰمَةِ ۝ **اَللّٰهُمَّ** صَلِّ عَلٰى سَيِّدِنَا مُحَمَّدٍ وَّعَلٰٓى اٰلِ سَيِّدِنَا مُحَمَّدٍ عَدَدَ مَا خَلَقْتَ فِيْ بِحَارِكَ السَّبْعَةِ مِمَّا لَا يَعْلَمُ عِلْمَهٗٓ اِلَّآ اَنْتَ وَمَآ اَنْتَ خَالِقُهٗٓ اِلٰى يَوْمِ الْقِيٰمَةِ ۝ **اَللّٰهُمَّ** صَلِّ عَلٰى سَيِّدِنَا مُحَمَّدٍ وَّعَلٰٓى اٰلِ سَيِّدِنَا مُحَمَّدٍ عَدَدَ الرَّمْلِ وَالْحَصٰى فِيْ مَشَارِقَ الْاَرْضِ وَ مَغَارِبِهَا ۝ **اَللّٰهُمَّ** صَلِّ عَلٰى سَيِّدِنَا مُحَمَّدٍ وَّعَلٰٓى اٰلِ سَيِّدِنَا مُحَمَّدٍ عَدَدَ مَا خَلَقْتَ مِنَ الْجِنِّ وَالْاِنْسِ وَمَآ اَنْتَ خَالِقُهٗٓ اِلٰى يَوْمِ الْقِيٰمَةِ ۝ **اَللّٰهُمَّ** صَلِّ عَلٰى سَيِّدِنَا مُحَمَّدٍ وَّعَلٰٓى اٰلِ سَيِّدِنَا مُحَمَّدٍ عَدَدَ اَنْفَاسِهِمْ وَاَلْفَاظِهِمْ وَاَلْحَاظِهِمْ مِّنْ يَّوْمِ خَلَقْتَ الدُّنْيَآ اِلٰى يَوْمِ الْقِيٰمَةِ ۝ **اَللّٰهُمَّ** صَلِّ عَلٰى سَيِّدِنَا مُحَمَّدٍ وَّعَلٰٓى اٰلِ سَيِّدِنَا مُحَمَّدٍ عَدَدَ طَيْرَانِ الْجِنِّ وَالْمَلٰٓئِكَةِ مِنْ يَّوْمِ خَلَقْتَ الدُّنْيَآ اِلٰى يَوْمِ الْقِيٰمَةِ ۝ **اَللّٰهُمَّ** صَلِّ عَلٰى سَيِّدِنَا مُحَمَّدٍ وَّعَلٰٓى اٰلِ سَيِّدِنَا مُحَمَّدٍ عَدَدَ الطُّيُوْرِ وَالْهَوَآمِّ وَعَدَدَ الْوُحُوْشِ وَالْاٰكَامِ فِيْ مَشَارِقِ الْاَرْضِ وَمَغَارِبِهَا ۝ **اَللّٰهُمَّ** صَلِّ عَلٰى سَيِّدِنَا مُحَمَّدٍ وَّعَلٰٓى اٰلِ سَيِّدِنَا

Muḥammad in every rolling cloud and sweeping wind from the day You created this world until the Day of Resurrection!

O God, bless our master Muḥammad and the family of our master Muḥammad in every drop of rain falling from the Your heavens to Your earth and in all the rain that will fall until the Day of Resurrection!

O God, bless our master Muḥammad in the movement of every branch, every tree, every leaf and every plant stirred by the wind and in the wind-stirred movement of everything else that You have created in the Abode of Safety from the day You created the world to the Day of Resurrection!

O God, bless our master Muḥammad and the family of our master Muḥammad in every bead of dew, in every drop of rain and in every plant from the day You created the world to the Day of Resurrection!

O God, bless our master Muḥammad and the family of our master Muḥammad in every star in the sky from the day You created this world until the Day of Resurrection!

O God, bless our master Muḥammad and the family of our master Muḥammad as much as You have created in Your Seven Seas, knowledge of which is Yours alone, and as much as that which You will create until the Day of Resurrection!

O God, bless our master Muḥammad and the family of our master Muḥammad in every grain of sand and in every pebble on the earth, East and West!

O God, bless our master Muḥammad and the family of our master Muḥammad in every jinn and human being You have created and in every one of them that You will create until the Day of Resurrection!

O God, bless our master Muḥammad and the family of our master Muḥammad in every one of their breaths, their utterances and their glances from the day You created this world until the Day of Resurrection!

O God, bless our master Muḥammad and the family of our master Muḥammad in the flying of the jinn and the angels from the day You created this world until the Day of Resurrection!

O God, bless our master Muḥammad and the family of our master Muḥammad in every bird and pest, in every wild beast and in every hill on the earth, East and West!

O God, bless our master Muḥammad and the family of our master

مُـحَمَّدٍ عَدَدَ الْاَحْيَآءِ وَالْاَمْوَاتِ ۝ **اَللّٰهُمَّ** صَـلِّ عَـلٰى سَيِّدِنَا مُحَمَّدٍ وَّعَلٰى اٰلِ سَيِّدِنَا مُحَمَّدٍ عَدَدَ مَآ اَظْلَمَ عَلَيْهِ الَّيْلُ وَاَشْرَقَ عَلَيْهِ النَّهَارُ مِنْ يَّوْمِ خَلَقْتَ الدُّنْيَآ اِلٰى يَوْمِ الْقِيٰمَةِ ۝ **اَللّٰهُمَّ** صَلِّ عَلٰى سَيِّدِنَا مُحَمَّدٍ وَّعَلٰى اٰلِ سَيِّدِنَا مُحَمَّدٍ عَدَدَ مَـنْ يَّـمْشِـىْ عَلٰى رِجْلَيْنِ وَمَنْ يَّمْشِىْ عَلٰٓى اَرْبَعٍ مِّنْ يَّوْمِ خَلَقْتَ الدُّنْيَآ اِلٰى يَوْمِ الْقِيٰمَةِ ۝ **اَللّٰهُمَّ** صَلِّ عَلٰى سَيِّدِنَا مُحَمَّدٍ وَّعَلٰى اٰلِ سَيِّدِنَا مُحَمَّدٍ عَدَدَ مَنْ صَلّٰى عَلَيْهِ مِنَ الْجِنِّ وَالْاِنْسِ وَالْمَلٰٓئِكَةِ مِنْ يَّوْمِ خَلَقْتَ الدُّنْيَآ اِلٰى يَوْمِ الْقِيٰمَةِ ۝ **اَللّٰهُمَّ** صَلِّ عَلٰى سَيِّدِنَا مُحَمَّدٍ وَّعَلٰٓى اٰلِ سَيِّدِنَا مُحَمَّدٍ عَدَدَ مَنْ يُّصَلِّىْ عَلَيْهِ ۝ **اَللّٰهُمَّ** صَـلِّ عَـلٰى سَيِّدِنَـا مُـحَـمَّـدٍ وَّعَلٰى اٰلِ سَيِّدِنَا مُحَمَّدٍ عَدَدَ مَنْ لَّمْ يُصَلِّ عَلَيْهِ ۝ **اَللّٰهُمَّ** صَـلِّ عَـلٰى سَيِّدِنَا مُحَمَّدٍ وَّعَلٰٓى اٰلِ سَيِّدِنَا مُحَمَّدٍ كَمَا يَجِبُ اَنْ يُّصَلّٰى عَلَيْهِ ۝ **اَللّٰهُمَّ** صَـلِّ عَلٰى سَيِّدِنَا مُحَمَّدٍ وَّعَلٰٓى اٰلِ سَيِّدِنَا مُحَمَّدٍ كَمَا يَنْبَغِىْ اَنْ يُّـصَلّٰى عَلَيْهِ ۝ **اَللّٰهُمَّ** صَـلِّ عَـلٰى سَيِّـدِنَا مُحَمَّدٍ وَّعَلٰى اٰلِ سَيِّدِنَا مُحَمَّدٍ حَتّٰـى لَا يَبْقٰى شَىْءٌ مِّنَ الصَّلٰوةِ عَلَيْهِ ۝ **اَللّٰهُمَّ** صَـلِّ عَلٰى سَيِّدِنَا مُحَمَّدٍ فِى الْاَوَّلِيْنَ ۝ وَصَلِّ عَلٰى سَيِّدِنَا مُحَمَّدٍ فِي الْاٰخِرِيْنَ ۝ **اَللّٰهُمَّ** صَلِّ عَلٰى سَيِّدِنَا مُحَمَّدٍ فِي الْمَلَاِ الْاَعْلٰى اِلٰى يَوْمِ الدِّيْنِ ۝ مَا شَآءَ اللّٰهُ لَا قُوَّةَ اِلَّا بِاللّٰهِ الْعَلِيِّ الْعَظِيْمِ ۝

اَلْحِزْبُ السَّادِسُ فِىْ يَوْمِ السَّبْتِ

اَللّٰهُمَّ صَلِّ عَـلٰى سَيِّدِنَـا مُـحَـمَّـدٍ وَّعَلٰٓى اٰلِ سَيِّدِنَا مُحَمَّدٍ وَّاَعْطِهِ الْوَسِيْلَةَ وَالْفَضِيْلَةَ وَالدَّرَجَةَ الرَّفِيْعَةَ وَابْعَثْهُ الْمَقَامَ مَّحْمُوْدَنِ الَّذِىْ وَعَدْتَّهٗ اِنَّكَ لَا تُخْلِفُ الْمِيْعَادَ ۝ **اَللّٰهُمَّ** عَـظِّـمْ شَـانَـهٗ وَبَيِّـنْ بُرْهَانَهٗ وَاَبْلِجْ حُجَّتَهٗ وَبَيِّنْ فَضِيْلَتَهٗ وَتَقَبَّلْ

Muḥammad in the living and in the dead!

O God, bless our master Muḥammad and the family of our master Muḥammad as much as all the night has covered in darkness and all the day has illuminated from the day You created this world until the Day of Resurrection!

O God, bless our master Muḥammad and the family of our master Muḥammad in every two-legged creature and in every four-legged creature from the day You created this world until the Day of Resurrection!

O God, bless our master Muḥammad and the family of our master Muḥammad as many times as the jinn, the human beings and the angels have asked You to bless him from the day You created this world until the Day of Resurrection!

O God, bless our master Muḥammad and the family of our master Muḥammad as many times as those who have asked for blessings upon him!

O God, bless our master Muḥammad and the family of our master Muḥammad as many times as those who have not asked for blessings upon him!

O God, bless our master Muḥammad and the family of our master Muḥammad as it is incumbent upon us to ask You to bless him!

O God, bless our master Muḥammad and the family of our master Muḥammad as it is fitting for him to be blessed!

O God, bless our master Muḥammad and the family of our master Muḥammad until all blessings are exhausted!

O God, bless our master Muḥammad among the first!

Bless our master Muḥammad among the last!

O God, bless our master Muḥammad in the Heavenly Assembly until the Day of Reckoning! And what God wills! There is no power save through God, the High, the Great

The Sixth Part to be Read on Saturday

O God, bless our liege Muḥammad and the family of our liege Muḥammad, and grant him the closest access, the pre-eminence, the lofty rank, and send him to the most praised station which You promised him for You do not renege on a promise!

O God, magnify his value, clarify his argument, embellish his proof, make evident his excellence and accept

شَفَاعَتَهٗ فِىۤ اُمَّتِهٖ وَاسْتَعْمِلْنَا بِسُنَّتِهٖ يَا رَبَّ الْعٰلَمِيْنَ ۝ وَ يَا رَبَّ الْعَرْشِ الْعَظِيْمِ ۝ اَللّٰهُمَّ يَا رَبِّ احْشُرْنَا فِىْ زُمْرَتِهٖ وَتَحْتَ لِوَآئِهٖ وَاسْقِنَا بِكَأْسِهٖ وَانْفَعْنَا بِمَحَبَّتِهٖۤ اٰمِيْنَ يَا رَبَّ الْعٰلَمِيْنَ ۝ اَللّٰهُمَّ يَا رَبِّ بَلِّغْهُ عَنَّآ اَفْضَلَ السَّلَامِ وَاجْزِهٖ عَنَّآ اَفْضَلَ مَا جَازَيْتَ بِهٖ نَبِيًّا عَنْ اُمَّتِهٖ يَا رَبَّ الْعٰلَمِيْنَ ۝ اَللّٰهُمَّ يَا رَبِّ اِنِّىۤ اَسْئَلُكَ اَنْ تَغْفِرَلِىْ وَتَرْحَمَنِىْ وَتَتُوْبَ عَلَىَّ وَتُعَافِيَنِىْ مِنْ جَمِيْعِ الْبَلَآءِ وَالْبَلْوَآءِ الْخَارِجِ مِنَ الْاَرْضِ وَالنَّازِلِ مِنَ السَّمَآءِ اِنَّكَ عَلٰى كُلِّ شَىْءٍ قَدِيْرٌ ۝ بِرَحْمَتِكَ وَاَنْ تَغْفِرَ لِلْمُؤْمِنِيْنَ وَالْمُؤْمِنَاتِ وَالْمُسْلِمِيْنَ وَالْمُسْلِمَاتِ الْاَحْيَآءِ مِنْهُمْ وَالْاَمْوَاتِ وَرَضِىَ اللّٰهُ عَنْ اَزْوَاجِهِ الطَّاهِرَاتِ اُمَّهَاتِ الْمُؤْمِنِيْنَ وَ رَضِىَ اللّٰهُ عَنْ اَصْحَابِهِ الْاَعْلَامِ اَئِمَّةِ الْهُدٰى وَمَصَابِيْحِ الدُّنْيَا وَعَنِ التَّابِعِيْنَ وَتَابِعِ التَّابِعِيْنَ لَهُمْ بِاِحْسَانٍ اِلٰى يَوْمِ الدِّيْنِ وَالْحَمْدُ لِلّٰهِ رَبِّ الْعٰلَمِيْنَ ۝

اِبْتِدَآءُ الثُّلُثِ الثَّالِثِ

اَللّٰهُمَّ رَبَّ الْاَرْوَاحِ وَالْاَجْسَادِ الْبَالِيَةِ اَسْئَلُكَ بِطَاعَةِ الْاَرْوَاحِ الرَّاجِعَةِ اِلٰى اَجْسَادِهَا وَبِطَاعَةِ الْاَجْسَادِ الْمُلْتَئِمَةِ بِعُرُوْقِهَا وَبِكَلِمَاتِكَ النَّافِذَةِ فِيْهِمْ وَاَخْذِكَ الْحَقَّ مِنْهُمْ وَالْخَلَآئِقُ بَيْنَ يَدَيْكَ يَنْتَظِرُوْنَ فَصْلَ قَضَآئِكَ وَيَرْجُوْنَ رَحْمَتَكَ وَيَخَافُوْنَ عِقَابَكَ اَنْ تَجْعَلَ النُّوْرَ فِىْ بَصَرِىْ وَذِكْرَكَ بِالَّيْلِ وَالنَّهَارِ عَلٰى لِسَانِىْ وَعَمَلًا صَالِحًا فَارْزُقْنِىْ ۝ اَللّٰهُمَّ صَلِّ عَلٰى سَيِّدِنَا مُحَمَّدٍ كَمَا صَلَّيْتَ عَلٰى سَيِّدِنَآ اِبْرٰهِيْمَ وَبَارِكْ عَلٰى سَيِّدِنَا مُحَمَّدٍ كَمَا بَارَكْتَ عَلٰى سَيِّدِنَآ اِبْرٰهِيْمَ ۝ اَللّٰهُمَّ اجْعَلْ صَلَوَاتِكَ وَبَرَكَاتِكَ عَلٰى سَيِّدِنَا مُحَمَّدٍ وَّعَلٰى اٰلِ سَيِّدِنَا مُحَمَّدٍ كَمَا جَعَلْتَهَا عَلٰى سَيِّدِنَآ اِبْرٰهِيْمَ وَعَلٰى اٰلِ سَيِّدِنَآ اِبْرٰهِيْمَ اِنَّكَ حَمِيْدٌ مَّجِيْدٌ ۝

his intercession for his nation and establish us on his way, O Lord of the Worlds! O Lord of the Mighty Throne!

O God, O Lord, gather us in his company and beneath his flag, have us drink from his drinking bowl and avail us of his love, Amen, O Lord of the Worlds!

O God, O Lord, bestow upon him, on our behalf, the best of peace, and reward him, on our behalf, better than You have rewarded any Prophet on behalf of his nation, O Lord of the Worlds!

O God, O Lord, I beseech You to forgive me, have mercy on me, accept my repentance and remove from me all earthly and heavenly trials and tribulations, for You are the Power of all things! Through Your Mercy, forgive the believing men and women and the submitted men and women, the living and the dead, and the Pleasure of God be with his pure wives, the Mothers of the Believers, and the pleasure of God be with his Companions, the eminent leaders of guidance and lamps of this lower life, and also with the Followers and the Followers of the Followers, salutations upon them until the Day of Resurrection, and praise be to God, the Lord of the Worlds!

(beginning of the third third)

O God , Lord of souls and mortal flesh, I ask You for the sake of the obedience of souls returning to their bodies (on the Day of Resurrection), and for the sake of the obedience of bodies becoming whole once again, and for the sake of Your Words which will order this and for the sake of Your exacting of Your rights over them, and for the sake of Your creatures who are before You waiting for the apportioning of Your Decree, hoping for Your Mercy and fearing Your punishment, I ask that You bestow light in my eyes, remembrance of You during the day and the night upon my tongue, and provide me with good actions!

O God, bless our master Muḥammad just as You blessed our master Abraham and sanctify our master Muḥammad just as You sanctified our master Abraham!

O God, grant Your blessings and Your favors to our master Muḥammad and the family of our master Muḥammad just as You granted them to our master Abraham and the family of our master Abraham, for You are the Praiseworthy, the Mighty!

وَبَارِكْ عَلٰى سَيِّدِنَا مُحَمَّدٍ وَّعَلٰى اٰلِ سَيِّدِنَا مُحَمَّدٍ كَمَا بَارَكْتَ عَلٰى سَيِّدِنَآ
اِبْرٰهِيْمَ وَعَلٰى اٰلِ سَيِّدِنَآ اِبْرٰهِيْمَ اِنَّكَ حَمِيْدٌ مَّجِيْدٌ ○ **اَللّٰهُمَّ** صَلِّ عَلٰى سَيِّدِنَا
مُحَمَّدٍ عَبْدِكَ وَرَسُوْلِكَ وَصَلِّ عَلَى الْمُؤْمِنِيْنَ وَالْمُؤْمِنَاتِ وَالْمُسْلِمِيْنَ
وَالْمُسْلِمَاتِ ○ **اَللّٰهُمَّ** صَلِّ عَلٰى سَيِّدِنَا مُحَمَّدٍ وَّعَلٰى اٰلِهٖ عَدَدَ مَآ اَحَاطَ بِهٖ
عِلْمُكَ وَاَحْصَاهُ كِتَابُكَ وَشَهِدَتْ بِهٖ مَلٰٓئِكَتُكَ صَلٰوةً دَآئِمَةً تَدُوْمُ بِدَوَامِ مُلْكِ
اللّٰهِ ○ **اَللّٰهُمَّ** اِنِّيْٓ اَسْئَلُكَ بِاَسْمَآئِكَ الْعِظَامِ مَا عَلِمْتُ مِنْهَا وَمَا لَمْ اَعْلَمْ
وَبِالْاَسْمَآءِ الَّتِيْ سَمَّيْتَ بِهَا نَفْسَكَ مَا عَلِمْتُ مِنْهَا وَمَا لَمْ اَعْلَمْ ○ اَنْ تُصَلِّيَ
عَلٰى سَيِّدِنَا مُحَمَّدٍ عَبْدِكَ وَنَبِيِّكَ وَ رَسُوْلِكَ عَدَدَ مَا خَلَقْتَ مِنْ قَبْلِ اَنْ تَكُوْنَ
السَّمَآءُ مَبْنِيَّةً وَّالْاَرْضُ مَدْحِيَّةً وَّ الْجِبَالُ مُرْسِيَّةً وَّالْعُيُوْنُ مُنْفَجِرَةً وَّالْاَنْهَارُ
مُنْهَمِرَةً وَّالشَّمْسُ مُشْرِقَةً وَّالْقَمَرُ مُضِيْئًا وَّ الْكَوَاكِبُ مُسْتَنِيْرَةً وَّالْبِحَارُ مَجْرِيَّةً
وَّالْاَشْجَارُ مُثْمِرَةً ○ **اَللّٰهُمَّ** صَلِّ عَلٰى سَيِّدِنَا مُحَمَّدٍ عَدَدَ عِلْمِكَ ○ وَصَلِّ عَلٰى
سَيِّدِنَا مُحَمَّدٍ عَدَدَ حِلْمِكَ ○ وَصَلِّ عَلٰى سَيِّدِنَا مُحَمَّدٍ عَدَدَ كَلِمَاتِكَ ○
وَصَلِّ عَلٰى سَيِّدِنَا مُحَمَّدٍ عَدَدَ نِعْمَتِكَ ○ وَصَلِّ عَلٰى سَيِّدِنَا مُحَمَّدٍ عَدَدَ
فَضْلِكَ ○ وَصَلِّ عَلٰى سَيِّدِنَا مُحَمَّدٍ عَدَدَ جُوْدِكَ ○ وَصَلِّ عَلٰى سَيِّدِنَا مُحَمَّدٍ
عَدَدَ سَمٰوٰتِكَ ○ وَصَلِّ عَلٰى سَيِّدِنَا مُحَمَّدٍ عَدَدَ اَرْضِكَ ○ وَصَلِّ عَلٰى سَيِّدِنَا
مُحَمَّدٍ عَدَدَ مَا خَلَقْتَ فِيْ سَبْعِ سَمٰوٰتِكَ مِنْ مَّلٰٓئِكَتِكَ ○ وَصَلِّ عَلٰى سَيِّدِنَا
مُحَمَّدٍ عَدَدَ مَا خَلَقْتَ فِيْٓ اَرْضِكَ مِنَ الْجِنِّ وَالْاِنْسِ وَ غَيْرِهِمَا مِنَ الْوَحْشِ
وَالطَّيْرِ وَغَيْرِهِمَا ○ وَصَلِّ عَلٰى سَيِّدِنَا مُحَمَّدٍ عَدَدَ مَا جَرٰى بِهِ الْقَلَمُ فِيْ عِلْمِ
غَيْبِكَ وَمَا يَجْرِيْ بِهٖٓ اِلٰى يَوْمِ الْقِيٰمَةِ وَصَلِّ عَلٰى سَيِّدِنَا مُحَمَّدٍ عَدَدَ الْقَطْرِ

And sanctify our master Muḥammad and the family of our master Muḥammad just as You sanctified our master Abraham and the family of our master Abraham, for You are the Praiseworthy, the Mighty!

O God, bless our master Muḥammad, Your servant and Your Messenger, and bless the believing men and women and the submitted men and women!

O God, bless our master Muḥammad and his family as much as all that is encompassed by Your Knowledge, all that is contained in Your Book and all that is witnessed by Your angels, blessings which are eternal and which last as long as the Kingdom of God lasts!

O God, I beseech You in Your Greatest Names, those which I know and those which I do not know, and in the Names that You have named Yourself, names I know not and names I shall never know, that You bless our master Muḥammad, Your servant, Your Prophet and Your Messenger, in all that You created before the sky was built, the earth was spread out, the mountains were anchored down, the springs burst forth, the rivers flowed out, the sun blazed forth, the moon shone out, the planets illuminated the sky, the oceans began to flow and the trees gave of their fruit!

O God, bless our master Muḥammad to the extent of Your Knowledge!

O God, bless our master Muḥammad to the extent of Your Forbearance!

O God, bless our master Muḥammad to the number of Your Words!

O God, bless our master Muḥammad to the number of Your Favors!

O God, bless our master Muḥammad to the extent of Your Grace!

O God, bless our master Muḥammad to the extent of Your Generosity!

O God, bless our master Muḥammad to the extent of Your Heavens!

O God, bless our master Muḥammad to the extent of Your Earth! And bless our master Muḥammad as many times as all the angels You have created in Your Seven Heavens! And bless our master Muḥammad as many times as all the jinn and humans, and beings other than them, and the beasts and the birds, and beings other than them, that You have created in Your Earth! And bless our master Muḥammad in all that the Pen has written in the Knowledge of the Unseen and in all that the Pen will write until the Day of Resurrection and bless our master

Muḥammad in every dewdrop and in every raindrop

وَالْمَطَرِ وَصَلِّ عَلٰى سَيِّدِنَا مُحَمَّدٍ عَدَدَ مَنْ يَّحْمَدُكَ وَيَشْكُرُكَ وَيُهَلِّلُكَ وَيُمَجِّدُكَ وَيَشْهَدُ اَنَّكَ اَنْتَ اللّٰهُ وَصَلِّ عَلٰى سَيِّدِنَا مُحَمَّدٍ عَدَدَ مَا صَلَّيْتَ عَلَيْهِ اَنْتَ وَمَلٰٓئِكَتُكَ ○ وَصَلِّ عَلٰى سَيِّدِنَا مُحَمَّدٍ عَدَدَ مَنْ صَلّٰى عَلَيْهِ مِنْ خَلْقِكَ وَصَلِّ عَلٰى سَيِّدِنَا مُحَمَّدٍ عَدَدَ مَنْ لَّمْ يُصَلِّ عَلَيْهِ مِنْ خَلْقِكَ ○ وَصَلِّ عَلٰى سَيِّدِنَا مُحَمَّدٍ عَدَدَ الْجِبَالِ وَالرِّمَالِ وَالْحَصٰى ○ وَصَلِّ عَلٰى سَيِّدِنَا مُحَمَّدٍ عَدَدَ الشَّجَرِ وَاَوْرَاقِهَا وَالْمَدَرِ وَاَثْقَالِهَا ○ وَصَلِّ عَلٰى سَيِّدِنَا مُحَمَّدٍ عَدَدَ كُلِّ سَنَةٍ وَّمَا تَخْلُقُ فِيْهَا وَمَا يَمُوْتُ فِيْهَا ○ وَصَلِّ عَلٰى سَيِّدِنَا مُحَمَّدٍ عَدَدَ مَا تَخْلُقُ كُلَّ يَوْمٍ وَّمَا يَمُوْتُ فِيْهِ اِلٰى يَوْمِ الْقِيٰمَةِ ○ **اَللّٰهُمَّ** وَصَلِّ عَلٰى سَيِّدِنَا مُحَمَّدٍ عَدَدَ السَّحَابِ الْجَارِيَةِ مَا بَيْنَ السَّمَآءِ وَالْاَرْضِ وَمَا تَمْطُرُ مِنَ الْمِيَاهِ ○ وَصَلِّ عَلٰى سَيِّدِنَا مُحَمَّدٍ عَدَدَ الرِّيَاحِ الْمُسَخَّرَاتِ فِيْ مَشَارِقِ الْاَرْضِ وَمَغَارِبِهَا وَ جَوْفِهَا وَ قِبْلَتِهَا ○ وَصَلِّ عَلٰى سَيِّدِنَا مُحَمَّدٍ عَدَدَ نُجُوْمِ السَّمَآءِ ○ وَصَلِّ عَلٰى سَيِّدِنَا مُحَمَّدٍ عَدَدَ مَا خَلَقْتَ فِيْ بِحَارِكَ مِنَ الْحِيْتَانِ وَالدَّوَآبِّ وَالْمِيَاهِ وَالرِّمَالِ وَغَيْرِ ذٰلِكَ ○ وَصَلِّ عَلٰى سَيِّدِنَا مُحَمَّدٍ عَدَدَ النَّبَاتِ وَالْحَصٰى ○ وَصَلِّ عَلٰى سَيِّدِنَا مُحَمَّدٍ عَدَدَ النَّمْلِ ○ وَصَلِّ عَلٰى سَيِّدِنَا مُحَمَّدٍ عَدَدَ الْمِيَاهِ الْعَذْبَةِ ○ وَصَلِّ عَلٰى سَيِّدِنَا مُحَمَّدٍ عَدَدَ الْمِيَاهِ الْمِلْحَةِ ○ وَصَلِّ عَلٰى سَيِّدِنَا مُحَمَّدٍ عَدَدَ نِعْمَتِكَ عَلٰى جَمِيْعِ خَلْقِكَ ○ وَصَلِّ عَلٰى سَيِّدِنَا مُحَمَّدٍ عَدَدَ نِقْمَتِكَ وَعَذَابِكَ عَلٰى مَنْ كَفَرَ بِسَيِّدِنَا مُحَمَّدٍ صَلَّى اللّٰهُ عَلَيْهِ وَسَلَّمَ ○ وَصَلِّ عَلٰى سَيِّدِنَا مُحَمَّدٍ عَدَدَ مَا دَامَتِ الدُّنْيَا وَالْاٰخِرَةُ ○ وَصَلِّ عَلٰى سَيِّدِنَا مُحَمَّدٍ عَدَدَ مَا دَامَتِ الْخَلَآئِقُ فِى الْجَنَّةِ ○ وَصَلِّ عَلٰى سَيِّدِنَا مُحَمَّدٍ

and bless our master **Muḥammad** as often as You are praised, as often as You are thanked, as often as Your Unity is declared, as often as You are magnified, as often as it is witnessed that You are indeed God, and bless our master **Muḥammad** as many times as You and Your angels have already blessed him! And bless our master **Muḥammad** as many times as all those from Your creation who have already asked for blessings upon him and as many times as all those from Your Creation who have not asked for blessings upon him! And bless our master Muḥammad in every mountain, in every grain of sand and in every stone! And bless our master **Muḥammad** in every tree and in every one of their leaves and in the soil and in its weight!

And bless our master **Muḥammad** as many times as there have been years and that which You have created in them and that which dies in them! And bless our master Muḥammad in all that You create every day and in all that dies every day until the Day of Resurrection!

O God, bless our master Muḥammad in every cloud sailing between the heavens and the earth and in every drop of their rain! And bless our master Muḥammad in every swirling wind in the East of the earth and in the West, in the North and in the South!

And bless our master **Muḥammad** as many times as there are stars in the sky!

And bless our master Muḥammad as many times as all the fish, all the sea-creatures, all the water and all the grains of sand and whatever else there is!

And bless our master Muḥammad in every plant and in every stone! And bless our master Muḥammad as abundantly as there is fresh water!

And bless our master Muḥammad as abundantly as there is saltwater! And bless our master Muḥammad as much as the entire Favor shown to the whole of Your creation!

And bless our master Muḥammad as much as Your vengeance and Your punishment on those who deny our master Muḥammad, God's blessings and peace be upon him!

And bless our master Muḥammad for as long as the duration of this world and the next!

And bless our master Muḥammad for as long as Your creatures will stay in the Garden!

And bless our master Muḥammad

عَدَدَ مَا دَامَتِ الْخَلَآئِقُ فِي النَّارِ ○ وَصَلِّ عَلى سَيِّدِنَا مُحَمَّدٍ عَلى قَدْرِ مَا تُحِبُّهٗ وَتَرْضَاهُ ○ وَصَلِّ عَلى سَيِّدِنَا مُحَمَّدٍ عَلى قَدْرِ مَا يُحِبُّكَ وَيَرْضَاكَ وَصَلِّ عَلى سَيِّدِنَا مُحَمَّدٍ اَبَدَالْاٰبِدِيْنَ وَاَنْزِلْهُ الْمَنْزِلَ الْمُقَرَّبَ عِنْدَكَ وَاَعْطِهِ الْوَسِيْلَةَ وَالْفَضِيْلَةَ وَالشَّفَاعَةَ وَالدَّرَجَةَ الرَّفِيْعَةَ وَابْعَثْهُ الْمَقَامَ الْمَحْمُوْدَ الَّذِيْ وَعَدْتَّهٗ اِنَّكَ لَا تُخْلِفُ الْمِيْعَادَ ○ **اَللّٰهُمَّ** اِنِّيْٓ اَسْئَلُكَ بِاَنَّكَ مَالِكِيْ وَسَيِّدِيْ وَ مَوْلَايَ وَثِقَتِيْ وَرَجَآئِيْٓ اَسْاَلُكَ بِحُرْمَةِ الشَّهْرِ الْحَرَامِ وَالْبَلَدِ الْحَرَامِ وَالْمَشْعَرِ الْحَرَامِ وَقَبْرِ نَبِيِّكَ عَلَيْهِ السَّلَامُ اَنْ تَهَبَ لِيْ مِنَ الْخَيْرِ مَا لَا يَعْلَمُ عِلْمَهٗٓ اِلَّآ اَنْتَ وَ تَصْرِفَ عَنِّيْ مِنَ السُّوْءِ مَا لَا يَعْلَمُ عِلْمَهٗٓ اِلَّآ اَنْتَ ○ **اَللّٰهُمَّ** يَا مَنْ وَّهَبَ لِسَيِّدِنَآ اٰدَمَ سَيِّدَنَا شِيْثَ ○ وَ لِسَيِّدِنَآ اِبْرٰهِيْمَ سَيِّدَنَآ اِسْمٰعِيْلَ وَ سَيِّدَنَآ اِسْحٰقَ ○ وَرَدَّ سَيِّدَنَا يُوْسُفَ عَلى سَيِّدِنَا يَعْقُوْبَ وَيَامَنْ كَشَفَ الْبَلَآءَ عَنْ سَيِّدِنَآ اَيُّوْبَ ○ وَيَامَنْ رَدَّ سَيِّدَنَا مُوْسٰى اِلٰىٓ اُمِّهٖ وَيَا زَآئِدَ سَيِّدِنَا الْخَضِرِ فِيْ عِلْمِهٖ ○ وَ يَا مَنْ وَّهَبَ لِسَيِّدِنَا دَاوٗدَ سَيِّدَنَا سُلَيْمٰنَ وَلِسَيِّدِنَا زَكَرِيَّا سَيِّدَنَا يَحْيٰىؑ ○ وَلِسَيِّدَتِنَا مَرْيَمَ سَيِّدَنَا عِيْسٰى وَ يَا حَافِظَ ابْنَةِ سَيِّدِنَا شُعَيْبٍ اَسْئَلُكَ اَنْ تُصَلِّيَ عَلى سَيِّدِنَا مُحَمَّدٍ وَّعَلى جَمِيْعِ النَّبِيِّيْنَ وَالْمُرْسَلِيْنَ وَ يَا مَنْ وَّهَبَ لِسَيِّدِنَا مُحَمَّدٍ صَلَّى اللّٰهُ عَلَيْهِ وَسَلَّمَ الشَّفَاعَةَ وَالدَّرَجَةَ الرَّفِيْعَةَ اَنْ تَغْفِرَلِيْ ذُنُوْبِيْ وَتَسْتُرَلِيْ عُيُوْبِيْ كُلَّهَا وَتُجِيْرَنِيْ مِنَ النَّارِ وَتُوْجِبَ لِيْ رِضْوَانَكَ وَاَمَانَكَ وَغُفْرَانَكَ وَاِحْسَانَكَ وَتُمَتِّعَنِيْ فِيْ جَنَّتِكَ مَعَ الَّذِيْنَ اَنْعَمْتَ عَلَيْهِمْ مِّنَ النَّبِيِّيْنَ وَالصِّدِّيْقِيْنَ وَالشُّهَدَآءِ وَالصَّالِحِيْنَ اِنَّكَ عَلى كُلِّ شَيْءٍ قَدِيْرٌ ○ وَصَلَّى اللّٰهُ عَلى سَيِّدِنَا مُحَمَّدٍ وَّعَلٰى اٰلِهٖ مَآ اَزْعَجَتِ الرِّيَاحُ سَحَابًا رُّكَامًا وَّذَاقَ كُلُّ ذِيْ رُوْحٍ حِمَامًا وَّ اَوْصِلِ

for as long as Your creatures will stay in the Fire! And bless our master Muḥammad equal to Your love for him and Your satisfaction with him! And bless our master Muḥammad equal to his love for You and his satisfaction with You and bless our master Muḥammad forever and ever and award him the closest position in Your Presence, and grant him the closest access, the pre-eminence, the Intercession and the lofty rank and send him to the most praised station which You promised him, for You do not renege a promise!

O God, I beseech You, for the sake of the fact that You are my King, my Lord, my Master, my Trust and my Hope, I beseech You for the honor of the Holy Month, the Holy Land, the Holy Sanctuary, and the tomb of Your Prophet, peace be upon him, that You bestow upon me Good, knowledge of which is Yours alone and that You remove from me Evil, knowledge of which is Yours alone!

O God, Who gave to our master Adam our master Seth! And to our master Abraham our master Ishmael and our master Isaac! And Who returned our master Joseph to our master Jacob and Who removed the trials from our master Job! And Who returned our master Moses to his nation and Who increased our master Khidr in knowledge! And Who gave to our master David our master Solomon and to our master Zechariah our master John the Baptist!

And Who gave to our lady Mary, our master Jesus and Who protected the daughter of Shuayb! I ask you to bless our master Muḥammad and all the Prophets and Messengers! And You Who gave to our master Muḥammad, God's blessings and peace be upon him, the great intercession and the lofty rank, I ask You to forgive me my sins, conceal all my failings, give me sanctuary from the Fire, grant me Your Pleasure and Your Safety and Your Forgiveness and Your Beneficence, and admit me into Your Garden along with those You have favored, the Prophets, the true ones, the martyrs and the righteous, for You are the Power of all existence!

And the blessings of God be upon our master Muḥammad and upon his family as often as the wind has stirred the gathered clouds and as
often as every thing possessed of a soul has tasted death and send

السَّلَامَ لِاَهْلِ السَّلَامِ فِىْ دَارِ السَّلَامِ تَحِيَّةً وَّسَلَامًا ۝ **اَللّٰهُمَّ** اَفْرِدْنِىْ لِمَا خَلَقْتَنِىْ لَهٗ وَلَا تَشْغَلْنِىْ بِمَا تَكَفَّلْتَ لِىْ بِهٖ وَلَا تَحْرِمْنِىْ وَاَنَا اَسْئَلُكَ وَلَا تُعَذِّبْنِىْ وَاَنَا اَسْتَغْفِرُكَ ۝ ثَلَاثًا ۝ **اَللّٰهُمَّ** صَلِّ عَلٰى سَيِّدِنَا مُحَمَّدٍ وَّعَلٰى اٰلِهٖ وَسَلِّمْ ۝ **اَللّٰهُمَّ** اِنِّىْٓ اَسْئَلُكَ وَاَتَوَجَّهُ اِلَيْكَ بِحَبِيْبِكَ الْمُصْطَفٰى عِنْدَكَ يَا حَبِيْبَنَا يَا سَيِّدَنَا مُحَمَّدً اِنَّا نَتَوَسَّلُ بِكَ اِلٰى رَبِّكَ فَاشْفَعْ لَنَا عِنْدَ الْمَوْلَى الْعَظِيْمِ يَا نِعْمَ الرَّسُوْلُ الطَّاهِرُ ۝ **اَللّٰهُمَّ** شَفِّعْهُ فِيْنَا بِجَاهِهٖ عِنْدَكَ ۝ ثَلَاثًا ۝ وَاجْعَلْنَا مِنْ خَيْرِ الْمُصَلِّيْنَ وَالْمُسْلِمِيْنَ عَلَيْهِ ۝ وَمِنْ خَيْرِ الْمُقَرَّبِيْنَ مِنْهُ وَالْوَارِدِيْنَ عَلَيْهِ وَمِنْ اَخْيَارِ الْمُحِبِّيْنَ فِيْهِ وَالْمَحْبُوْبِيْنَ لَدَيْهِ ۝ وَفَرِّحْنَا بِهٖ فِىْ عَرَصَاتِ الْقِيٰمَةِ ۝ وَاجْعَلْهُ لَنَا دَلِيْلًا اِلٰى جَنَّةِ النَّعِيْمِ بِلَا مَئُوْنَةٍ وَّلَا مَشَقَّةٍ وَّلَا مُنَاقَشَةِ الْحِسَابِ وَاجْعَلْهُ مُقْبِلًا عَلَيْنَا ۝ وَلَا تَجْعَلْهُ غَاضِبًا عَلَيْنَا ۝ وَاغْفِرْلَنَا وَلِوَالِدِيْنَا وَلِجَمِيْعِ الْمُسْلِمِيْنَ الْاَحْيَآءِ مِنْهُمْ وَالْمَيِّتِيْنَ وَاٰخِرُ دَعْوٰنَا اَنِ الْحَمْدُ لِلّٰهِ رَبِّ الْعٰلَمِيْنَ ۝

اِبْتِدَآءُ الرُّبْعِ الرَّابِعِ

فَاَسْئَلُكَ يَآ اَللّٰهُ يَآ اَللّٰهُ يَآ اَللّٰهُ يَا حَىُّ يَا قَيُّوْمُ يَا ذَا الْجَلَالِ وَالْاِكْرَامِ لَآ اِلٰهَ اِلَّآ اَنْتَ سُبْحٰنَكَ اِنِّىْ كُنْتُ مِنَ الظّٰلِمِيْنَ ۝ اَسْئَلُكَ بِمَا حَمَلَ كُرْسِيُّكَ مِنْ عَظْمَتِكَ وَجَلَالِكَ وَبَهَآئِكَ وَقُدْرَتِكَ وَسُلْطَانِكَ وَبِحَقِّ اَسْمَآئِكَ الْمَخْزُوْنَةِ الْمَكْنُوْنَةِ الْمُطَهَّرَةِ الَّتِىْ لَمْ يَطَّلِعْ عَلَيْهَآ اَحَدٌ مِّنْ خَلْقِكَ وَبِحَقِّ الْاِسْمِ الَّذِىْ وَضَعْتَهٗ عَلَى الَّيْلِ فَاَظْلَمَ وَعَلَى النَّهَارِ فَاسْتَنَارَ وَعَلَى السَّمٰوٰتِ فَاسْتَقَلَّتْ ۝ وَعَلَى الْاَرْضِ فَاسْتَقَرَّتْ ۝ وَعَلَى الْبِحَارِ فَانْفَجَرَتْ ۝ وَعَلَى الْعُيُوْنِ فَنَبَعَتْ ۝ وَعَلَى السَّحَابِ فَاَمْطَرَتْ ۝ وَاَسْئَلُكَ بِالْاَسْمَآءِ الْمَكْتُوْبَةِ فِىْ جَبْهَةِ سَيِّدِنَا

abundant peace and salutations to the people of peace in the abode of peace!

O God, keep me for what You created me for and do not let me be occupied with what You provide me with and do not deprive me and I ask You not to punish me and I seek Your forgiveness! (**three times**)

O God, bless and grant peace to our master Muḥammad and his family!

O God, I ask You and turn my face to You, for the sake of Your beloved Muṣṭafā in Your Presence, O our beloved, O our master Muḥammad, I seek your mediation to Your Lord to intercede for us with the great master, O what a pure Messenger!

O God, grant us his intercession for the sake of his honor in Your Presence! (**three times**)

And make us the best of those who ask for blessings and peace upon him! And the best of those who are near to him and who are received by him! And the best of those who are in love with him and are loved in his presence! And have mercy on us because of him in the courtyards of the Day of Resurrection! And make him, for us, a sign to the Garden of delights, burdenless, trouble free, unopposed and make him our welcomer! Let him not be angry with us! And forgive us and our parents and all the submitted ones (the Muslims), living and dead, and our final prayer is praise be to God, Lord of the Worlds!

(beginning of the fourth quarter)

So I ask You, **O God, O God, O God,**

O Life, O Everlasting, O Master of Majesty and honor, there is no god but You, Glory to You, I am one lost in the darkness! I ask You for the sake of that which shoulders Your Throne from Your Might Oceans, Your Majesty Oceans, Your Beauty Oceans, Your Power Oceans, Your Strength Oceans, and for the sake of the reality of Your guarded and hidden and pure Names, which no created being can attain to, and for the sake of the reality of the Name which when laid upon the night it darkens, when laid upon the day it lightens, when laid upon the heavens they rise, when laid upon the earth it is made firm, when laid upon the seas they roll, when laid upon the springs they burst forth and when laid upon the clouds they rain! I ask You in the names written on the forehead of our master

جِبْرِيْلَ عَلَيْهِ السَّلَامُ ○ وَبِالْاَسْمَآءِ الْمَكْتُوْبَةِ فِىْ جَبْهَةِ سَيِّدِنَآ اِسْرَافِيْلَ عَلَيْهِ السَّلَامُ ○ وَعَلٰى جَمِيْعِ الْمَلٰٓئِكَةِ وَاَسْئَلُكَ بِالْاَسْمَآءِ الْمَكْتُوْبَةِ حَوْلَ الْعَرْشِ وَبِالْاَسْمَآءِ الْمَكْتُوْبَةِ حَوْلَ الْكُرْسِيِّ ○ وَاَسْئَلُكَ بِاسْمِكَ الْعَظِيْمِ الَّذِىْ سَمَّيْتَ بِهٖ نَفْسَكَ وَ اَسْئَلُكَ بِحَقِّ اَسْمَآئِكَ كُلِّهَا مَا عَلِمْتُ مِنْهَا وَمَا لَمْ اَعْلَمْ ○ وَاَسْئَلُكَ بِالْاَسْمَآءِ الَّتِىْ دَعَاكَ بِهَا سَيِّدُنَآ اٰدَمُ عَلَيْهِ السَّلَامُ ○ وَبِالْاَسْمَآءِ الَّتِىْ دَعَاكَ بِهَا سَيِّدُنَا نُوْحٌ عَلَيْهِ السَّلَامُ ○ وَبِالْاَسْمَآءِ الَّتِىْ دَعَاكَ بِهَا سَيِّدُنَا صَالِحٌ عَلَيْهِ السَّلَامُ ○ وَبِالْاَسْمَآءِ الَّتِىْ دَعَاكَ بِهَا سَيِّدُنَا يَعْقُوْبُ عَلَيْهِ السَّلَامُ ○ وَبِالْاَسْمَآءِ الَّتِىْ دَعَاكَ بِهَا سَيِّدُنَا يُوْسُفُ عَلَيْهِ السَّلَامُ ○ وَبِالْاَسْمَآءِ الَّتِىْ دَعَاكَ بِهَا سَيِّدُنَا يُوْنُسُ عَلَيْهِ السَّلَامُ ○ وَبِالْاَسْمَآءِ الَّتِىْ دَعَاكَ بِهَا سَيِّدُنَا مُوْسٰى عَلَيْهِ السَّلَامُ ○ وَبِالْاَسْمَآءِ الَّتِىْ دَعَاكَ بِهَا سَيِّدُنَا هٰرُوْنَ عَلَيْهِ السَّلَامُ ○ وَ بِالْاَسْمَآءِ الَّتِىْ دَعَاكَ بِهَا سَيِّدُنَا شُعَيْبٌ عَلَيْهِ السَّلَامُ ○ وَبِالْاَسْمَآءِ الَّتِىْ دَعَاكَ بِهَا سَيِّدُنَآ اِبْرَاهِيْمُ عَلَيْهِ السَّلَامُ ○ وَبِالْاَسْمَآءِ الَّتِىْ دَعَاكَ بِهَا سَيِّدُنَآ اِسْمٰعِيْلُ عَلَيْهِ السَّلَامُ ○ وَبِالْاَسْمَآءِ الَّتِىْ دَعَاكَ بِهَا سَيِّدُنَا دَاوٗدُ عَلَيْهِ السَّلَامُ ○ وَبِالْاَسْمَآءِ الَّتِىْ دَعَاكَ بِهَا سَيِّدُنَا سُلَيْمٰنُ عَلَيْهِ السَّلَامُ ○ وَبِالْاَسْمَآءِ الَّتِىْ دَعَاكَ بِهَا سَيِّدُنَا زَكَرِيَّا عَلَيْهِ السَّلَامُ ○ وَبِالْاَسْمَآءِ الَّتِىْ دَعَاكَ بِهَا سَيِّدُنَا يَحْيٰى عَلَيْهِ السَّلَامُ ○ وَبِالْاَسْمَآءِ الَّتِىْ دَعَاكَ بِهَا سَيِّدُنَا يُوْشَعُ عَلَيْهِ السَّلَامُ ○ وَبِالْاَسْمَآءِ الَّتِىْ دَعَاكَ بِهَا سَيِّدُنَا الْخَضِرُ عَلَيْهِ السَّلَامُ ○ وَبِالْاَسْمَآءِ الَّتِىْ دَعَاكَ بِهَا سَيِّدُنَآ اِلْيَاسُ عَلَيْهِ السَّلَامُ ○ وَبِالْاَسْمَآءِ الَّتِىْ دَعَاكَ بِهَا سَيِّدُنَا الْيَسَعُ عَلَيْهِ السَّلَامُ ○ وَبِالْاَسْمَآءِ الَّتِىْ دَعَاكَ بِهَا سَيِّدُنَا ذُوالْكِفْلِ عَلَيْهِ السَّلَامُ ○ وَبِالْاَسْمَآءِ الَّتِىْ دَعَاكَ بِهَا

Gabriel, peace be upon him! I ask you in the Names written on the forehead of our master Israfil, peace be upon him,and upon all the angels! And I ask You in the Names written around the Throne and in the Names written around the Footstool!

O God, I ask You in the most majestic names with which You have named Yourself, and in the reality of all Your Names those of which I am aware and those of which I am not aware! And I ask You, **O God**, in the names in which our master Adam peace be upon him called You! And I ask You, **O God**, in the names in which our master Noah, peace be upon him, called You! And I ask You,

O God, in the names in which our master Salih, peace be upon him, called You! And I ask You, **O God**, in the names in which our master Jacob, peace be upon him, called You. And I ask You, **O God**, in the names in which our master Joseph, peace be upon him, called You. And I ask You, **O God**, in the names in which our master Jonah, peace be upon him, called You! And I ask You, **O God**, in the names in which our master Moses, peace be upon him, called You! And I ask You,

O God, in the names in which our master Aaron, peace be upon him, called You! And I ask You, **O God**, in the names in which our master Shuayb, peace be upon him, called You! And I ask You, **O God**, in the names in which our master Abraham, peace be upon him, called You! And I ask You, **O God**, in the names in which our master Ishmael, peace be upon him, called You! And I ask You, **O God**, in the names in which our master David, peace be upon him, called You! And I ask You, **O God**, in the names in which our master Solomon, peace be upon him, called You! And I ask You, **O God**, in the names in which our master Zechariah, peace be upon him, called You! And I ask You,

O God, in the names in which our master John the Baptist, peace be upon him, called You!

And I ask You, **O God**, in the names in which our master Joshua, peace be upon him, called You! And I ask You, **O God**, in the names in which our master Khidr, peace be upon him, called You! And I ask You, **O God**, in the names in which our master Elias, peace be upon him, called You! And I ask You, **O God**, in the names in which our master Esau, peace be upon him, called You! And I ask You,

O God, in the names in which our master Dhu Kifl, peace be upon him, called You!

And I ask You, **O God**, in the names in which our master

سَيِّدُنَا عِيْسٰى عَلَيْهِ السَّلَامُ۝ وَبِالْاَسْمَآءِ الَّتِىْ دَعَاكَ بِهَا سَيِّدِنَا مُحَمَّدٌ صَلَّى اللّٰهُ عَلَيْهِ وَسَلَّمَ نَبِيُّكَ وَرَسُوْلُكَ وَحَبِيْبُكَ وَصَفِيُّكَ يَا مَنْ قَالَ وَقَوْلُهُ الْحَقُّ وَاللّٰهُ خَلَقَكُمْ وَمَا تَعْمَلُوْنَ وَلَا يَصْدُرُ عَنْ اَحَدٍ مِّنْ عَبِيْدِهٖ قَوْلٌ وَّلَا فِعْلٌ وَلَا حَرْكَةٌ وَلَا سَكُوْنٌ اِلَّا وَقَدْ سَبَقَ فِىْ عِلْمِهٖ وَقَضَآئِهٖ وَقَدَرِهٖ كَيْفَ يَكُوْنُ كَمَآ اَلْهَمْتَنِىْ وَقَضَيْتَ لِىْ بِجَمْعِ هٰذَا الْكِتٰبُ وَيَسَّرْتَ عَلَيَّ فِيْهِ الطَّرِيْقَ وَالْاَسْبَابَ وَنَفَيْتَ عَنْ قَلْبِىْ فِىْ هٰذَا النَّبِيِّ الْكَرِيْمِ الشَّكَّ وَالْاِرْتِيَابَ وَغَلَّبْتَ حُبَّهٗ عِنْدِىْ عَلٰى حُبِّ جَمِيْعِ الْاَقْرِبَآءِ وَ الْاَحِبَّآءِ اَسْئَلُكَ يَآ اَللّٰهُ يَآ اَللّٰهُ يَآ اَللّٰهُ اَنْ تَرْزُقَنِىْ وَكُلَّ مَنْ اَحَبَّهٗ وَاتَّبَعَهٗ شَفَاعَتَهٗ وَ مُرَافَقَتَهٗ يَوْمَ الْحِسَابِ مِنْ غَيْرِ مُنَاقَشَةٍ وَّلَا عَذَابٍ وَّلَا تَوْبِيْخٍ وَّلَا عِتَابٍ وَّاَنْ تَغْفِرَلِىْ ذُنُوْبِىْ وَتَسْتُرَعُيُوْبِىْ يَا وَهَّابُ يَا غَفَّارُ۝ وَاَنْ تُنَعِّمَنِىْ بِالنَّظَرِ اِلٰى وَجْهِكَ الْكَرِيْمِ فِىْ جُمْلَةِ الْاَحْبَابِ يَوْمَ الْمَزِيْدِ وَالثَّوَابِ۝ وَ اَنْ تَتَقَبَّلَ مِنِّىْ عَمَلِىْ وَاَنْ تَعْفُوَ عَمَّآ اَحَاطَ عِلْمُكَ بِهٖ مِنْ خَطِيْئَتِىْ وَنِسْيَانِىْ وَ زَلَلِىْ وَاَنْ تُبَلِّغَنِىْ مِنْ زِيَارَةِ قَبْرِهٖ وَالتَّسْلِيْمِ عَلَيْهِ وَعَلٰى صَاحِبَيْهِ غَايَةَ اَمَلِىْ بِمَنِّكَ وَفَضْلِكَ وَجُوْدِكَ وَ كَرَمِكَ يَا رَئُوْفُ يَا رَحِيْمُ يَا وَلِيُّ۝ وَاَنْ تُجَازِيَهٗ عَنِّىْ وَعَنْ كُلِّ مَنْ اٰمَنَ بِهٖ وَاتَّبَعَهٗ مِنَ الْمُسْلِمِيْنَ وَالْمُسْلِمَاتِ الْاَحْيَآءِ مِنْهُمْ وَالْاَمْوَاتِ اَفْضَلَ وَاَتَمَّ وَ اَعَمَّ مَا جَازَيْتَ بِهٖٓ اَحَدًا مِّنْ خَلْقِكَ يَا قَوِيُّ يَا عَزِيْزُ يَا عَلِيُّ وَ اَسْئَلُكَ اللّٰهُمَّ بِحَقِّ مَآ اَقْسَمْتُ بِهٖ عَلَيْكَ اَنْ تُصَلِّيَ عَلٰى سَيِّدِنَا مُحَمَّدٍ وَّعَلٰى اٰلِ سَيِّدِنَا مُحَمَّدٍ عَدَدَ مَا خَلَقْتَ مِنْ قَبْلِ اَنْ تَكُوْنَ السَّمَآءُ مَبْنِيَّةً وَّالْاَرْضُ مَدْحِيَّةً وَّالْجِبَالُ عُلْوِيَّةً وَّالْعُيُوْنُ مُنْفَجِرَةً وَّالْبِحَارُ مُسَخَّرَةً وَّالْاَنْهَارُ مُنْهَمِرَةً وَّالشَّمْسُ مُضْحِيَّةً وَّالْقَمَرُ مُضِيئًا وَّالنَّجْمُ مُنِيرًا وَّلَا يَعْلَمُ اَحَدٌ حَيْثُ تَكُوْنُ اِلَّآ

Jesus, son of Mary, peace be upon him, called You!

And I ask You, **O God**, in the names in which our master Muḥammad, the blessings and peace of God be upon him, called You, Your Prophet, Your Messenger, Your Friend!

O He who said, and His word is true, 'And God created You and what you do'! There is no action, no word, no movement and no inactivity which originates from His servants, but that it has already been preordained in His Knowledge, His Destiny and His Decree!

As I was inspired and destined to compile this book and the method and means were facilitated for me, and all doubts and misgivings about this noble Prophet were removed from my heart, and love for him overcame the love for all relations and loved ones, I ask You, O God, O God, O God, that You grant me, and all who love him and follow him, his intercession and his company on the Day of Account, without any disputing, any punishment, any reproach, any censure, and forgive me my sins and conceal my failings, O Granter, O Forgiver! And Favor me with a glance at Your Noble Face among the dear ones on the Day of Excess and Reward!

And accept from me my actions and annul all of my failings, lapses and mistakes which You have knowledge of and grant me a visit to his tomb and peace be upon him and his Companions to the utmost limit of my hope from Your Favor, Your Grace, Your Generosity, Your Nobility, O Gracious, O Merciful, O Sovereign!

And reward him on my behalf and on behalf of every Muslim man and woman, living or dead, who believes in him and follows him, better than, more perfect than and more extensively than You have rewarded anyone from Your creation, O Powerful, O Mighty, O Sublime!

And I ask You, **O God**, by the reality of my swearing by You, that You bless our master Muḥammad and the family of our master Muḥammad in all that You created before the sky was built, the earth was spread out, the mountains were raised, the springs burst forth, the oceans were subdued, the rivers streamed out, the sun shone forth, the moon beamed and the stars illuminated the sky and no one knew where You were but

اَنْتَ ۝ وَاَنْ تُصَلِّيَ عَلَيْهِ وَ عَلَى اٰلِهٖ عَدَدَ كَلَامِكَ ۝ وَاَنْ تُصَلِّيَ عَلَيْهِ وَ عَلَى اٰلِهٖ عَدَدَ اٰيَاتِ الْقُرْاٰنِ وَحُرُوْفِهٖ وَاَنْ تُصَلِّيَ عَلَيْهِ وَعَلَى اٰلِهٖ عَدَدَ مَنْ يُّصَلِّيْ عَلَيْهِ وَاَنْ تُصَلِّيَ عَلَيْهِ وَعَلَى اٰلِهٖ عَدَدَ مَنْ لَّمْ يُصَلِّ عَلَيْهِ وَاَنْ تُصَلِّيَ عَلَيْهِ وَعَلَى اٰلِهٖ مِلْءَ اَرْضِكَ وَاَنْ تُصَلِّيَ عَلَيْهِ وَعَلَى اٰلِهٖ عَدَدَ مَا جَرٰى بِهِ الْقَلَمُ فِيْٓ اُمِّ الْكِتٰبِ ۝ وَ اَنْ تُصَلِّيَ عَلَيْهِ وَعَلَى اٰلِهٖ عَدَدَ مَا خَلَقْتَ فِيْ سَبْعِ سَمٰوٰتِكَ ۝ وَاَنْ تُصَلِّيَ عَلَيْهِ وَعَلَى اٰلِهٖ عَدَدَ مَآ اَنْتَ خَالِقُهٗ فِيْهِنَّ اِلٰى يَوْمِ الْقِيٰمَةِ فِيْ كُلِّ يَوْمٍ اَلْفَ مَرَّةٍ ۝ وَاَنْ تُصَلِّيَ عَلَيْهِ وَعَلَى اٰلِهٖ عَدَدَ قَطْرِ الْمَطَرِ وَكُلِّ قَطْرَةٍ قَطَرَتْ مِنْ سَمَآئِكَ اِلٰى اَرْضِكَ مِنْ يَّوْمِ خَلَقْتَ الدُّنْيَآ اِلٰى يَوْمِ الْقِيٰمَةِ فِيْ كُلِّ يَوْمٍ اَلْفَ مَرَّةٍ ۝

اَلْحِزْبُ السَّابِعُ فِيْ يَوْمِ الْاَحَدِ

وَاَنْ تُصَلِّيَ عَلَيْهِ وَعَلَى اٰلِهٖ عَدَدَ مَنْ سَبَّحَكَ وَقَدَّسَكَ وَسَجَدَ لَكَ وَ عَظَّمَكَ مِنْ يَّوْمِ خَلَقْتَ الدُّنْيَآ اِلٰى يَوْمِ الْقِيٰمَةِ فِيْ كُلِّ يَوْمٍ اَلْفَ مَرَّةٍ ۝ وَاَنْ تُصَلِّيَ عَلَيْهِ وَعَلَى اٰلِهٖ عَدَدَ كُلِّ سَنَةٍ خَلَقْتَهُمْ فِيْهَا مِنْ يَّوْمِ خَلَقْتَ الدُّنْيَآ اِلٰى يَوْمِ الْقِيٰمَةِ فِيْ كُلِّ يَوْمٍ اَلْفَ مَرَّةٍ ۝ وَاَنْ تُصَلِّيَ عَلَيْهِ وَعَلَى اٰلِهٖ عَدَدَ السَّحَابِ الْجَارِيَةِ ۝ وَاَنْ تُصَلِّيَ عَلَيْهِ وَعَلَى اٰلِهٖ عَدَدَ الرِّيَاحِ الذَّارِيَةِ مِنْ يَّوْمِ خَلَقْتَ الدُّنْيَآ اِلٰى يَوْمِ الْقِيٰمَةِ فِيْ كُلِّ يَوْمٍ اَلْفَ مَرَّةٍ ۝ وَاَنْ تُصَلِّيَ عَلَيْهِ وَعَلَى اٰلِهٖ عَدَدَ مَا هَبَّتِ الرِّيَاحُ عَلَيْهِ وَحَرَّكَتْهُ مِنَ الْاَغْصَانِ وَالْاَشْجَارِ وَاَوْرَاقِ الثِّمَارِ وَالْاَزْهَارِ وَعَدَدَ مَا خَلَقْتَ عَلٰى قَرَارِ اَرْضِكَ وَمَا بَيْنَ سَمٰوٰتِكَ مِنْ يَّوْمِ خَلَقْتَ الدُّنْيَآ اِلٰى يَوْمِ الْقِيٰمَةِ فِيْ كُلِّ يَوْمٍ اَلْفَ مَرَّةٍ ۝ وَاَنْ تُصَلِّيَ عَلَيْهِ وَعَلَى اٰلِهٖ عَدَدَ اَمْوَاجِ بِحَارِكَ مِنْ يَّوْمِ خَلَقْتَ الدُّنْيَآ اِلٰى يَوْمِ الْقِيٰمَةِ فِيْ كُلِّ يَوْمٍ اَلْفَ مَرَّةٍ ۝ وَاَنْ تُصَلِّيَ عَلَيْهِ وَعَلَى اٰلِهٖ

You!

And bless him and his family as many times as the number of Your words!

And bless him and his family as many times as there are verses and letters in the Quran! And bless him and his family as many times as those who ask You to bless him and bless him and his family as many times as those who neglect to ask You to bless him!

And bless him and his family as much as the earth and bless him and his family as much as the Pen has written in the Mother of the Book!

And bless him and his family as much as You have created in Your Seven Heavens! And bless him and his family as much as You will create in them until the Day of Resurrection and every day a thousand times!

And bless him and his family in every single drop of rain and in the totality of all the rain which has fallen from Your sky to the earth from the day You created this world until the Day of Resurrection and every day a thousand times!

The Seventh Part to be Read on Sunday

And bless him and his family as many times as Your glorifiers, Your worshippers, Your prostrated servants and Your magnifiers, from the day You created this world until the Day of Resurrection every day a thousand times!

And bless him and his family as many times as the years in which You created them (ie. those who glorify You, etc.), from the day You created this world until the Day of Resurrection every day a thousand times!

And bless him and his family in every sweeping cloud! And bless him and his family in every gusting wind from the day You created this world until the Day of Resurrection every day a thousand times!

And bless him and his family in the movement of every branch, every tree, every leaf, every fruit and every flower stirred by the wind, and in everything created on the earth and in everything within Your heavens stirred by the wind from the day You created this world until the Day of Resurrection every day a thousand times!

And bless him and his family in every ocean wave from the day You created this world until the Day of Resurrection every day a thousand times! And bless him and his family

عَدَدَ الرَّمْلِ وَالْحَصٰى وَ كُلِّ حَجَرٍ وَّ مَدَرٍ خَلَقْتَهٗ فِيْ مَشَارِقِ الْاَرْضِ وَمَغَارِبِهَا سَهْلِهَا وَ جِبَالِهَا وَاَوْدِيَتِهَا مِنْ يَّوْمِ خَلَقْتَ الدُّنْيَآ اِلٰى يَوْمِ الْقِيٰمَةِ فِيْ كُلِّ يَوْمٍ اَلْفَ مَرَّةٍ ○ وَاَنْ تُصَلِّيَ عَلَيْهِ وَعَلٰى اٰلِهٖ عَدَدَ نَبَاتِ الْاَرْضِ فِيْ قِبْلَتِهَا وَجَوْفِهَا وَشَرْقِهَا وَ غَرْبِهَا وَسَهْلِهَا وَ جِبَالِهَا مِنْ شَجَرٍ وَّثَمَرٍ وَّ اَوْرَاقٍ وَّزَرْعٍ وَّجَمِيْعِ مَآ اَخْرَجَتْ وَمَا يَخْرُجُ مِنْهَا مِنْ نَّبَاتِهَا وَبَرَكَاتِهَا مِنْ يَّوْمِ خَلَقْتَ الدُّنْيَآ اِلٰى يَوْمِ الْقِيٰمَةِ فِيْ كُلِّ يَوْمٍ اَلْفَ مَرَّةٍ ○ وَاَنْ تُصَلِّيَ عَلَيْهِ وَعَلٰى اٰلِهٖ عَدَدَ مَا خَلَقْتَ مِنَ الْاِنْسِ وَالْجِنِّ وَالشَّيَاطِيْنِ وَمَآ اَنْتَ خَالِقُهٗ مِنْهُمْ اِلٰى يَوْمِ الْقِيٰمَةِ فِيْ كُلِّ يَوْمٍ اَلْفَ مَرَّةٍ ○ وَاَنْ تُصَلِّيَ عَلَيْهِ وَعَلٰى اٰلِهٖ عَدَدَ كُلِّ شَعْرَةٍ فِيْٓ اَبْدَانِهِمْ وَ وُجُوْهِهِمْ وَعَلٰى رُءُوْسِهِمْ مُنْذُ خَلَقْتَ الدُّنْيَآ اِلٰى يَوْمِ الْقِيٰمَةِ فِيْ كُلِّ يَوْمٍ اَلْفَ مَرَّةٍ ○ وَاَنْ تُصَلِّيَ عَلَيْهِ وَعَلٰى اٰلِهٖ عَدَدَ اَنْفَاسِهِمْ وَاَلْفَاظِهِمْ وَاَلْحَاظِهِمْ مِّنْ يَّوْمِ خَلَقْتَ الدُّنْيَآ اِلٰى يَوْمِ الْقِيٰمَةِ فِيْ كُلِّ يَوْمٍ اَلْفَ مَرَّةٍ ○ وَاَنْ تُصَلِّيَ عَلَيْهِ وَعَلٰى اٰلِهٖ عَدَدَ طَيَرَانِ الْجِنِّ وَخَفَقَانِ الْاِنْسِ مِنْ يَّوْمِ خَلَقْتَ الدُّنْيَآ اِلٰى يَوْمِ الْقِيٰمَةِ فِيْ كُلِّ يَوْمٍ اَلْفَ مَرَّةٍ ○ وَاَنْ تُصَلِّيَ عَلَيْهِ وَعَلٰى اٰلِهٖ عَدَدَ كُلِّ بَهِيْمَةٍ خَلَقْتَهَا عَلٰى اَرْضِكَ صَغِيْرَةً وَّ كَبِيْرَةً فِيْ مَشَارِقِ الْاَرْضِ وَمَغَارِبِهَا مِمَّا عُلِمَ وَمِمَّا لَا يَعْلَمُ عِلْمَهٗٓ اِلَّآ اَنْتَ مِنْ يَّوْمِ خَلَقْتَ الدُّنْيَآ اِلٰى يَوْمِ الْقِيٰمَةِ فِيْ كُلِّ يَوْمٍ اَلْفَ مَرَّةٍ ○ وَاَنْ تُصَلِّيَ عَلَيْهِ وَعَلٰى اٰلِهٖ عَدَدَ مَنْ صَلّٰى عَلَيْهِ وَعَدَدَ مَنْ لَّمْ يُصَلِّ عَلَيْهِ وَعَدَدَ مَنْ يُّصَلِّيْ عَلَيْهِ اِلٰى يَوْمِ الْقِيٰمَةِ فِيْ كُلِّ يَوْمٍ اَلْفَ مَرَّةٍ ○ وَاَنْ تُصَلِّيَ عَلَيْهِ وَعَلٰى اٰلِهٖ عَدَدَ الْاَحْيَآءِ وَالْاَمْوَاتِ وَعَدَدَ مَا خَلَقْتَ مِنْ حِيْتَانٍ وَّطَيْرٍ وَّنَمْلٍ وَّنَحْلٍ وَّ حَشَرَاتٍ ○ وَاَنْ تُصَلِّيَ عَلَيْهِ وَعَلٰى اٰلِهٖ فِي الَّيْلِ اِذَا يَغْشٰى وَالنَّهَارِ اِذَا تَجَلّٰى ○

in every grain of sand, in every stone, in every rock and in every cloud You have created in the East and in the West, on lowland and on highland, and in the valleys from the day You created this world until the Day of Resurrection every day a thousand times!

And bless him and his family in every tree, every fruit, every leaf and every plant of the earth, in the South and in the North, in the East and in the West, on the plains and in the hills, and in everything You have produced from it and in everything You will produce from it from the day You created this world until the Day of Resurrection every day a thousand times!

And bless him and his family in every human being, every jinn and every devil You have created from the day You created this world until the Day of Resurrection every day a thousand times!

And bless him and his family in every hair on their bodies, on their faces, and on their heads since the time You created this world until the Day of Resurrection every day a thousand times!

And bless him and his family in every one of their breaths, in every one of their utterances and in every one of their glances, from the day You created this world until the Day of Resurrection every day a thousand times!

And bless him and his family in every flight of a jinn and in every human heartbeat from the day You created this world until the Day of Resurrection every day a thousand times!

And bless him and his family in every large and every small creature created by You in the West and in the East of Your earth, those which are known and those of whom knowledge is Yours alone from the day You created this world until the Day of Resurrection every day a thousand times!

And bless him and his family as many times as those who have asked for blessings upon him and as many times as those who have not and as many times as those who will ask until the Day of Resurrection every day a thousand times!

And bless him and his family in every soul, alive and dead, in every insect, in every bird, in every ant, in every bee and in every beast You have created!

And bless him and his family in every darkening night and in every brightening day!

وَانْ تُصَلِّيَ عَلَيْهِ وَعَلٰى اٰلِهٖ فِى الْاٰخِرَةِ وَالْاُوْلٰى ۞ وَانْ تُصَلِّيَ عَلَيْهِ وَعَلٰى اٰلِهٖ مُنْذُ كَانَ فِي الْمَهْدِ صَبِيًّا اِلٰى اَنْ صَارَ كَهْلاً مَّهْدِيًّا فَقَبَضْتَهٗ اِلَيْكَ عَدْلاً مَّرْضِيًّا لِّتَبْعَثَهٗ شَفِيْعًا حَفِيًّا ۞ وَانْ تُصَلِّيَ عَلَيْهِ وَعَلٰى اٰلِهٖ عَدَدَ خَلْقِكَ وَرِضٰى نَفْسِكَ وَزِنَةَ عَرْشِكَ وَ مِدَادَ كَلِمَاتِكَ وَانْ تُعْطِيَهُ الْوَسِيْلَةَ وَالْفَضِيْلَةَ وَالدَّرَجَةَ الرَّفِيْعَةَ وَالْحَوْضَ الْمَوْرُوْدَ وَالْمَقَامَ الْمَحْمُوْدَ وَالْعِزَّ الْمَمْدُوْدَ وَانْ تُعَظِّمَ بُرْهَانَهٗ وَ اَنْ تُشَرِّفَ بُنْيَانَهٗ وَانْ تَرْفَعَ مَكَانَهٗ وَ اَنْ تَسْتَعْمِلَنَا يَا مَوْلٰنَا بِسُنَّتِهٖ وَ اَنْ تُمِيْتَنَا عَلٰى مِلَّتِهٖ ۞ وَ اَنْ تَحْشُرَنَا فِىْ زُمْرَتِهٖ وَتَحْتَ لِوَآئِهٖ وَ اَنْ تَجْعَلَنَا مِنْ رُّفَقَآئِهٖ وَ اَنْ تُوْرِدَنَا حَوْضَهٗ وَ اَنْ تَسْقِيَنَا بِكَاْسِهٖ وَ اَنْ تَنْفَعَنَا بِمَحَبَّتِهٖ وَ اَنْ تَتُوْبَ عَلَيْنَا وَ اَنْ تُعَافِيَنَا مِنْ جَمِيْعِ الْبَلَآءِ وَالْبَلْوَآءِ وَالْفِتَنِ مَا ظَهَرَ مِنْهَا وَمَا بَطَنَ وَ اَنْ تَرْحَمَنَا وَ اَنْ تَعْفُوَ عَنَّا وَ تَغْفِرَلَنَا وَلِجَمِيْعِ الْمُؤْمِنِيْنَ وَالْمُؤْمِنَاتِ وَالْمُسْلِمِيْنَ وَالْمُسْلِمَاتِ الْاَحْيَآءِ مِنْهُمْ وَالْاَمْوَاتِ وَالْحَمْدُ لِلّٰهِ رَبِّ الْعٰلَمِيْنَ ۞ وَهُوَ حَسْبِىْ وَنِعْمَ الْوَكِيْلُ وَلَا حَوْلَ وَلَا قُوَّةَ اِلَّا بِاللّٰهِ الْعَلِيِّ الْعَظِيْمِ ۞ **اَللّٰهُمَّ** صَلِّ عَلٰى سَيِّدِنَا مُحَمَّدٍ وَّعَلٰى اٰلِ سَيِّدِنَا مُحَمَّدٍ مَّا سَجَعَتِ الْحَمَآئِمُ وَحَمَتِ الْحَوَآئِمُ وَسَرَحَتِ الْبَهَآئِمُ وَنَفَعَتِ التَّمَآئِمُ وَشُدَّتِ الْعَمَآئِمُ وَنَمَتِ النَّوَآئِمُ ۞ **اَللّٰهُمَّ** صَلِّ عَلٰى سَيِّدِنَا مُحَمَّدٍ وَّعَلٰى اٰلِ سَيِّدِنَا مُحَمَّدٍ مَّآ اَبْلَجَ الْاَصْبَاحُ وَهَبَّتِ الرِّيَاحُ وَ دَبَّتِ الْاَشْبَاحُ وَتَعَاقَبَ الْغُدُوُّ وَالرَّوَاحُ وَتُقُلِّدَتِ الصِّفَاحُ وَاعْتُقِلَتِ الرِّمَاحُ وَصَحَّتِ الْاَجْسَادُ وَالْاَرْوَاحُ ۞ **اَللّٰهُمَّ** صَلِّ عَلٰى سَيِّدِنَا مُحَمَّدٍ وَّعَلٰى اٰلِ سَيِّدِنَا مُحَمَّدٍ مَّا دَارَتِ الْاَفْلَاكُ وَدَجَتِ الْاَحْلَاكُ وَ سَبَّحَتِ الْاَمْلَاكُ ۞ **اَللّٰهُمَّ** صَلِّ عَلٰى سَيِّدِنَا مُحَمَّدٍ وَّعَلٰى اٰلِ سَيِّدِنَا مُحَمَّدٍ كَمَا صَلَّيْتَ عَلٰى

And bless him and his family in the end and in the beginning! And bless him and his family from the time he was in the cradle until his time of maturity when You took him to Yourself, justly satisfied, and until You finally send him as a welcome intercessor!

And bless him and his family in all of Your creation, to the extent of Your Pleasure, in the decoration of Your Throne, in the ink of Your Words, and grant him the closest access, the pre-eminence, the lofty rank, the oft-visited pool, the most praised station, and the greatest standing, and enhance his proof, ennoble his stature, raise his station, and have us, O Lord, follow his way and have us die following his religion!

And resurrect us in his company, beneath his flag, put us in his assembly, water us at his pool, have us drink from his drinking bowl, grant us his love, accept our repentance, remove from us all trials and tribulations, inner and outer discord, and have mercy on us, pardon us and forgive us along with all the believing men and women and submitted men and women, the living and the dead, and praise be to God, Lord of the Worlds!

And He suffices me and He is the best of Protectors and there is no help or power save in God, the High, the Mighty!

O God, bless our master Muḥammad and the family of our master Muḥammad in the cooing of doves, in the circling of beasts around water holes, in the grazing of cattle, in the wearing of amulets, in the winding of turbans and in the sleeping of slumberers!

O God, bless our master Muḥammad and the family of our master Muḥammad in the breaking dawns, in the blowing winds, in the creeping shades, in the succeeding morns and eves, in the girding on of armor, in the impounding of lances, and in the healing of bodies and souls!

O God, bless our master Muḥammad and the family of our master Muḥammad in the rotation of the celestial bodies, in the overshadowing of darkness and in the glorifying of angels!

O God, bless our master Muḥammad and the family of our
master Muḥammad just as You blessed

سَيِّدِنَآ اِبْرٰهِيْمَ وَبَارِكْ عَلٰى سَيِّدِنَا مُحَمَّدٍ وَّعَلٰى اٰلِ سَيِّدِنَا مُحَمَّدٍ كَمَا بَارَكْتَ عَلٰى سَيِّدِنَآ اِبْرٰهِيْمَ فِى الْعٰلَمِيْنَ اِنَّكَ حَمِيْدٌ مَّجِيْدٌ ○ **اَللّٰهُمَّ** صَلِّ عَلٰى سَيِّدِنَا مُحَمَّدٍ وَّعَلٰى اٰلِ سَيِّدِنَا مُحَمَّدٍ مَّا طَلَعَتِ الشَّمْسُ وَمَا صُلِّيَتِ الْخَمْسُ وَمَا تَاَلَّقَ بَرْقٌ وَّ تَدَفَّقَ وَدْقٌ وَّمَا سَبَّحَ رَعْدٌ○ **اَللّٰهُمَّ** صَلِّ عَلٰى سَيِّدِنَا مُحَمَّدٍ وَّعَلٰى اٰلِ سَيِّدِنَا مُحَمَّدٍ مَّا مِلْءَ السَّمٰوٰتِ وَالْاَرْضِ وَمِلْءَ مَا بَيْنَهُمَا وَمِلْءَ مَا شِئْتَ مِنْ شَيْءٍ بَعْدُ ○ **اَللّٰهُمَّ** كَمَا قَامَ بِاَعْبَاءِ الرِّسَالَةِ وَاسْتَنْقَذَ الْخَلْقَ مِنَ الْجَهَالَةِ وَجَاهَدَ اَهْلَ الْكُفْرِ وَالضَّلَالَةِ وَدَعَا اِلٰى تَوْحِيْدِكَ وَقَاسَى الشَّدَآئِدَ فِىْٓ اِرْشَادِ عَبِيْدِكَ فَاَعْطِهِ اللّٰهُمَّ سُؤْلَهٗ وَبَلِّغْهُ مَاْمُوْلَهٗ وَاٰتِهِ الْوَسِيْلَةَ وَالْفَضِيْلَةَ وَالدَّرَجَةَ الرَّفِيْعَةَ وَابْعَثْهُ الْمَقَامَ الْمَحْمُوْدَ الَّذِىْ وَعَدْتَّهٗٓ اِنَّكَ لَا تُخْلِفُ الْمِيْعَادَ ○ **اَللّٰهُمَّ** وَاجْعَلْنَا مِنَ الْمُتَّبِعِيْنَ لِشَرِيْعَتِهِ الْمُتَّصِفِيْنَ بِمَحَبَّتِهِ الْمُهْتَدِيْنَ بِهَدْيِهٖ وَسِيْرَتِهٖ وَتَوَفَّنَا عَلٰى سُنَّتِهٖ وَلَا تَحْرِمْنَا فَضْلَ شَفَاعَتِهٖ وَاحْشُرْنَا فِىْٓ اَتْبَاعِهِ الْغُرِّ الْمُحَجَّلِيْنَ وَاَشْيَاعِهِ السَّابِقِيْنَ وَ اَصْحَابِ الْيَمِيْنِ يَآ اَرْحَمَ الرَّاحِمِيْنَ ○ **اَللّٰهُمَّ** صَلِّ عَلٰى مَلٰٓئِكَتِكَ وَالْمُقَرَّبِيْنَ وَعَلٰى اَنْبِيَآئِكَ وَالْمُرْسَلِيْنَ وَعَلٰى اَهْلِ طَاعَتِكَ اَجْمَعِيْنَ وَاجْعَلْنَا بِالصَّلٰوةِ عَلَيْهِمْ مِّنَ الْمَرْحُوْمِيْنَ ○ **اَللّٰهُمَّ** صَلِّ عَلٰى سَيِّدِنَا مُحَمَّدِ نِ الْمَبْعُوْثِ مِنْ تِهَامَةَ وَالْاٰمِرِ بِالْمَعْرُوْفِ وَالْاِسْتِقَامَةِ وَالشَّفِيْعِ لِاَهْلِ الذُّنُوْبِ فِىْ عَرَصَاتِ الْقِيٰمَةِ ○ **اَللّٰهُمَّ** اَبْلِغْ عَنَّا نَبِيَّنَا وَ شَفِيْعَنَا وَحَبِيْبَنَا اَفْضَلَ الصَّلٰوةِ وَالتَّسْلِيْمِ وَابْعَثْهُ الْمَقَامَ الْمَحْمُوْدَ الْكَرِيْمَ وَاٰتِهِ الْفَضِيْلَةَ وَالْوَسِيْلَةَ وَالدَّرَجَةَ الرَّفِيْعَةَ الَّتِىْ وَعَدْتَّهٗ فِى الْمَوْقِفِ الْعَظِيْمِ○ وَصَلِّ اللّٰهُمَّ عَلَيْهِ صَلٰوةً دَآئِمَةً مُّتَّصِلَةً تَتَوَالٰى وَتَدُوْمُ ○ **اَللّٰهُمَّ** صَلِّ عَلَيْهِ وَعَلٰى اٰلِهٖ مَا لَاحَ بَارِقٌ وَّ

our master Abraham, and sanctify our master Muḥammad and the family of our master Muḥammad just as You sanctified our master Abraham in all the worlds, for You are indeed the Praiseworthy, the Mighty!

O God, bless our master Muḥammad and the family of our master Muḥammad in the rising sun, in the performing of the five daily prayers, in lightning which strikes, in the falling rain and in the pealing of thunder!

O God, bless our master Muḥammad and the family of our master Muḥammad to the fullness of the heavens and the earth and to the fullness of whatever is between them and to the fullness of whatever You may have created elsewhere!

O God, as he bore the responsibility of the Message, delivered creation from ignorance, struggled against the people of unbelief and error, called to Your Unity, endured hardships in guiding Your servants, then grant him,

O God, his wishes, fulfill his hopes, and give him the closest access, the pre-eminence, the lofty rank, and send him to the most praised station which You promised him, for You never renege on a promise!

O God, make us the followers of his law, those known for their love of him, those guided by his guidance and life, and have us die following his way, and do not deny us the favor of his intercession, and resurrect us among his followers, those shining with light, his foremost companions, the companions of the right hand, O Most Merciful of the Merciful!

O God, bless Your angels, Your archangels, Your Prophets and Your Messengers, all the people obedient to You, and may our asking for such blessings be a mercy for us!

O God, bless our master Muḥammad, the envoy from Tihama, the commander and upholder of justice, the intercessor for the people of sin on the courtyards of the Day of Resurrection!

O God, send to our Prophet, our advocate and our beloved, on our behalf, the finest blessings and peace, and send him to the most praised and noble station, and grant him the pre-eminence, the closest access and the lofty rank which You have promised him on the Great Day of Standing!

And bless him, **O God**, with blessings eternal, continual, continuous and everlasting! **O God**, bless him and his family in the

lightning which strikes,

ذَرَّشَارِقٌ وَّ وَقَبَ غَاسِقٌ وَانْهَمَرَ وَادِقٌ وَّصَلِّ عَلَيْهِ وَعَلٰى اٰلِهٖ مِلْءَ اللُّوْحِ وَالْفَضَآءِ وَمِثْلَ نُجُوْمِ السَّمَآءِ وَعَدَدَ الْقَطْرِ وَالْحَصٰى وَصَلِّ عَلَيْهِ وَعَلٰى اٰلِهٖ صَلٰوةً لَّا تُعَدُّ وَلَا تُحْصٰى ۝ **اَللّٰهُمَّ** صَلِّ عَلَيْهِ زِنَةَ عَرْشِكَ وَمَبْلَغَ رِضَاكَ وَمِدَادَ كَلِمَاتِكَ وَمُنْتَهٰى رَحْمَتِكَ ۝ **اَللّٰهُمَّ** صَلِّ عَلَيْهِ وَعَلٰى اٰلِهٖ وَاَزْوَاجِهٖ وَذُرِّيَّتِهٖ وَبَارِكْ عَلَيْهِ وَعَلٰى اٰلِهٖ وَاَزْوَاجِهٖ وَذُرِّيَّتِهٖ كَمَا صَلَّيْتَ وَبَارَكْتَ عَلٰى سَيِّدِنَآ اِبْرٰهِيْمَ وَعَلٰى اٰلِ سَيِّدِنَآ اِبْرٰهِيْمَ اِنَّكَ حَمِيْدٌ مَّجِيْدٌ ۝ وَجَازِهٖ عَنَّآ اَفْضَلَ مَا جَازَيْتَ نَبِيًّا عَنْ اُمَّتِهٖ وَاجْعَلْنَا مِنَ الْمُهْتَدِيْنَ بِمِنْهَاجِ شَرِيْعَتِهٖ وَاهْدِنَا بِهَدْيِهٖ وَتَوَفَّنَا عَلٰى مِلَّتِهٖ وَاحْشُرْنَا يَوْمَ الْفَزَعِ الْاَكْبَرِ مِنَ الْاٰمِنِيْنَ فِيْ زُمْرَتِهٖ وَاَمِتْنَا عَلٰى حُبِّهٖ وَحُبِّ اٰلِهٖ وَاَصْحَابِهٖ وَذُرِّيَّتِهٖ ۝ **اَللّٰهُمَّ** صَلِّ عَلٰى سَيِّدِنَا مُحَمَّدٍ اَفْضَلِ اَنْبِيَآئِكَ وَاَكْرَمِ اَصْفِيَآئِكَ وَاِمَامِ اَوْلِيَآئِكَ وَخَاتِمِ اَنْبِيَآئِكَ وَحَبِيْبِ رَبِّ الْعٰلَمِيْنَ وَشَهِيْدِ الْمُرْسَلِيْنَ وَشَفِيْعِ الْمُذْنِبِيْنَ وَسَيِّدِ وُلْدِ اٰدَمَ اَجْمَعِيْنَ الْمَرْفُوْعِ الذِّكْرِ فِي الْمَلٰٓئِكَةِ الْمُقَرَّبِيْنَ الْبَشِيْرِ النَّذِيْرِ السِّرَاجِ الْمُنِيْرِ الصَّادِقِ الْاَمِيْنِ الْحَقِّ الْمُبِيْنِ الرَّءُوْفِ الرَّحِيْمِ الْهَادِيْٓ اِلَى الصِّرَاطِ الْمُسْتَقِيْمِ الَّذِيْٓ اٰتَيْتَهٗ سَبْعًا مِّنَ الْمَثَانِيْ وَالْقُرْاٰنَ الْعَظِيْمَ نَبِيِّ الرَّحْمَةِ وَهَادِي الْاُمَّةِ اَوَّلِ مَنْ تَنْشَقُّ عَنْهُ الْاَرْضُ وَيَدْخُلُ الْجَنَّةَ وَالْمُؤَيَّدِ بِسَيِّدِنَا جِبْرِيْلَ وَسَيِّدِنَا مِيْكَآئِيْلَ الْمُبَشَّرِ بِهٖ فِي التَّوْرٰةِ وَالْاِنْجِيْلِ الْمُصْطَفَى الْمُجْتَبَى الْمُنْتَخَبِ اَبِي الْقَاسِمِ سَيِّدِنَا **مُحَمَّدِ** بْنِ عَبْدِ اللّٰهِ ابْنِ عَبْدِالْمُطَّلِبِ بْنِ هَاشِمٍ ۝ **اَللّٰهُمَّ** صَلِّ عَلٰى مَلٰٓئِكَتِكَ وَالْمُقَرَّبِيْنَ الَّذِيْنَ يُسَبِّحُوْنَ الَّيْلَ وَالنَّهَارَ لَا يَفْتُرُوْنَ وَلَا يَعْصُوْنَ اللّٰهَ مَآ اَمَرَهُمْ وَيَفْعَلُوْنَ مَا يُؤْمَرُوْنَ ۝ **اَللّٰهُمَّ** وَكَمَا اصْطَفَيْتَهُمْ سُفَرَآءَ اِلٰى رُسُلِكَ وَاُمَنَآءَ عَلٰى وَحْيِكَ وَشُهَدَآءَ عَلٰى خَلْقِكَ

in the day which dawns, in the night which obscures and in the rain which pours! And bless him and his family to the fullness of the Tablet and the Cosmos, and in every star in the sky and in every raindrop and in every stone, and bless him and his family with blessings innumerable and incalculable!

O God, bless him in the decoration of Your Throne, to the full extent of Your Pleasure, in the Ink of Your Words and to the bounds of Your Mercy!

O God, bless him and his family, his wives and his descendants, and sanctify him and his family, his wives and his descendants just as You blessed and sanctified our master Abraham and the family of our master Abraham, for You are indeed Praiseworthy, Mighty! And reward him, on our behalf, better than You have rewarded any Prophet on behalf of his nation, and place us among those guided by the way of his law, guide us through his guidance, have us pass away following his religion, and resurrect us on the Day of the Greatest Terror among the faithful in his company and have us die loving him and loving his family, his companions and his descendants!

O God, bless our master Muḥammad, the finest of Your Prophets, the noblest of Your friends, the leader of Your saints, the Seal of Your Prophets, the beloved of the Lord of the Worlds, the witness for the Messengers, the advocate of the sinners, the master of all the children of Adam, the one mentioned highly among the highest angels, the news-bringer, the warner, the shining lamp, the truthful one, the trustworthy one, the clear truth, the compassionate and merciful one, the guide to the straight path and to whom You granted the seven oft-mentioned verses and the mighty Quran, the Prophet of mercy, the guide of the nation, the first upon whom the earth breathed and the first to enter the Garden, the one supported by our master Gabriel and our master Michael, the one announced in the Torah and in the Gospel, the chosen one, the elected one, the selected one, Father of Qasim, our master Muḥammad, son of ᶜAbd Allāh, son of ᶜAbd al-Muṭṭalib, son of Hashim!

O God, bless Your highest angels who glorify you ceaselessly, night and day, and who never disobey God in what He has ordered and who carry out what they have been ordered to do!

O God, just as You have chosen them to be envoys to Your Messengers, guardians of Your revelation and witnesses over

Your Creation,

وَخَرَقْتَ لَهُمْ كُنُفَ حُجُبِكَ وَاَطْلَعْتَهُمْ عَلٰى مَكْنُوْنِ غَيْبِكَ وَاخْتَرْتَ مِنْهُمْ خَزَنَةً لِّجَنَّتِكَ وَحَمَلَةً لِّعَرْشِكَ وَجَعَلْتَهُمْ مِّنْ اَكْثَرِ جُنُوْدِكَ وَفَضَّلْتَهُمْ عَلَى الْوَرٰى وَاَسْكَنْتَهُمُ السَّمٰوٰتِ الْعُلٰى وَنَزَّهْتَهُمْ عَنِ الْمَعَاصِىْ وَالدَّنَآءٰتِ وَقَدَّسْتَهُمْ عَنِ النَّقَآئِصِ وَالْاٰفَاتِ فَصَلِّ عَلَيْهِمْ صَلٰوةً دَآئِمَةً تَزِيْدُهُمْ بِهَا فَضْلاً وَّتَجْعَلُنَا لِاسْتِغْفَارِهِمْ بِهَآ اَهْلاً ۝ **اَللّٰهُمَّ** وَصَلِّ عَلٰى جَمِيْعِ اَنْبِيَآئِكَ وَرُسُلِكَ الَّذِيْنَ شَرَحْتَ صُدُوْرَهُمْ وَاَوْدَعْتَهُمْ حِكْمَتَكَ وَطَوَّقْتَهُمْ نُبُوَّتَكَ وَاَنْزَلْتَ عَلَيْهِمْ كُتُبَكَ وَهَدَيْتَ بِهِمْ خَلْقَكَ وَدَعَوْا اِلٰى تَوْحِيْدِكَ وَشَوَّقُوْآ اِلٰى وَعْدِكَ وَ خَوَّفُوْا مِنْ وَّعِيْدِكَ وَاَرْشَدُوْآ اِلٰى سَبِيْلِكَ وَقَامُوْا بِحُجَّتِكَ وَدَلِيْلِكَ وَسَلِّمِ اللّٰهُمَّ عَلَيْهِ تَسْلِيْمًا وَّهَبْ لَنَا بِالصَّلٰوةِ عَلَيْهِمْ اَجْرً عَظِيْمًا ۝ **اَللّٰهُمَّ** صَلِّ عَلٰى سَيِّدِنَا مُحَمَّدٍ وَّعَلٰى اٰلِ سَيِّدِنَا مُحَمَّدٍ صَلٰوةً دَآئِمَةً مَّقْبُوْلَةً تُؤَدِّىْ بِهَا عَنَّا حَقَّهُ الْعَظِيْمَ ۝ **اَللّٰهُمَّ** صَلِّ عَلٰى سَيِّدِنَا مُحَمَّدٍ صَاحِبِ الْحُسْنِ وَالْجَمَالِ وَالْبَهْجَةِ وَالْكَمَالِ وَالْبَهَآءِ وَالنُّوْرِ وَالْوِلْدَانِ وَالْحُوْرِ وَالْغُرَفِ وَالْقُصُوْرِ وَاللِّسَانِ الشَّكُوْرِ وَالْقَلْبِ الْمَشْكُوْرِ وَالْعِلْمِ الْمَشْهُوْرِ وَالْجَيْشِ الْمَنْصُوْرِ وَالْبَنِيْنَ وَالْبَنَاتِ وَ الْاَزْوَاجِ الطَّاهِرَاتِ وَالْعُلُوِّ عَلَى الدَّرَجَاتِ وَالزَّمْزَمِ وَالْمَقَامِ وَالْمَشْعَرِ الْحَرَامِ وَاجْتِنَابِ الْاٰثَامِ وَتَرْبِيَةِ الْاَيْتَامِ وَالْحَجِّ وَ تِلَاوَةِ الْقُرْاٰنِ وَتَسْبِيْحِ الرَّحْمٰنِ وَصِيَامِ رَمَضَانَ وَاللِّوَآءِ الْمَعْقُوْدِ وَالْكَرَمِ وَالْجُوْدِ وَالْوَفَآءِ بِالْعُهُوْدِ صَاحِبِ الرَّغْبَةِ وَالتَّرْغِيْبِ وَالْبَغْلَةِ وَالنَّجِيْبِ وَالْحَوْضِ وَالْقَضِيْبِ النَّبِيِّ الْاَوَّابِ النَّاطِقِ بِالصَّوَابِ الْمَنْعُوْتِ فِى الْكِتَابِ النَّبِيِّ عَبْدِ اللّٰهِ النَّبِيِّ كَنْزِ اللّٰهِ النَّبِيِّ حُجَّةِ اللّٰهِ النَّبِيِّ مَنْ اَطَاعَهٗ فَقَدْ اَطَاعَ اللّٰهَ وَمَنْ عَصَاهُ فَقَدْ عَصَى اللّٰهَ النَّبِيِّ

and have allowed them to pass through the folds of Your Veils, and have given them access to Your hidden unseen realms, and have chosen them to be the guardians of Your Garden and bearers of Your Throne, and have made them the most numerous of Your Soldiers, and have favored them over mortal men, and have populated the high heavens with them, and have freed them from disobedience and baseness, and have sanctified them from shortcomings and misfortunes, so bless them eternally and may this request serve as a means of increasing their favor and a means of their asking forgiveness for us!

O God, bless all of Your Prophets and Messengers whose hearts You have opened, to whom You have entrusted Your Wisdom, whom You have empowered with Your prophethood, to whom You have revealed Your Books, by whom Your Creation has been guided, who have called to Your Unity, who have looked forward to Your Promise and feared Your Threat, who have guided to Your Path, who have upheld Your Proof and Your Evidence, and grant them abundant peace,

O God, and through this request for them bestow upon us a mighty reward!

O God, bless our master **Muḥammad** and the family of our master **Muḥammad** blessings eternally acceptable and which discharge us of his overwhelming rights over us!

O God, bless our master **Muḥammad**, the possessor of beauty and handsomeness, of splendor and perfection, of radiance and light, of youthful servants and houris, of chambers and palaces, of a grateful tongue and a praiseworthy heart, of renowned knowledge and the victorious army, of sons and daughters, of pure wives, of the highest of ranks, of the spring of Zamzam, of the Station of Abraham, of the Holy Sanctuary, of infallibility, of an orphan's upbringing, of the pilgrimage, of the Quranic recitation, of glorification of the Merciful, of the Ramadan fast, of the flag, of nobility and generosity, the fulfiller of promises, the possessor of longing for God, the one who kindled such longing in others, the owner of the mule (his mount), of noble birth, of the pool, of the scepter, the Prophet of return, the speaker with reward, the one mentioned in the Book, the Prophet-servant of God, the Prophet-treasure of God, the Prophet-proof of God, the Prophet obedience to whom is the same as obedience to God, and to whom disobedience is the same

as disobedience to the Arabian

الْعَرَبِيِّ الْقُرَشِيِّ الزَّمْزَمِيِّ الْمَكِّيِّ التِّهَامِيِّ صَاحِبِ الْوَجْهِ الْجَمِيْلِ وَالطَّرْفِ
الْكَحِيْلِ وَالْخَدِّ الْاَسِيْلِ وَالْكَوْثَرِ وَالسَّلْسَبِيْلِ قَاهِرِ الْمُضَآدِّيْنَ مُبِيْدِ الْكٰفِرِيْنَ
وَقَاتِلِ الْمُشْرِكِيْنَ قَآئِدِ الْغُرِّ الْمُحَجَّلِيْنَ اِلٰى جَنَّاتِ النَّعِيْمِ وَجَوَارِ الْكَرِيْمِ
صَاحِبِ سَيِّدِنَا جِبْرِيْلَ عَلَيْهِ السَّلَامُ وَرَسُوْلِ رَبِّ الْعٰلَمِيْنَ وَشَفِيْعِ الْمُذْنِبِيْنَ
وَغَايَةِ الْغَمَامِ ۝ وَمِصْبَاحِ الظَّلَامِ وَالْقَمَرِ التَّمَامِ صَلَّى اللّٰهُ عَلَيْهِ وَعَلٰى اٰلِهِ
الْمُصْطَفِيْنَ مِنْ اَطْهَرِ جِبِلَّةٍ صَلٰوةً دَآئِمَةً عَلَى الْاَبَدِ غَيْرَ مُضْمَحِلَّةٍ صَلَّى اللّٰهُ
عَلَيْهِ وَعَلٰى اٰلِهِ صَلٰوةً يَّتَجَدَّدُ بِهَا حُبُوْرُهٗ وَيُشَرَّفُ بِهَا فِى الْمِيْعَادِ بَعْثُهٗ وَنُشُوْرُهٗ
فَصَلَّى اللّٰهُ عَلَيْهِ وَعَلٰى اٰلِهِ الْاَنْجُمِ الطَّوَالِعِ صَلٰوةً تَجُوْدُ عَلَيْهِمْ اَجْوَدَ الْغُيُوْثِ
الْهَوَامِعِ اَرْسَلَهٗ مِنْ اَرْجَحِ الْعَرَبِ مِيْزَانًا وَّاَوْضَحِهَا بَيَانًا وَّاَفْصَحِهَا لِسَانًا وَّ
اَشْمَخِهَآ اِيْمَانًا وَّاَعْلٰهَا مَقَامًا وَّاَحْلٰهَا كَلَامًا وَّاَوْفٰهَا ذِمَامًا وَّاَصْفٰهَا رِغَامًا ۝
فَاَوْضَحَ الطَّرِيْقَةَ وَنَصَحَ الْخَلِيْقَةَ وَشَهَّرَ الْاِسْلَامَ وَكَسَّرَ الْاَصْنَامَ وَاَظْهَرَ
الْاَحْكَامَ وَحَظَرَ الْحَرَامَ وَعَمَّ بِالْاِنْعَامِ صَلَّى اللّٰهُ عَلَيْهِ وَعَلٰى اٰلِهِ فِىْ كُلِّ مَحْفِلٍ
وَّمَقَامٍ اَفْضَلَ الصَّلٰوةِ وَالسَّلَامِ صَلَّى اللّٰهُ عَلَيْهِ وَعَلٰى اٰلِهِ عَوْدًا وَّبَدْءًا ۝ صَلٰوةً
تَكُوْنُ ذَخِيْرَةً وَّوِرْدًا صَلَّى اللّٰهُ عَلَيْهِ وَعَلٰى اٰلِهِ صَلٰوةً تَآمَّةً زَاكِيَةً وَّصَلَّى اللّٰهُ
عَلَيْهِ وَعَلٰى اٰلِهِ صَلٰوةً يَّتْبَعُهَا رَوْحٌ وَّ رَيْحَانٌ وَّ يَعْقُبُهَا مَغْفِرَةٌ وَّ رِضْوَانٌ ۝ وَّصَلَّى
اللّٰهُ عَلٰى اَفْضَلِ مَنْ طَابَ مِنْهُ النِّجَارُ وَسَمَا بِهِ الْفَخَارُ وَاسْتَنَارَتْ بِنُوْرِ جَبِيْنِهِ
الْاَقْمَارُ ۝ وَتَضَآئَلَتْ عِنْدَ جُوْدِ يَمِيْنِهِ الْغَمَآئِمُ وَالْبِحَارُ سَيِّدِنَا وَنَبِيِّنَا **مُحَمَّدِ**نِ
الَّذِىْ بِبَاهِرِ آيَاتِهٖٓ اَضَآئَتِ الْاَنْجَادُ وَ الْاَغْوَارُ وَبِمُعْجِزَاتِ اٰيَاتِهٖ نَطَقَ الْكُتُبُ
وَتَوَاتَرَتِ الْاَخْبَارُ صَلَّى اللّٰهُ عَلَيْهِ وَعَلٰى اٰلِهِ وَاَصْحَابِهِ الَّذِيْنَ هَاجَرُوْ لِنُصْرَتِهٖ

Prophet, the Qurayshi Prophet, the Zamzami Prophet, the Meccan Prophet the Tihami Prophet, the possessor of the handsome face, the naturally mascared eyebrows, the noble cheeks, and the springs of *kawthar* and *salsabil*, the conqueror of the Arabic speaking peoples, the destroyer of the unbelievers, the slayer of the polytheists, the guide to the divine garden and vicinity of the benevolent (God) for those with shining faces and shining limbs, the companion of our master Gabriel, peace be upon him, the Messenger of the Lord of the Worlds, the advocate for sinners even though their sins reach the limits of the clouds, the lamp of the darkness and the full moon, may God's blessings be upon him and his most purely chosen family, blessings eternal and everlasting, never diminishing, the blessings of God be upon him and his family! Blessings by means of which his happiness is renewed, his sending and his resurrection on the Promised Day are honored! Bless him and his family, the rising stars, blessings more generous than abundant pouring rains!

Send them to the one who of all the Arabs is more just, more eloquent, greater in faith, higher in station, more articulate in words, more careful of the rights of others and purer in his aversion for others (ie. his enemies)! For he enlightened the Path and advised creation, made Islam known and smashed the idols, made justice appear and forbid the prohibited, and spread favors to the whole world, the blessings of God be upon him and his family at every gathering and every spot, the best of God's blessings and peace be upon him and his family over and over again! Blessings which are a source of treasure, the blessings of God be upon him and his family, complete and pure blessings, and the blessings of God be upon him and his family, blessings ensued by fragrances and scents, succeeded by forgiveness and satisfaction!

And the blessings of God be upon the one through whom the lineage (of mankind) was most permeated with goodness, and because of whom (the notion of) Glory was exalted, and through the light of whose cheeks the moons were illuminated! And the generosity of his right hand illuminated the clouds and seas, our master and Prophet Muḥammad, who by the splendor of his signs illuminated the highlands and the lowlands, and by the miracles of his signs the Book was enunciated and the good news was transmitted, the blessings of God be upon him

and his family, and his Companions who emigrated to help him

وَنَصَرُوْهُ فِيْ هِجْرَتِهٖ فَنِعْمَ الْمُهَاجِرُوْنَ وَنِعْمَ الْاَنْصَارُ صَلٰوةً نَّامِيَةً دَآئِمَةً مَّا سَجَعَتْ فِيْۤ اَيْكِهَا الْاَطْيَارُ وَهَمَعَتْ بِوَبْلِهَا الدِّيْمَةُ الْمِدْرَارُ ضَاعَفَ اللّٰهُ عَلَيْهِ دَآئِمَ صَلَوَاتِهٖ ○ **اَللّٰهُمَّ** صَلِّ عَلٰى سَيِّدِنَا مُحَمَّدٍ وَّعَلٰى اٰلِهِ الطَّيِّبِيْنَ الْكِرَامِ صَلٰوةً مَّوْصُوْلَةً دَآئِمَةَ الْاِتِّصَالِ بِدَوَامِ ذِى الْجَلَالِ وَالْاِكْرَامِ ○ **اَللّٰهُمَّ** صَلِّ عَلٰى سَيِّدِنَا مُحَمَّدِنِ الَّذِىْ هُوَ قُطْبُ الْجَلَالَةِ وَشَمْسُ النُّبُوَّةِ وَالرِّسَالَةِ وَالْهَادِىْ مِنَ الضَّلَالَةِ وَالْمُنْقِذُ مِنَ الْجَهَالَةِ صَلَّى اللّٰهُ عَلَيْهِ وَسَلَّمَ صَلٰوةً دَآئِمَةَ الْاِتِّصَالِ وَالتَّوَالِىْ مُتَعَاقِبَةً ۢ بِتَعَاقُبِ الْاَيَّامِ وَاللَّيَالِىْ ○

اَلْحِزْبُ الثَّامِنُ فِىْ يَوْمِ الْاِثْنَيْنِ

اَللّٰهُمَّ صَلِّ عَلٰى سَيِّدِنَا مُحَمَّدِنِ النَّبِيِّ الزَّاهِدِ رَسُوْلِ الْمَلِكِ الصَّمَدِ الْوَاحِدِ صَلَّى اللّٰهُ عَلَيْهِ وَسَلَّمَ صَلٰوةً دَآئِمَةً اِلٰى مُنْتَهَى الْاَبَدِ بِلَا انْقِطَاعٍ وَّلَا نَفَادٍ صَلٰوةً تُنْجِيْنَا بِهَا مِنْ حَرِّ جَهَنَّمَ وَبِئْسَ الْمِهَادُ ○ **اَللّٰهُمَّ** صَلِّ عَلٰى سَيِّدِنَا مُحَمَّدِنِ النَّبِيِّ الْاُمِّيِّ وَعَلٰى اٰلِهٖ وَسَلِّمْ صَلٰوةً لَّا يُحْصٰى لَهَا عَدَدٌ وَّلَا يُعَدُّ لَهَا مَدَدٌ ○ **اَللّٰهُمَّ** صَلِّ عَلٰى سَيِّدِنَا مُحَمَّدٍ صَلٰوةً تُكْرِمُ بِهَا مَثْوَاهُ وَتُبَلِّغُ بِهَا يَوْمَ الْقِيٰمَةِ مِنَ الشَّفَاعَةِ رِضَاهُ ○ **اَللّٰهُمَّ** صَلِّ عَلٰى سَيِّدِنَا مُحَمَّدِنِ النَّبِيِّ الْاَصِيْلِ السَّيِّدِ النَّبِيْلِ الَّذِىْ جَآءَ بِالْوَحْيِ وَالتَّنْزِيْلِ وَاَوْضَحَ بَيَانَ التَّاْوِيْلِ وَ جَآئَهُ الْاَمِيْنُ سَيِّدُنَا جِبْرِيْلُ عَلَيْهِ السَّلَامُ بِالْكَرَامَةِ وَالتَّفْضِيْلِ وَاَسْرٰى بِهِ الْمَلِكُ الْجَلِيْلُ فِى اللَّيْلِ الْبَهِيْمِ الطَّوِيْلِ فَكَشَفَ لَهٗ عَنْ اَعْلَى الْمَلَكُوْتِ وَاَرَاهُ سَنَآءَ الْجَبَرُوْتِ وَنَظَرَ اِلٰى قُدْرَةِ الْحَيِّ الدَّآئِمِ الْبَاقِى الَّذِىْ لَا يَمُوْتُ ○ صَلَّى اللّٰهُ عَلَيْهِ وَسَلَّمَ صَلٰوةً مَّقْرُوْنَةً ۢ بِالْجَمَالِ وَالْحُسْنِ وَالْكَمَالِ وَالْخَيْرِ وَالْاِفْضَالِ ○ **اَللّٰهُمَّ** صَلِّ عَلٰى سَيِّدِنَا

and helped him to emigrate, and blessed be the Emigrants and blessed be the Helpers, blessings which grow and are eternal for as long as birds coo in the forests, rain streams down in abundance, and multiply the eternal blessings upon him!

O God, bless our master Muḥammad and his good and noble family with blessings which are perpetual and eternally bound up with the duration of the Owner of Majesty and Nobility!

O God, bless our master Muḥammad who is the pole of majesty, the sun of prophethood and the message, the guide away from error and the critic of ignorance, the blessings and peace of God be upon him, eternal blessings bound up with, and successively repeating in accordance with, the alternation of days and nights!

The Eighth Part to be Read on Monday

O God, bless our master Muḥammad, the ascetic Prophet, the Messenger of the Only Eternal King, and God's blessings and peace be upon him, blessings which are eternal, and which reach the farthest limit of eternity, with no break and depletion, blessings which save us from the heat of hellfire, an evil resting place!

O God, bless and grant peace to our master Muḥammad, the unlettered Prophet, and his family, blessings which are uncountable and blessings whose supply is not impeded!

O God, bless our master Muḥammad, blessings which ennoble his abode and blessings which procure on the Day of Judgment pleasure from his intercession!

O God, bless our master Muḥammad, the Prophet of noble origin, the highbred master, who came with inspiration and revelation, and who clarified the meaning of interpretation, and to whom came the faithful one, our master Gabriel, peace be upon him, with honor and dignity, and who journeyed with him to the King, the Glorious One, on the long dark Night and revealed to him the heights of the kingdoms of heaven and showed him the supremacy of the Omnipotence of the heavens, and who saw the Power of the Living, the Eternal, the Abiding, the One Who never dies! God's blessings and peace be upon him, blessings which are permeated with beauty, with charm, with perfection, with goodness and with favor!

O God, bless our master

مُحَمَّدٍ وَّعَلٰى اٰلِ سَيِّدِنَا مُحَمَّدٍ عَدَدَ الْاَقْطَارِ ۝ وَصَلِّ عَلٰى سَيِّدِنَا مُحَمَّدٍ وَّعَلٰى اٰلِ سَيِّدِنَا مُحَمَّدٍ عَدَدَ وَرَقِ الْاَشْجَارِ ۝ وَصَلِّ عَلٰى سَيِّدِنَا مُحَمَّدٍ وَّعَلٰى اٰلِ سَيِّدِنَا مُحَمَّدٍ عَدَدَ زَبَدِ الْبِحَارِ ۝ وَصَلِّ عَلٰى سَيِّدِنَا مُحَمَّدٍ وَّعَلٰى اٰلِ سَيِّدِنَا مُحَمَّدٍ عَدَدَ الْاَنْهَارِ ۝ وَصَلِّ عَلٰى سَيِّدِنَا مُحَمَّدٍ وَّعَلٰى اٰلِ سَيِّدِنَا مُحَمَّدٍ عَدَدَ رَمْلِ الصَّحَارٰى وَالْقِفَارِ ۝ وَصَلِّ عَلٰى سَيِّدِنَا مُحَمَّدٍ وَّعَلٰى اٰلِ سَيِّدِنَا مُحَمَّدٍ عَدَدَ ثِقْلِ الْجِبَالِ وَالْاَحْجَارِ ۝ وَصَلِّ عَلٰى سَيِّدِنَا مُحَمَّدٍ وَّعَلٰى اٰلِ سَيِّدِنَا مُحَمَّدٍ عَدَدَ اَهْلِ الْجَنَّةِ وَاَهْلِ النَّارِ ۝ وَصَلِّ عَلٰى سَيِّدِنَا مُحَمَّدٍ وَّعَلٰى اٰلِ سَيِّدِنَا مُحَمَّدٍ عَدَدَ الْاَبْرَارِ وَالْفُجَّارِ ۝ وَصَلِّ عَلٰى سَيِّدِنَا مُحَمَّدٍ وَّعَلٰى اٰلِ سَيِّدِنَا مُحَمَّدٍ عَدَدَ مَا يَخْتَلِفُ بِهِ الَّيْلُ وَالنَّهَارُ ۝ وَاجْعَلِ اللّٰهُمَّ صَلَاتَنَا عَلَيْهِ حِجَابًا مِّنْ عَذَابِ النَّارِ وَسَبَبًا لِّاِبَاحَةِ دَارِالْقَرَارِ اِنَّكَ اَنْتَ الْعَزِيْزُ الْغَفَّارُ ۝ وَصَلَّى اللّٰهُ عَلٰى سَيِّدِنَا مُحَمَّدٍ وَّعَلٰى اٰلِهِ الطَّيِّبِيْنَ وَذُرِّيَّتِهِ الْمُبَارَكِيْنَ وَصَحَابَتِهِ الْاَكْرَمِيْنَ وَاَزْوَاجِهٖ اُمَّهَاتِ الْمُؤْمِنِيْنَ صَلٰوةً مَّوْصُوْلَةً تَتَرَدَّدُ اِلٰى يَوْمِ الدِّيْنِ ۝ **اَللّٰهُمَّ** صَلِّ عَلٰى سَيِّدِ الْاَبْرَارِ وَزَيْنِ الْمُرْسَلِيْنَ الْاَخْيَارِ وَاَكْرَمِ مَنْ اَظْلَمَ عَلَيْهِ الَّيْلُ وَاَشْرَقَ عَلَيْهِ النَّهَارُ ۝ ثَلَاثًا ۝ **اَللّٰهُمَّ** يَاذَا الْمَنِّ الَّذِىْ لَا يُكَافٰى امْتِنَانُهٗ وَالطَّوْلِ الَّذِىْ لَا يُجَازٰى اِنْعَامُهٗ وَ اِحْسَانُهٗ نَسْاَلُكَ بِكَ وَلَا نَسْاَلُكَ بِاَحَدٍ غَيْرِكَ اَنْ تُطْلِقَ اَلْسِنَتَنَا عِنْدَ السُّؤَالِ وَ تُوَفِّقَنَا لِصَالِحِ الْاَعْمَالِ وَتَجْعَلَنَا مِنَ الْاٰمِنِيْنَ يَوْمَ الرَّجْفِ وَالزَّلَازِلِ يَا ذَالْعِزَّةِ وَالْجَلَالِ ۝ اَسْاَلُكَ يَا نُوْرَ النُّوْرِ قَبْلَ الْاَزْمِنَةِ وَالدُّهُوْرِ ۝ اَنْتَ الْبَاقِىْ بِلَا زَوَالٍ الْغَنِىُّ بِلَا مِثَالٍ الْقُدُّوْسُ الطَّاهِرُ الْعَلِىُّ الْقَاهِرُ الَّذِىْ لَا يُحِيْطُ بِهٖ مَكَانٌ وَّ لَا يَشْتَمِلُ عَلَيْهِ زَمَانٌ ۝ اَسْئَلُكَ بِاَسْمَآئِكَ الْحُسْنٰى كُلِّهَا وَبِاَعْظَمِ

Muḥammad and the family of our master Muḥammad as many times as there are drops of rain!

And bless our master Muḥammad and the family of our master Muḥammad as many times as there are leaves on the trees! And bless our master Muḥammad and the family of our master Muḥammad in as much abundance as there is foam upon the sea!

And bless our master Muḥammad and the family of our master Muḥammad as many times as there are rivers! And bless our master Muḥammad and the family of our master Muḥammad as many times as there are grains of sand in the desert and in the wilderness!

And bless our master Muḥammad and the family of our master Muḥammad as much as the weight of all mountains and all rocks!And bless our master Muḥammad and the family of our master Muḥammad as many times as there are dwellers of the Garden and dwellers of the Fire! And bless our master Muḥammad and the family of our master Muḥammad as many times as there are righteous ones and as many times as there are corrupt ones!And bless our master Muḥammad and the family of our master Muḥammad as many times as the night has alternated with the day!

And make, **O God**, our asking for blessings upon him a shield which gives us protection from the punishment of the Fire and a means of us gaining permission to enter the Abode of Permanence, for You are the Mighty, the Forgiving! And God's blessings and peace be upon our master Muḥammad and upon his virtuous family, his blessed descendants, his honored Companions and his wives, Mothers of the Believers, blessings which are continual and frequent until the Day of Judgment!

O God, bless the Master of the righteous, the adornment of the Messengers, the choicest and noblest ever to have been cloaked in the darkness of the night or bathed in the light of the day! (**three times**)

O God, O Master of Favor, whose strength and might are unequalled, and whose favor and virtue are beyond compare, we ask You and nobody else but You, to loosen our tongues in beseeching You, and grant us success in doing good works, and make us among the trustworthy ones on the Day of Convulsions and Earthquakes, O Master of Might and Glory! I ask You, O Light of the Light which was before Time and Eternity! You are the Abiding with no ending, the Rich with no equal, the Holy, the Pure, the High, the Powerful, the One Who is neither encompassed by space nor contained by time! I ask You in all of Your most

beautiful names and in the Greatest

اَسْمَآئِكَ اِلَيْكَ وَاَشْرَفِهَا عِنْدَكَ مَنْزِلَةً وَّاَجْزَلِهَا عِنْدَكَ ثَوَابًا وَّ اَسْرَعِهَا مِنْكَ
اِجَابَةً وَّبِاسْمِكَ الْمَخْزُوْنِ الْمَكْنُوْنِ الْجَلِيْلِ الْاَجَلِّ الْكَبِيْرِ الْاَكْبَرِ الْعَظِيْمِ
الْاَعْظَمِ الَّذِىْ تُحِبُّهٗ وَتَرْضٰى عَمَّنْ دَعَاكَ بِهٖ وَتَسْتَجِيْبُ لَهٗ دُعَآءَهٗ ○ اَسْئَلُكَ
اللّٰهُمَّ بِلَآ اِلٰهَ اِلَّآ اَنْتَ الْحَنَّانُ الْمَنَّانُ بَدِيْعُ السَّمٰوٰتِ وَالْاَرْضِ ذُوالْجَلَالِ
وَالْاِكْرَامِ عٰلِمُ الْغَيْبِ وَالشَّهَادَةِ الْكَبِيْرُ الْمُتَعَالِ ○ وَ اَسْئَلُكَ بِاسْمِكَ الْعَظِيْمِ
الْاَعْظَمِ الَّذِىْٓ اِذَا دُعِيتَ بِهٖٓ اَجَبْتَ وَاِذَا سُئِلْتَ بِهٖٓ اَعْطَيْتَ وَاَسْئَلُكَ بِاسْمِكَ
الَّذِىْ يَذِلُّ لِعَظْمَتِهِ الْعُظَمَآءُ وَالْمُلُوْكُ وَالسِّبَاعُ وَالْهَوَآمُّ وَكُلُّ شَىْءٍ خَلَقْتَهٗ يَآ
اللّٰهُ يَا رَبِّ اسْتَجِبْ دَعْوَتِىْ يَا مَنْ لَّهُ الْعِزَّةُ وَالْجَبَرُوْتُ يَا ذَاالْمُلْكِ وَالْمَلَكُوْتِ
يَا مَنْ هُوَ حَيٌّ لَّا يَمُوْتُ سُبْحَانَكَ رَبِّ مَآ اَعْظَمَ شَانُكَ وَ اَرْفَعَ مَكَانُكَ اَنْتَ
رَبِّىْ يَا مُتَقَدِّسًا فِىْ جَبَرُوْتِهٖٓ اِلَيْكَ اَرْغَبُ وَاِيَّاكَ اَرْهَبُ يَا عَظِيْمُ يَا كَبِيْرُ يَا جَبَّارُ
يَا قَادِرُ يَا قَوِىُّ تَبَارَكْتَ يَا عَظِيْمُ تَعَالَيْتَ يَا عَلِيْمُ سُبْحَانَكَ يَا عَظِيْمُ سُبْحَانَكَ
يَا جَلِيْلُ اَسْئَلُكَ بِاسْمِكَ الْعَظِيْمِ التَّآمِّ الْكَبِيْرِ اَنْ لَّا تُسَلِّطَ عَلَيْنَا جَبَّارًا عَنِيْدًا وَّلَا
شَيْطَانًا مَّرِيْدًا وَّلَآ اِنْسَانًا حَسُوْدًا وَّلَا ضَعِيفًا مِّنْ خَلْقِكَ وَلَا شَدِيْدًا وَّلَا بَآرًّا
وَّلَا فَاجِرًا وَّلَا عَبِيْدًا وَّلَا عَنِيْدًا ○ **اَللّٰهُمَّ** اِنِّىْٓ اَسْئَلُكَ فَاِنِّىْٓ اَشْهَدُ اَنَّكَ اَنْتَ اللّٰهُ
الَّذِىْ لَآ اِلٰهَ اِلَّآ اَنْتَ الْوَاحِدُ الْاَحَدُ الصَّمَدُ الَّذِىْ لَمْ يَلِدْ وَلَمْ يُوْلَدْ وَلَمْ يَكُنْ لَّهٗ
كُفُوًا اَحَدٌ ؕ يَا هُوَ يَامَنْ لَّا هُوَ اِلَّا هُوَ يَا مَنْ لَّآ اِلٰهَ اِلَّا هُوَ يَآ اَزَلِىُّ يَآ اَبَدِىُّ يَا
دَهْرِىُّ يَا دَيْمُوْمِىُّ يَا مَنْ هُوَ الْحَىُّ الَّذِىْ لَا يَمُوْتُ يَآ اِلٰهَنَا وَاِلٰهَ كُلِّ شَىْءٍ اِلٰهًا
وَّاحِدًا لَّآ اِلٰهَ اِلَّآ اَنْتَ ○ **اَللّٰهُمَّ** فَاطِرَ السَّمٰوٰتِ وَالْاَرْضِ عٰلِمَ الْغَيْبِ وَالشَّهَادَةِ
الرَّحْمٰنُ الرَّحِيْمُ الْحَىُّ الْقَيُّوْمُ الدَّيَّانُ الْحَنَّانُ الْمَنَّانُ الْبَاعِثُ الْوَارِثُ ذَالْجَلَالِ

of Your names, and for the sake of the rank most noble to You, and for the sake of the reward most plentiful with You, and for the sake of the promptest response from You, and in Your Protected and Hidden Name, the Most Exalted of the Exalted, the Greatest of the Great, the Most Magnificent of the Magnificent, the One Who responds to and satisfies him who calls upon You in them and whose prayer is accepted!

I ask You, O God, there is no god but You, the Compassionate, the Benefactor, the Creator of the Heavens and the Earth, Master of Glory and honor, Knower of the Unseen and the Seen, the Great, the Exalted!

I ask You in Your Greatest Name, in which, when we pray, our prayer is granted, and in which, when we make a request, our request is granted!

And I ask You in the name which humbles with its might the mighty ones, the kings, the lions, the reptiles and every thing You have created!

O God, O Lord, accept my prayer! O You to Whom is the majesty and omnipotence, O Master of Sovereignty and Kingdoms, O You Who are the Living Who never dies, glory to You! Lord, What is greater than Your Rank, higher than Your Position? You are my Lord! O Holy One in His Omnipotence, I beseech You and I fear You! O Great, O Majestic, O Powerful, O Almighty, O Strong, You have blessed Yourself! O Great One, You have exalted Yourself! O Knowing One, glory to You!

O Great One, glory to You! O Splendid One, I ask You in Your great, perfect and majestic name, not to give dominion over me to the tyrant, the stubborn one, rebellious Satan, an envious man, the weak among Your creation, the oppressive one, the ruinous one, the corrupt one, the enslaved one, or the willful one! O God, I ask You and I bear witness that You are God, and there is no god but You, the One, the Only, the Eternal, the One Who neither begets nor is begotten, and there is nothing like Him.

O He! O the One Who there is no other he but He!

O the One Who there is no god but He!

O my Infinity! O my Eternity!

O my Destiny! O my Everlasting! O the One Who is the Living Who does not die! O our God and God of every thing, God, Alone, there is no god but You!

O God, Creator of the Heavens and the Earth, Knower of the Unseen and the Seen, the Compassionate, the Merciful, the Living, the Everlasting, the Judge, the Benefactor, the Munificent, the Reviver, the

Inheritor, the Master of Glory

وَالْإِكْرَامِ۝ قُلُوْبُ الْخَلَآئِقِ بِيَدِكَ نَوَاصِيْهِمْ اِلَيْكَ فَاَنْتَ تَزْرَعُ الْخَيْرَ فِيْ قُلُوْبِهِمْ وَتَمْحُو الشَّرَّ اِذَاشِئْتَ مِنْهُمْ۝ فَاَسْئَلُكَ اللّٰهُمَّ اَنْ تَمْحُوَ مِنْ قَلْبِيْ كُلَّ شَيْءٍ تَكْرَهُهٗ وَاَنْ تَحْشُوَ قَلْبِيْ مِنْ خَشْيَتِكَ وَمَعْرِفَتِكَ وَ رَهْبَتِكَ وَالرَّغْبَةَ فِيْمَا عِنْدَكَ وَالْاَمْنَ وَالْعَافِيَةَ وَاعْطِفْ عَلَيْنَا بِالرَّحْمَةِ وَالْبَرَكَةِ مِنْكَ وَاَلْهِمْنَا الصَّوَابَ وَالْحِكْمَةَ۝ فَنَسْئَلُكَ اللّٰهُمَّ عِلْمَ الْخَآئِفِيْنَ وَاِنَابَةَ الْمُخْبِتِيْنَ وَاِخْلَاصَ الْمُوْقِنِيْنَ وَشُكْرَ الصَّابِرِيْنَ وَتَوْبَةَ الصِّدِّيْقِيْنَ ۝ وَنَسْئَلُكَ اللّٰهُمَّ بِنُوْرِ وَجْهِكَ الَّذِيْ مَلَاَ اَرْكَانَ عَرْشِكَ اَنْ تَزْرَعَ فِيْ قَلْبِيْ مَعْرِفَتَكَ حَتّٰٓى اَعْرِفَكَ حَقَّ مَعْرِفَتِكَ كَمَا يَنْبَغِيْٓ اَنْ تُعْرَفَ بِهٖ وَصَلَّى اللّٰهُ عَلٰى سَيِّدِنَا مُحَمَّدٍ خَاتِمِ النَّبِيّٖنَ وَاِمَامِ الْمُرْسَلِيْنَ وَعَلٰى اٰلِهٖ وَصَحْبِهٖ وَسَلَّمَ تَسْلِيْمًا وَّالْحَمْدُ لِلّٰهِ رَبِّ الْعٰلَمِيْنَ۝

اَللّٰهُمَّ اغْفِرْ لِمُؤَلِّفِهٖ وَارْحَمْهُ وَاجْعَلْهُ مِنَ الْمَحْشُوْرِيْنَ فِيْ زُمْرَةِ النَّبِيّٖنَ وَالصِّدِّيْقِيْنَ وَالشُّهَدَآءِ وَالصَّالِحِيْنَ بِفَضْلِكَ يَا رَحْمٰنُ۝ وَاغْفِرِ اللّٰهُمَّ لَنَا وَلِوَالِدَيْنَا وَلِاَسَاتِذَتِنَا وَلِمَشَآئِخِنَا وَلِجَمِيْعِ الْمُؤْمِنِيْنَ وَالْمُؤْمِنَاتِ وَالْمُسْلِمِيْنَ وَالْمُسْلِمَاتِ الْاَحْيَآءِ مِنْهُمْ وَالْاَمْوَاتِ بِرَحْمَتِكَ يَآ اَرْحَمَ الرَّاحِمِيْنَ۝ وَاَنْ تَتُوْبَ عَلَيْهِ اِنَّكَ غَفُوْرٌ رَّحِيْمٌ۝ اَللّٰهُمَّ اٰمِيْنَ يَا رَبَّ الْعٰلَمِيْنَ۝

ثُمَّ تُقْرَاُ هٰذِهِ الْكَلِمَاتِ اَرْبَعَةَ عَشَرَ مَرَّةً وَّهِيَ هٰذِهٖ۝

اَللّٰهُمَّ صَلِّ عَلٰى بَدْرِ التَّمَامِ۝ **اَللّٰهُمَّ** صَلِّ عَلٰى نُوْرِ الظَّلَامِ۝ **اَللّٰهُمَّ** صَلِّ عَلٰى مِفْتَاحِ دَارِ السَّلَامِ۝ **اَللّٰهُمَّ** صَلِّ عَلَى الشَّفِيْعِ فِيْ جَمِيْعِ الْاَنَامِ۝

ثُمَّ تُقْرَاُ هٰذِهِ الْاَبْيَاتُ الْمَنْسُوْبَةُ لِلْمُؤَلِّفِ:-

يَا رَحْمَةَ اللّٰهِ اِنِّيْ خَآئِفٌ وَّجِلٌ ۝

and Honor! The hearts of all creatures are between Your hands, we entrust them to You, for You cause goodness to grow in their hearts and You erase the evil from them as You like!

So I ask You, **O God**, that You erase from my heart everything that You hate and fill my heart with fear of You, knowledge of You, awe of You, longing for what is with You, and security and well-being, and have pity on us with mercy and blessings from You, and inspire in us that which is proper and wise!

And I ask You, **O God**, for the knowledge of those who fear, the repentance of the humble, the sincerity of those who are certain, the gratitude of the patient, and the penitence of the truthful ones!

And we ask You, **O God**, by the light of Your Face which fills every corner of Your Throne, that You cause to grow in my heart knowledge of You until I know You, Your True Knowledge, in a way that You should be known, and the blessings and abundant peace of God be upon our master Muḥammad, the Seal of the Prophets and Leader of the Messengers, and upon his family and Companions, and praise be to God, the Lord of the Worlds!

O God, forgive the author and have mercy upon him and make him among those who are gathered together in the company of the Prophets and truthful ones, and martyrs and righteous ones, through Your Favor, O Compassionate One!

And forgive us, **O God**, and our parents, our masters, our sheikhs and all the believing men and women, and surrendering men and women, alive and dead, through Your mercy, O Most Merciful of the Merciful! And accept his repentance for You are the Forgiving, the Merciful!

O God, Amen, O Lord of the worlds!

(Then recite the following phrases fourteen times each)

O God, bless the perfect full moon! **O God**, bless the light of the darkness! **O God**, bless the key to the abode of peace! **O God**, bless the intercessor of all of creation!

(Then recite the following verses ascribed to the author)

O Mercy of God! I am afraid, filled with dread, O Grace of God!

يَا نِعْمَةَ اللّٰهِ اِنِّىْ مُفْلِسٌ عَانٍ ○
وَلَيْسَ لِىْ عَمَلٌ اَلْقٰى الْعَلِيْمَ بِهٖ ○
سِوٰى مَحَبَّتِكَ الْعُظْمٰى وَاِيْمَانِىْ ○
فَكُنْ اَمَانِىَ مِنْ شَرِّ الْحَيٰوةِ وَمِنْ ○
شَرِّ الْمَمَاتِ وَمِنْ اِحْرَاقِ جُثْمَانِىْ ○
وَكُنْ غِنَاىَ الَّذِىْ مَا بَعْدَهٗ فَلَسٌ ○
وَكُنْ فَكَاكِىَ مِنْ اَغْلَالِ عِصْيَانِىْ ○
تَحِيَّةُ الصَّمَدِ الْمَوْلٰى وَرَحْمَتُهٗ ○
مَا غَنَّتِ الْوُرْقُ فِىْ اَوْرَاقِ اَغْصَانٍ ○
عَلَيْكَ يَا عُرْوَتِىَ الْوُثْقٰى وَيَا سَنَدِىْ ○
اَلْاَوْفٰى وَمَنْ مَّدْحُهٗ رَوْحِىْ وَرَيْحَانِىْ ○

ثُمَّ تُقْرَأُ الْفَاتِحَةُ لِلْمُؤَلِّفِ وَهٰذَا الدُّعَآءُ
يُقْرَأُ عَقِيْبَ خَتْمِ دَلَآئِلِ الْخَيْرٰتِ○

بِسْمِ اللّٰهِ الرَّحْمٰنِ الرَّحِيْمِ○

اَللّٰهُمَّ اشْرَحْ بِالصَّلٰوةِ عَلَيْهِ صُدُوْرَنَا ○ وَيَسِّرْبِهَآ اُمُوْرَنَا ○ وَفَرِّجْ بِهَا هُمُوْمَنَا ○ وَاكْشِفْ بِهَا غُمُوْمَنَا ○ وَاغْفِرْبِهَا ذُنُوْبَنَا ○ وَاقْضِ بِهَا دُيُوْنَنَا ○ وَاَصْلِحْ بِهَآ اَحْوَالَنَا○ وَبَلِّغْ بِهَآ اٰمَالَنَا○ وَتَقَبَّلْ بِهَا تَوْبَتَنَا○ وَاغْسِلْ بِهَا حُوْبَتَنَا○ وَانْصُرْ بِهَا حُجَّتَنَا ○ وَطَهِّرْ بِهَآ اَلْسِنَتَنَا ○ وَاٰنِسْ بِهَا وَحْشَتَنَا ○ وَارْحَمْ بِهَا غُرْبَتَنَا ○ وَاجْعَلْهَا نُوْرًا بَيْنَ اَيْدِيْنَا وَمِنْ خَلْفِنَا○ وَعَنْ اَيْمَانِنَا○ وَعَنْ شَمَآئِلِنَا○ وَمِنْ فَوْقِنَا

I am ruined, help me!
And I have no good acts with which to meet The Knowing!
Save great love for You and my faith!
Be my protection from the evil of life and from
The evil of death and from the burning of my mortal frame!
And fulfill my every need saving me from ruin!
And be my release from the fetters of disobedience!
Salutations of the Eternal, the Master, and His Mercy,
As abundant as the leaves in the leafiness of the boughs,
Upon you, O Trusty Handhold, O my Support!
The Faithful One and upon whomever praises him
spiritually and fragrantly!

(Then recite the *Fatihah* for the author and the following supplication which is the seal of *The Guide to Goodness*)

In the name of God, The Merciful, the Compassionate

O God, through our asking for blessings upon him expand our hearts! And thereby ease our affairs! And dispel our anxieties! And remove our sorrows!

And thereby forgive our sins! And relieve our debts! And improve our states!And thereby fulfill our hopes!

And accept our repentance!

And cleanse our misdeeds! And thereby help our pleas! And purify our tongues!

And end our loneliness! And thereby relieve our separation!

And make it a light in front of us and behind us! To our right!

And to our left! And above us

وَمِنْ تَحْتِنَا ۝ وَفِى حَيَاتِنَا وَمَوْتِنَا ۝ وَفِى قُبُوْرِنَا وَحَشْرِنَا وَنَشْرِنَا وَظِلًّا فِى الْقِيٰمَةِ عَلٰى رُءُوْسِنَا ۝ وَثَقِّلْ بِهَا مَوَازِيْنَ حَسَنَاتِنَا ۝ وَاَدِمْ بَرَكَاتِهَا عَلَيْنَا حَتّٰى نَلْقٰى نَبِيَّنَا وَسَيِّدَنَا مُحَمَّدًا صَلَّى اللّٰهُ عَلَيْهِ وَعَلٰى اٰلِهٖ وَسَلَّمَ وَنَحْنُ اٰمِنُوْنَ مُطْمَئِنُّوْنَ فَرِحُوْنَ مُسْتَبْشِرُوْنَ ۝ وَلَا تُفَرِّقْ بَيْنَنَا وَبَيْنَهٗ حَتّٰى تُدْخِلَنَا مَدْخَلَهٗ وَتُؤْوِيْنَآ اِلٰى جِوَارِهِ الْكَرِيْمِ مَعَ الَّذِيْنَ اَنْعَمْتَ عَلَيْهِمْ مِّنَ النَّبِيّيْنَ وَالصِّدِّيْقِيْنَ وَالشُّهَدَآءِ وَالصّٰلِحِيْنَ وَحَسُنَ اُولٰٓئِكَ رَفِيْقًا ۝ **اَللّٰهُمَّ** اِنَّآ اٰمَنَّا بِهٖ صَلَّى اللّٰهُ عَلَيْهِ وَسَلَّمَ وَلَمْ نَرَهٗ فَمَتِّعْنَا اللّٰهُمَّ فِى الدَّارَيْنِ بِرُؤْيَتِهٖ وَثَبِّتْ قُلُوْبَنَا عَلٰى مَحَبَّتِهٖ ۝ وَاسْتَعْمِلْنَا عَلٰى سُنَّتِهٖ ۝ وَتَوَفَّنَا عَلٰى مِلَّتِهٖ ۝ وَاحْشُرْنَا فِى زُمْرَتِهِ النَّاجِيَةِ وَحِزْبِهِ الْمُفْلِحِيْنَ ۝ وَانْفَعْنَا بِمَا انْطَوَتْ عَلَيْهِ قُلُوْبَنَا مِنْ مَّحَبَّتِهٖ صَلَّى اللّٰهُ عَلَيْهِ وَسَلَّمَ يَوْمَ لَا جَدَّ وَلَا مَالَ وَلَا بَنِيْنَ ۝ وَاَوْرِدْنَا حَوْضَهُ الْاَصْفٰى ۝ وَاسْقِنَا بِكَاْسِهِ الْاَوْفٰى ۝ وَيَسِّرْ عَلَيْنَا زِيَارَةَ حَرَمِكَ وَحَرَمِهٖ مِنْ قَبْلِ اَنْ تُمِيْتَنَا ۝ وَاَدِمْ عَلَيْنَا الْاِقَامَةَ بِحَرَمِكَ وَحَرَمِهٖ صَلَّى اللّٰهُ عَلَيْهِ وَسَلَّمَ اِلٰٓى اَنْ نَّتَوَفّٰى ۝ **اَللّٰهُمَّ** اِنَّا نَسْتَشْفِعُ بِهٖٓ اِلَيْكَ اِذْ هُوَ اَوْجَهُ الشُّفَعَآءُ اِلَيْكَ ۝ وَنُقْسِمُ بِهٖ عَلَيْكَ اِذْ هُوَ اَعْظَمُ مَنْ اُقْسِمَ بِحَقِّهٖ عَلَيْكَ ۝ وَنَتَوَسَّلُ بِهٖٓ اِلَيْكَ اِذْ هُوَ اَقْرَبُ الْوَسَآئِلِ اِلَيْكَ ۝ نَشْكُوْآ اِلَيْكَ يَا رَبِّ قَسْوَةَ قُلُوْبِنَا ۝ وَكَثْرَةَ ذُنُوْبِنَا ۝ وَطُوْلَ اٰمَالِنَا ۝ وَفَسَادَ اَعْمَالِنَا ۝ وَتَكَاسُلَنَا عَنِ اطَّاعَاتِ ۝ وَهُجُوْمَنَا عَلَى الْمُخَالَفَاتِ ۝ فَنِعْمَ الْمُشْتَكٰٓى اِلَيْهِ اَنْتَ يَا رَبِّ بِكَ نَسْتَنْصِرُ عَلٰٓى اَعْدَآئِنَا ۝ وَاَنْفُسِنَا فَانْصُرْنَا ۝ وَعَلٰى فَضْلِكَ نَتَوَكَّلُ فِى صَلَاحِنَا فَلَا تَكِلْنَآ اِلٰى غَيْرِكَ يَا رَبَّنَا ۝ **اَللّٰهُمَّ** وَاِلٰى جَنَابِ رَسُوْلِكَ صَلَّى اللّٰهُ عَلَيْهِ وَسَلَّمَ نَنْتَسِبُ فَلَا تُبْعِدْنَا ۝ وَبِبَابِكَ نَقِفُ فَلَا

and beneath us!

And in our lives and in our deaths! And in our graves and in our gathering and in our resurrection and shade for us on the Day of Judgment over our heads!

And weigh down the scales thereby with good actions! And repeat its blessing on us until we meet with our Prophet our master Muḥammad, God's blessings and peace be upon him and his family, and we are believing, we are certain, we are overjoyed and we are the receivers of good news!

And do not separate us from him until You make us enter through his entrance hall and accommodate us in his noble neighborhood with those You have favored among the Prophets, the truthful ones, the martyrs and the righteous ones, and what a fine company they are! **O God**, we have believed in him, the blessings and peace of God be upon him, without seeing him, so make us enjoy, **O God**, a vision of him in the two realms and keep our hearts always in love with him!And establish us upon his way!

And cause us to die following his religion! And resurrect us in his secure company and party of success! And avail us of that love of him, the blessings and peace of God be upon him, which is locked away in our hearts on the day when there will be no ancestors, no wealth and no sons (that is, to speak up for us)! And have us drink at his purest pool! To drink from his fullest chalice!

And facilitate for us a visit to Your Sacred Place (Mecca) and his sacred place (Medina) before you cause us to die! And make our stay at Your Sacred Place and his sacred place, the blessings and peace of God be upon him, last until we pass away!

O God, we seek his intercession with You, for his is the most lauded intercession with You! And we entreat You through him for he is the greatest one to entreat You! We seek access to You through him for his is the closest access to You! We complain to You, O Lord, about the hardness of our hearts!And the abundance of our sins!

And the extent of our hopes! And the imperfection of our actions! And our laziness to do good deeds!And our haste to commit bad deeds! Bestow upon this plaintiff, You, O Lord, victory over our enemies! And help our souls! And through Your Grace make us rely solely on our good acts and not upon anything else, O our Lord!

O God, we associate ourselves with the honor of Your Messenger, the blessings and peace of God be upon him, so do not distance us! And we

stop at Your Door so do

تَطْرُدْنَا ○ وَاِيَّاكَ نَسْئَلُ فَلَا تُخَيِّبْنَا ○ **اَللّٰهُمَّ** ارْحَمْ تَضَرُّعَنَا وَاٰمِنْ خَوْفَنَا ○ وَتَقَبَّلْ اَعْمَالَنَا وَاَصْلِحْ اَحْوَالَنَا ○ وَاجْعَلْ بِطَاعَتِكَ اِشْتِغَالَنَا ○ وَاِلَى الْخَيْرِ مَآلِنَا ○ وَحَقِّقْ بِالزِّيَادَةِ اٰمَالَنَا ○ وَاخْتِمْ بِالسَّعَادَةِ اٰجَالَنَا ○ هٰذَا ذُلُّنَا ظَاهِرٌ بَيْنَ يَدَيْكَ وَحَالُنَا لَا يَخْفٰى عَلَيْكَ ○ اَمَرْتَنَا فَتَرَكْنَا ○ وَنَهَيْتَنَا فَارْتَكَبْنَا ○ وَلَا يَسَعُنَآ اِلَّا عَفْوُكَ ○ فَاعْفُ عَنَّا يَا خَيْرَ مَأْمُوْلٍ ○ وَاَكْرَمَ مَسْئُوْلٍ ○ اِنَّكَ عَفُوٌّ غَفُوْرٌ رَّحِيْمٌ يَّآ اَرْحَمَ الرَّاحِمِيْنَ ○ وَصَلَّى اللّٰهُ عَلٰى سَيِّدِنَا مُحَمَّدٍ وَّعَلٰٓى اٰلِهٖ وَصَحْبِهٖ وَسَلَّمَ تَسْلِيْمًا وَّالْحَمْدُ لِلّٰهِ رَبِّ الْعَالَمِيْنَ ○

بِـــــــالْـــــــخَيْـــــــرِ

تَـــــــمَّـــــــتْ

not turn us away!

And we ask You alone so do not disappoint us!

O God, have mercy upon our imploring and allay our fear!

Accept our actions and make us righteous! Make obedience to You our main occupation!

And make us use our wealth only for good! And fulfill our hopes and more!

And seal our final destinations with happiness!

Thus is our lowliness made clear before You and our condition is not hidden from You!

You have commanded us and we have been remiss! You have forbidden us and we have transgressed! Nothing is wider than Your Clemency!

So pardon us, O Best Fulfiller of Hopes!

And Most Generous Requestee!

For You are the Pardoner, the Forgiver, the Merciful, O Most Merciful of the Merciful!

And the blessings and abundant peace of God be upon our master Muḥammad and upon his family and Companions and praise be to God, Lord of the Worlds!

Completed with Goodness

دُعائے اِعْتِصَام

بِسْمِ اللّٰهِ الرَّحْمٰنِ الرَّحِيْمِ○

اَللّٰهُ لَآ اِلٰهَ اِلَّا هُوَ الْحَيُّ الْقَيُّوْمُ لَا تَاْخُذُهٗ سِنَةٌ وَّلَا نَوْمٌ لَّهٗ مَا فِي السَّمٰوٰتِ وَمَا فِي الْاَرْضِ مَنْ ذَا الَّذِيْ يَشْفَعُ عِنْدَهٗٓ اِلَّا بِاِذْنِهٖ يَعْلَمُ مَا بَيْنَ اَيْدِيْهِمْ وَمَا خَلْفَهُمْ وَلَا يُحِيْطُوْنَ بِشَيْءٍ مِّنْ عِلْمِهٖٓ اِلَّا بِمَا شَآءَ وَسِعَ كُرْسِيُّهُ السَّمٰوٰتِ وَالْاَرْضَ وَلَا يَـُٔوْدُهٗ حِفْظُهُمَا وَهُوَ الْعَلِيُّ الْعَظِيْمُ ○ لَآ اِكْرَاهَ فِي الدِّيْنِ قَدْ تَّبَيَّنَ الرُّشْدُ مِنَ الْغَيِّ فَمَنْ يَّكْفُرْ بِالطَّاغُوْتِ وَيُؤْمِنْۢ بِاللّٰهِ فَقَدِ اسْتَمْسَكَ بِالْعُرْوَةِ الْوُثْقٰى لَا انْفِصَامَ لَهَا وَاللّٰهُ سَمِيْعٌ عَلِيْمٌ ○ اَللّٰهُ وَلِيُّ الَّذِيْنَ اٰمَنُوْا يُخْرِجُهُمْ مِّنَ الظُّلُمٰتِ اِلَى النُّوْرِ وَالَّذِيْنَ كَفَرُوْٓا اَوْلِيٰٓـؤُهُمُ الطَّاغُوْتُ يُخْرِجُوْنَهُمْ مِّنَ النُّوْرِ اِلَى الظُّلُمٰتِ اُولٰٓئِكَ اَصْحٰبُ النَّارِ هُمْ فِيْهَا خٰلِدُوْنَ ○

ایکبار اِعْتَصَمْتُ بِاللّٰهِ الْفَتَّاحِ الْقَابِضِ اَعُوْذُ بِاللّٰهِ السَّمِيْعِ الْعَلِيْمِ مِنَ الشَّيْطٰنِ الرَّجِيْمِ ○ بِسْمِ اللّٰهِ الرَّحْمٰنِ الرَّحِيْمِ ○ وَاِذَا جَآءَكَ الَّذِيْنَ يُؤْمِنُوْنَ بِاٰيٰتِنَا فَقُلْ سَلٰمٌ عَلَيْكُمْ كَتَبَ رَبُّكُمْ عَلٰى نَفْسِهِ الرَّحْمَةَ اَنَّهٗ مَنْ عَمِلَ مِنْكُمْ سُوْٓءًا بِجَهَالَةٍ ثُمَّ تَابَ مِنْۢ بَعْدِهٖ وَاَصْلَحَ فَاَنَّهٗ غَفُوْرٌ رَّحِيْمٌ ○ وَكَذٰلِكَ نُفَصِّلُ الْاٰيٰتِ وَلِتَسْتَبِيْنَ سَبِيْلُ الْمُجْرِمِيْنَ ○ قُلْ اِنِّيْ نُهِيْتُ اَنْ اَعْبُدَ الَّذِيْنَ تَدْعُوْنَ مِنْ دُوْنِ اللّٰهِ قُلْ لَّآ اَتَّبِعُ اَهْوَآءَكُمْ قَدْ ضَلَلْتُ اِذًا وَّمَآ اَنَا مِنَ الْمُهْتَدِيْنَ ○ ثُمَّ اَنْزَلَ عَلَيْكُمْ مِّنْۢ بَعْدِ الْغَمِّ اَمَنَةً نُّعَاسًا يَّغْشٰى طَآئِفَةً مِّنْكُمْ وَطَآئِفَةٌ قَدْ اَهَمَّتْهُمْ اَنْفُسُهُمْ يَظُنُّوْنَ بِاللّٰهِ غَيْرَ الْحَقِّ ظَنَّ الْجَاهِلِيَّةِ يَقُوْلُوْنَ هَلْ لَّنَا مِنَ الْاَمْرِ مِنْ شَيْءٍ قُلْ اِنَّ الْاَمْرَ كُلَّهٗ لِلّٰهِ يُخْفُوْنَ فِيْٓ اَنْفُسِهِمْ مَّا لَا يُبْدُوْنَ لَكَ يَقُوْلُوْنَ لَوْ

The Supplication of Refuge

In the Name of God, the Merciful, the Compassionate

"God, there is no god but He, the Living, the Self-Subsisting, Eternal, No slumber can seize him, nor sleep. His are all things in the heavens and on earth.

"Who is there can intercede in His Presence except as He permits? He knows what appears to His creatures before or after or behind them.

"Nor shall they compass aught of His knowledge except as He wills. His throne extends over the heavens and the earth. And He feels no fatigue in guarding and preserving them. For He is the Most High, the Supreme.

"Let there be no compulsion in religion. Truth stands out clear from error. Whoever rejects evil and believes in God has grasped the most trustworthy handhold that never breaks.

"And God hears and knows all things.God is the protector of those who have faith. From the depths of darkness He will lead them forth into light. Of those who reject faith the patrons are the evil ones. From light they will lead them forth into the depths of darkness. They will be companions of the Fire, to dwell therein." (*Surah al-Baqarah*, 255-257).

When those come to you who believe in Our Signs say: "Peace be upon you, Your Lord has ascribed for himself (the rule) of Mercy. Verily, if any of you did evil in ignorance, and thereafter repented, and amended (his behavior). Lo, He is Oft-forgiving, Most Merciful." Thus do we explain the signs in detail. That the way of the sinners may be shown up.

Say: *"I am forbidden to worship those—others than God—whom you call upon." Say: "I will not follow your vain desires. If I did, I would stray from the path, and be not of the company of those who receive guidance."* (*Surah al-Anam*, 54-56).

After the excitement of the distress, he sent down calm on a band of you, overcome with slumber, whilst another band was stirred to anxiety by their own feelings, moved by wrong suspicions due to ignorance.

They said: "What affair is this of ours?" Say: "Indeed this affair is wholly God's." They hide in their minds what they dare not reveal to you.

They say to themselves:

كَانَ لَنَا مِنَ الْاَمْرِ شَيْءٌ مَّا قُتِلْنَا هٰهُنَا ۗ قُلْ لَّوْ كُنْتُمْ فِيْ بُيُوْتِكُمْ لَبَرَزَ الَّذِيْنَ
كُتِبَ عَلَيْهِمُ الْقَتْلُ اِلٰى مَضَاجِعِهِمْ ۚ وَلِيَبْتَلِيَ اللّٰهُ مَا فِيْ صُدُوْرِكُمْ وَلِيُمَحِّصَ
مَا فِيْ قُلُوْبِكُمْ ۗ وَاللّٰهُ عَلِيْمٌ ۢ بِذَاتِ الصُّدُوْرِ ۝ مُحَمَّدٌ رَّسُوْلُ اللّٰهِ ۗ وَالَّذِيْنَ مَعَهٗٓ
اَشِدَّآءُ عَلَى الْكُفَّارِ رُحَمَآءُ بَيْنَهُمْ تَرٰىهُمْ رُكَّعًا سُجَّدًا يَّبْتَغُوْنَ فَضْلًا مِّنَ اللّٰهِ
وَرِضْوَانًا ۫ سِيْمَاهُمْ فِيْ وُجُوْهِهِمْ مِّنْ اَثَرِ السُّجُوْدِ ۗ ذٰلِكَ مَثَلُهُمْ فِي التَّوْرٰىةِ ۛۖ
وَمَثَلُهُمْ فِي الْاِنْجِيْلِ ۛ كَزَرْعٍ اَخْرَجَ شَطْاَهٗ فَاٰزَرَهٗ فَاسْتَغْلَظَ فَاسْتَوٰى عَلٰى
سُوْقِهٖ يُعْجِبُ الزُّرَّاعَ لِيَغِيْظَ بِهِمُ الْكُفَّارَ ۗ وَعَدَ اللّٰهُ الَّذِيْنَ اٰمَنُوْا وَعَمِلُوا
الصّٰلِحٰتِ مِنْهُمْ مَّغْفِرَةً وَّاَجْرًا عَظِيْمًا ۝ اَلِفْ بَا تَا ثَا جِيْمْ حَا خَا دَالْ ذَالْ رَا
زَا سِيْنْ شِيْنْ صَادْ ضَادْ طَا ظَا عَيْنْ غَيْنْ فَا قَافْ كَافْ لَامْ مِيْمْ نُوْنْ وَاوْ هَا
يَا ۝ يَا رَبِّ سَهِّلْ وَيَسِّرْ وَلَا تُعَسِّرْ عَلَيْنَا يَارَبِّ ۝

"If we had had anything to do with this affair we should not have been in the slaughter here."

Say: *"Even if you had remained in your homes, those for whom death was decreed would certainly have gone forth to the place of their death.*

"But all this was that God might test what is in your hearts. For God knows well the secrets of your hearts." (*Surah ale-Imran*, 154).

Muḥammad is the Apostle of God. And those who are with him are strong against unbelievers, compassionate amongst each other. You will see them bow and prostrate themselves, seeking Grace from God and His good pleasure.

On their faces are their marks, the traces of prostration. This is their similitude in the Torah.

And their similitude in the Gospel is like a seed which sends forth its blade, then makes it strong. It then becomes thick, and it stands on its own stem, filling the sowers with wonder and delight.

As a result, it fills the unbelievers with rage at them. *"God has promised those among them who believe and do righteous deeds forgiveness and a great reward."* (*Surah al-Fath*, 29)—*alif, ba, ta, tha, jeem, ha, kha, dal, dhal, ra, za, seen, sheen, sad, dad, tta, zaa, ᶜain, ghain, qaf, kaf, lam, meem, nun, waw, heh, ya.*

O my Lord, give us ease and relieve us and do not burden us, O my Lord!